GW00503259

# ON THE LIST: 1990S

### The 111 Best Music Lists of the 1990s

by Jason Preston

On The List: 1990s. Copyright © 2020 by Jason Preston.

All rights reserved. Printed in the United States of America by Skinner Publishing in Los Angeles, California. No part of this book may be reproduced or transmitted in any form or by any means, electronic or mechanical, including photocopying, recording, or by any information retrieval system, without permission in writing from the copyright owner.

Portions of this book previously appeared on
www.goodbadunknown.com

The Good, The Bad, and the Unknown © Jason Preston
Layout and Publishing by Geoff Skinner
Cover Design and Photographs by Kevin Marcus
Edited by Brian Serven
Copyedit by Lisa J. Lord

Library of Congress Control Number:
ISBN-13: 979-8666330425
ISBN-10: 8666330425

0 1 2

# DEDICATION

*For Ellis & Hadley...*
*I wouldn't have done this without you*

# CHAPTERS

# INTRODUCTION

If I had to define the '90s with one singular image, it would be a naked baby diving into a swimming pool, chasing a dollar bill on a fishing hook. We all know it. We've all seen it. It's the most infamous album cover of the decade. It's the cover of Nirvana's album, *Nevermind*. I remember the first time I saw the cover, and honestly, when I saw it, I had no idea what it was.

It was the fall of 1991, my first week of college at UCLA, and my parents were dropping me off at school. Coincidentally, my neighbor growing up was a senior at UCLA, so there was one familiar face on campus. After checking out my dorm room, my parents and I went to visit him. When we arrived at his apartment, he was ecstatic. He had just made a music purchase. He held up a CD long box and said, "Look what I just got." First of all, for those who don't know, a long box is a 12-inch long cardboard case that CDs were sold in because record stores were originally equipped with racks made for vinyl records. They were too deep to display CDs. In order to display the CDs in the vinyl racks, record labels encased the CDs in long cardboard boxes with the album covers printed on them. Long boxes were only around for a couple of years, but that's not important right now. What is important is my friend was holding up Nirvana's *Nevermind*. This was my introduction to Nirvana and the impact their music would have on my decade.

We were almost two years into the '90s, twenty percent of the decade had already gone by, and we were just learning about the band that would be considered the most important artist of the decade. And while history has dictated Nirvana's

11

decade-defining stature, Nirvana didn't define the '90s. They are a small piece of a larger movement. Nirvana was only around for about two and a half years, from the fall of 1991 until the spring of 1994. The rest of the decade was a fluctuating crowd of personalities all running in circles like a zombie feeding frenzy. While grunge was the most famous style in the '90s, it wasn't the only one. The first part of the '90s was dominated by boy bands and metal groups. Grunge took over for the next two years, followed by pop punk and ska. Britpop had its turn for a couple of years until we ended the decade with metal music and boy bands again. And while all these prevailing styles were stealing up the airwaves, you also had hip-hop taking off on its own starship. You had the swing revival, DJs, alt-country, indie, folk, electronica, dance, R&B, trip hop, and the biggest soundtracks you've ever heard. Ultimately, the style of the '90s was...no style. And while the '90s didn't care about identity, for me, it's the decade where I figured out who I was. At the beginning of the decade, I was a high school student who wasn't even old enough to drive. By the end of the decade, I was working in Hollywood on the biggest movie of all time and the most popular show on television. Since I am the yardstick by how all these bands will be judged, let's get to the most important question: Who am I?

*       *       *

My name is Jason Paul Preston. I am a writer, director, TV and film producer, voice-over actor, radio DJ, blogger, music promoter, and musicologist. I've run radio stations. I created my own awards show. I've been nominated for Emmys. I've won film festivals. I was a DJ on the first global radio station. I programmed the first RPG game for a web browser. I worked on one of the decade's most popular television shows (*Friends*) and the biggest box office film of all time (*Titanic*).  And one time, Michael Jackson touched me.  How did I get my start?

I graduated high school in the summer of 1991 and went on to attend UCLA as a history major.  After graduation, I continued my education and transferred to UCLA's film school for my master's degree with a concentration in screenwriting.  While at school, I worked constantly.  I had a full-time job at a movie theater in Westwood.  The Fox Village Theater (owned by Mann Theaters at the time) wasn't just any theater; it was one of the most iconic movie theaters in Los Angeles. On my first day on the job, I worked the world premiere for *Batman Returns*.  During the first run of the film, Michael Jackson came to see it three times.  On one occasion, as he was exiting out the back of the theater, I held the door open for him, and he patted me on the shoulder. True story.  Over my three years at the theater, I worked some of the biggest movie premieres of the decade and even snuck into some after parties.  Besides my movie theater job, I also was an intern at different production companies, working my way into the industry.  I worked at ICM talent agency. I read scripts and did coverage for Gary Foster Productions when they were making *Sleepless in Seattle*.  I did the same for Lightstorm Entertainment while they were prepping *Titanic*.  I was even there the day that Leonardo DiCaprio came into the office to meet with James Cameron regarding his role in the movie.  I'll never forget staring down the hallway and seeing Leo sitting in the office with no idea that I was witnessing an iconic Hollywood moment.

When I wasn't interning around town, I was a DJ at the campus radio station, KLA.  I didn't have my first show until my junior year when I co-hosted a show about rare tracks. During my senior year, I became the General Manager, and when I moved on to grad school, I continued as a manager until I graduated in 1998.

Working in radio came with perks. I could get tickets to any live show I wanted to see in Los Angeles. The record labels would comp me tickets to anything. If I wanted any new CDs, they'd send me a box. If I wanted T-shirts, stickers, any sort of swag, all I had to do was ask. I wasn't just an important student on campus; I had become a player in the big leagues. Record labels were kissing my ass to get me to play their music. It was a lot for a college kid to handle, but I took advantage of it every chance I could. I went to shows three times a week, went backstage, and met the artists. I saw great festivals, intense club shows, exclusive private events, and dozens of record release parties. It was a dream.

In my final year of grad school, I had picked up a new skill: programming HTML for web browsers. Since it was a rare skill at the time, I landed a job at Universal Studios, working with their web team, where I helped program the first first-person game for a web browser based on their new movie-themed ride, *Jurassic Park*. I was pretty good at this programming stuff, which made graduation quite difficult.

When entering the work-force after graduation, I had three paths I could take: film, radio, or the internet. I applied to KROQ but didn't get the job. The web company I had worked for replaced me. So when I was offered a production job on a TV show called *Jesse* by BKC (Bright, Kaufman, Crane), the creators of *Friends* and *Veronica's Closet*, it wasn't just the best choice; it was the only choice. I worked for one year at *Jesse*, spending Friday nights working on the set of

*Friends.* The following season, I jumped to the one-hour drama, *Family Law.* Even though my day job was in TV, I kept my hand in the music industry by writing album and concert reviews. On Friday nights I hosted a radio show for Spike Radio, the first global radio station.

My decade had been a blur. In ten short years, I had accomplished more than most people do in a lifetime. It was chaotic, but all my accomplishments came out of my endurance to perform. This type of success was indicative of the decade. There was a feeling of community-like we were all on the same team. We rooted for each other to succeed and our failures didn't hold us back. We didn't blame others for our struggles or challenges: it was no one's fault, it just was. During the '90s, if there was a problem, we just figured it out. People were friendlier. Material things didn't matter as much. Success was measured in authenticity rather than wealth. The more real something was, the more we loved it. It was as if we finally figured out what mattered.

The culture of the '90s is perfectly captured in its music. It wasn't about success; it was about authenticity. We didn't care about sounding perfect; we wanted it to be flawed. The imperfections are what made the music more human. It made us feel more connected to it. You heard this from all corners of the music industry. The music had become more honest. It felt human, like it was one of us. Music became more diverse with as many facets as there are different people. The music in the '90s was our livelihood, it was our mantra, it was our social glue. It defined us as much as we defined it. Let me explain.

*       *       *

We all love leftovers. There's nothing better than a Thanksgiving sandwich the day after Thanksgiving. Turkey with stuffing, cranberries, mashed potatoes, layered with gravy all between two fluffy pieces of bread. Food heaven. Two days after Thanksgiving, the leftovers are still pretty good. Three days after, tolerable. Four days after, edible. Five days after, you start thinking, what else can I have? As much as we love leftovers, they're still not as good as the food on the day it was made.

The music that came out in the first couple of years of the '90s sounded like '80s leftovers. They were the second string, the knockoffs, the less interesting copycats of what came before. The music sounded like the industry was merely dumping what bands they had left on their shelves from the previous decade. And while leftovers can be pretty good, it's not the same.

For example, hard rock and metal dominated most of the '80s. Despite a handful of decent albums, the quality of the music in the early '90s paled in comparison to the monstrous legacy of Guns N' Roses, Def Leppard, Bon Jovi, and Mötley Crüe in the '80s. What we were left with were the Bullet Boys, Mr. Big, and Trixter. I hate to admit it, but I saw Trixter in concert. It was dark times my friends, very dark. But what were my options? The musical world was ruled by MC Hammer, Vanilla Ice, and Milli Vanilli. Even Michael Bolton was an A-list rock star. Yes, these years for music were that bleak.

There was hope though, and you could see the swell coming if you knew where to look.

Alternative rock (or modern rock in the '80s) had been growing in popularity. In the early '90s, the first of these bands broke through, setting the stage for bigger things to come. Sonic Youth's *Goo*, Alice in Chains' *Facelift*, and Jane's Addiction's *Ritual De Lo Habitual* found success because music fans needed something fresh, something new, something challenging rather than the carbon copies of a now-gone era. These bands were new voices with new perspectives. Then, in August 1991, the world would go through an awakening.

In a brief span of just two months, between August 1st, 1991 and September 30th, 1991, the following decade-defining albums were released: Metallica - *The Black Album*, Red Hot Chili Peppers - *Blood Sugar Sex Magik*, Massive Attack - *Blue Lines*, Soundgarden - *Badmotorfinger*, Cypress Hill - *Cypress Hill*, Guns N' Roses - *Use Your Illusion*, A Tribe Called Quest - *The Low End Theory*, Primal Scream - *Screamadelica*, Pearl Jam - *Ten*, and of course, Nirvana - *Nevermind*. All ten of these releases are in my top 111 albums of the decade. Six of them are in the top 25 and three of them are in the top 11. This moment in time, this two-month period produced more genre-defining music than at any other time during the decade, if not ever. This release pocket is important because it revolutionized everything. And the revolution was televised.

Enter MTV. MTV was a 24-hour cable channel that played nothing but music videos from all the musical artists you needed to know about. Our generation watched MTV all the time. That's not an exaggeration. We literally had MTV on all the time. When you woke up, when you slept, when you were doing homework, in bars, stores, restaurants, everywhere you went, MTV was playing. MTV was our 24-

hour news service because what MTV was playing was the only news we cared about. They were the yardstick for what music was culturally relevant. They defined what we should listen to and they ignored what we should avoid. When grunge broke, it was all about Seattle. The next year, it was all about Compton. Then, Manchester. Then, Berkeley. Then, Orange County, New York, and Chapel Hill. We absorbed all of it. If MTV thought it was cool then that's all we needed to know to incorporate it into our lives, creating a music revolution that encapsulated all of society. Until the spring of 1994, the world was pretty great.

Our generation had seemingly taken over the world. From the indie movie explosion with filmmakers like Quentin Tarantino, Kevin Smith, Robert Rodriguez, and Richard Linklater, to the way we dressed, to the new President of the United States, to television shows about nothing; it was Gen-X's world and you were all lucky to be living in it. I don't know how to truly describe those years. Remember the day you received your driver's license and all the opportunities were wide open? It was like that. It was like having your first party in your apartment and not having to worry about your parents coming home. It was like your first crush. Actually, it was like having your first crush like you back. For the first time in my life, I felt heard. I felt like my generation mattered. I felt like I mattered. And, then with a snap, it ended.

Then it would all change drastically, overnight.

In April 1994, Kurt Cobain committed suicide.

At that time, Nirvana wasn't the biggest band in the world. Pearl Jam was more popular. Pearl Jam sold more albums, they sold out more concerts, and they had more songs playing on the radio. Don't get me wrong, arguing over Pearl Jam or Nirvana, is like arguing over Batman or Superman. They were both adored, loved, and idolized...but Pearl Jam was bigger. Cobain wasn't the John Lennon of our generation. The Beatles were bigger than Jesus, remember? The difference was, Cobain was one of us. He was a regular guy. This is why we liked him so much. He was just himself. He was authentic. The '90s were defined by authenticity. That authenticity allowed us to connect to the music on a more personal level. When Cobain died, it was like a piece of us died. It was like losing a friend. The two and a half years of ignorant bliss ended in an instant and the '90s were never the same, nor were we. Cobain was a symbol of the fragility of our way of life. The facade of the '90s had collapsed, and now we were on our own.

The next few years of the '90s felt different. Grunge still held strong for another few years with huge albums by The Smashing Pumpkins, Stone Temple Pilots, and Soundgarden but something was off. The authenticity from the first wave of grunge was raw and unrefined. These new offerings, which came from the bands of the first wave, felt more produced. They were no longer regular people making music, they were now-famous rock stars making music.

For the next few years, music was a runaway car, racing down the highway, with no idea where it was going and not a road map to be found. Because there was no direction, every direction became possible. There was a new punk revolution that was led by Green Day, Offspring, and Rancid. There was the everything but the kitchen sink music of Beck, the blow up the world defiance from Rage Against The Machine, and the party your ass off jubilation from the

Red Hot Chili Peppers. We had Britpop with Oasis and Blur. Ska bands with No Doubt and Sublime. We had a 1930s Swing revival complete with bowling shirts and black and white shoes. Even hip-hop evolved through multiple phases, from gangsta rap to hardcore to G-Funk. We opened the doors for all bands and all styles. The musical jukebox of the late '90s is so eclectic, if you picked music at random, it would sound less chaotic. By losing Nirvana, we lost our direction. So by the end of the decade, we went back to what was comfortable: the reemergence of pop with cookie-cutter boy bands and the return of metal in its "nü" form.

We never were able to recapture that feeling we had at the beginning of the decade, but what we gained was so much bigger. What we learned from the grunge, the rap, and the indie scene was that what we were looking for was around us at all times. We weren't looking for the next Nirvana. We weren't looking for the next Dr. Dre. What we were looking for was authenticity; in the lyrics, in the music, in the artists themselves. By searching for this element, we uncovered so many unique and ground-breaking bands who would have never had exposure otherwise. To me, this is everything. This is why the '90s are so important. The decade is defined by the underdogs, by the outsiders, by the long shots. This was the decade where everyone had a chance, and you felt it. You felt it in the air. You felt more than any other time that you could accomplish anything. It's no wonder Gen-X would change the world with the tech revolution. We did because no one told us we couldn't.

There was one genre in the decade that embodies this sentiment more than any other. That genre is electronica (also known as EDM). The electronica scene was its own world. Like alternative music in the '80s, electronica was largely ignored by the mainstream world. It was a blossoming underground scene that thrived on independence. Electronica raves didn't take place in clubs; they were in warehouses, airport hangars, and abandoned buildings. Without the restraints of mainstream regulation, the electronica scene flourished, creating some of the decade's most innovative music. And the greatest thing about it, if you didn't know about it, you didn't know about it. It was like belonging to a secret club, which kept it pure and intoxicating.

The greatest thing about the music of the '90s is that the fans were in control. We dictated what we wanted to hear rather than letting the labels and radio stations tell what they wanted us to hear. We felt in control, and you could hear it in the music.

*      *      *

The best example I have to sum up the decade happened to me in the spring of 1999. I was visiting a friend who was in the Peace Corps in Bolivia. He took me to stay at a village just inside the Amazon jungle, where he was living. No more than 500 people lived in this village. I roomed with a nice Bolivian family who spoke very little English. They had a son who could sing and play guitar. They raved about how talented their son was, that he was a great singer and a great guitar player. One night, the son finally pulled out his guitar and began playing. I instantly recognized the song as "Polly" by Nirvana. I didn't have the heart to tell his parents that their son did not write the song. I just congratulated him and gave him a knowing wink. Truth is, he actually sounded pretty good. My take away from this was that the music of the '90s was so powerful and so meaningful that it permeated culture, that it translated to other communities across the globe, and that in the middle of the Amazon jungle, they knew who Nirvana was.

*       *       *

This is the third book in my On The List series. Even though it's released third, it's actually the second book chronologically. Each time I've written one of these books, I've tried to put a unique spin on it. The first book, about music in the 2000s, was based on my music blog from that era. The book largely mirrors the blog posts and blogosphere style music writing of that time. The second book is about the 1980s, which concentrated on that decade's music along with the events and pop culture of that era. This book revolves around the 1990s. Since it was such a pivotal decade for me, this book will be about me. It will be about my experiences and how they relate to the bands in this book. There will be some very direct connections, some tangent stories and some bands where there's just a deep admiration. Overall, the bands and music discussed here largely represent my experiences in the '90s. These are the bands I loved, these are the bands I collected, that I listened to, that I followed, that I saw in concert; these are the bands who drove my music passion. These will be the albums that I owned and the songs I listened to on repeat. There will be plenty of very popular artists as well as some very obscure ones. There will be dozens of bands that didn't make the book. Some of the excluded artists I just never listened to, some are artists I loathed, and some are artists I liked, but I just ran out of space in the book. So if your favorite artist isn't in here, it's not that they didn't deserve to be included in the book; they just weren't a huge part of my life at the time. These are the bands and music that shaped my decade.

As I've mentioned in my other books, these lists are not definitive and change each time I listen to them. But I do have rules. For a band to be included in the book, they must have released three albums during the decade, not including live albums or greatest hits. And since EPs were big in the '90s, every two EPs that a band released counts as one album. Every song listed had to have been released in the '90s. You won't see "Personal Jesus" by Depeche Mode because it was released in 1989, even though its parent album, *Violator*, didn't come out until 1990. But since I made the rules and I'm writing the book, I can do anything I want. Rules are meant to be broken.

Ultimately, this book is about fun. Read it with a flannel shirt, some Doc Martens, and a Discman and I promise that you'll have such a good time that you'll forget to feed your Tamagotchi.

So, who wants to have some fun?

# THE 111 BEST ALBUMS OF THE DECADE

In creating this top 111, I chose albums that are not just impactful albums on the decade as a whole, but albums that impacted my life personally. That said, this isn't just a list of my favorites but a list of albums that were greatly relevant at that time, that affected the generation, in turn affecting me. These are only official studio albums. No compilations, so no Beta Band *The Three E.P.s*. No live albums, so no Nirvana *Unplugged In New York*. No soundtracks, so no *Singles* soundtrack. No compilations, so no *No Alternative*. And, no greatest hits because that would be cheating.

## The 111 Best Albums of the '90s:

1. **Pearl Jam** - *Ten* (1991) - Nirvana's *Nevermind* will historically be labeled as the album that changed the musical world, but in 1991, Pearl Jam's *Ten* was bigger. Everybody owned this disc. It was in everyone's car. It was on everyone's CD shelf. Even people who didn't like rock bought this album. Pearl Jam dominated radio and MTV. This album was so popular, every song was being played on the radio. The band actually stopped releasing singles in fear of getting too big. While it was Nirvana's hipster cool that opened the door for grunge, it was Pearl Jam who carried it forward unto the masses.

2. **Nirvana** - *In Utero* (1993) - Though *Nevermind* brought us Nirvana and inspired a generation, *In Utero* is just a better album. Don't get me wrong, *Nevermind* is fantastic, but it's the album the record label wanted

the band to make. *In Utero* is the album Kurt Cobain wanted to make. *In Utero* finds Cobain dealing with the weight of being the unwilling leader of the generation to wrestling with tumultuous married life and the infancy of parenthood. All the while battling drug addiction and just trying to make it on stage every night. He was the anti-rock star. *In Utero* is an anti-rock album. It is the closest we will ever get to look inside the mind, heart, and soul of Cobain. *Nevermind* is who we wanted him to be, *In Utero* is who he was.

3. **Beastie Boys** - *Check Your Head* (1992) - It was more than an album, it was our creed, it was our motto, it was our anthem. If you didn't have this album memorized, your Gen-X membership would be revoked.

4. **Rage Against The Machine** - *Rage Against The Machine* (1992) - No album has aged with more potency than Rage Against The Machine's debut. It was the battle cry of woke culture before woke culture was even born. Decades later, the music and the message are more relevant than ever.

5. **Wu-Tang Clan** - *Enter The Wu-Tang (36 Chambers)* (1993) - Nine rappers walk into a record label and pitch an album filled with comic book references, the aesthetic of kung fu films, numerology, and doesn't adhere to any song structure. Loud/RCA records gave it the green light and gave us one of the best hip-hop records of all time.

6. **The Smashing Pumpkins** - *Mellon Collie And The Infinite Sadness* (1995) - This is a sprawling 28-song odyssey into a vast extraordinary dreamworld. Billy Corgan's opus is a never-ending treasure chest of riches. Each song had its own individual journey,

with new gems to uncover with each listen. A luminous album that ruled all music and made the Pumpkins the biggest band in the world.

7. **Tool** - *Aenima* (1996) - Any hard rock album that includes a man shouting a cookie recipe in German, samples Bill Hicks, and promotes giving California an enema means this band is messed up in the most creative way. Is it metal? Is it rock? Is it alternative? It's Tool.

8. **Radiohead** - *The Bends* (1995) - Many will argue that *OK Computer* is more important, influential, and ground-breaking. While much of that is true, *The Bends* is just a perfect rock album from beginning to end. It was this album's flawless sensibilities that gave birth to the creative magnitude for *OK Computer*.

9. **Nirvana** - *Nevermind* (1991) - There's a lot written about the album, that it defined a generation, that it reinvented rock music. None of it is true. The album is spectacular. Hell, it's in the top 11. But its potency wasn't in reinventing the wheel. What *Nevermind* did was take everything that was emotionally happening in the world, all of our frustrations, and put it to song. *Nevermind* didn't revolutionize anything, it just captured the emotional state of society in the perfect snapshot.

10. **Nas** - *Illmatic* (1994) - It was serious, it was intelligent, it changed perception, it opened eyes, it rethought what a rap could be. And it inspired every rap album that followed it.

11. **Massive Attack** - *Blue Lines* (1991) - Combining rap, rock, reggae, funk, and dance, Massive Attack's muggy rave unto the light fantastic is such a rare offering that it defied all genres and created its own. Welcome to the birth of trip hop.

12. **Red Hot Chili Peppers** - *Blood Sugar Sex Magik* (1991) - As part of the 1991 alternative rock revolution, this is the Chili Peppers funktified recipe for a musical feast, their appetite for celebration.

13. **Jane's Addiction** - *Ritual De Lo Habitual* (1990) - *Ritual De Lo Habitual* is a landmark piece of music that ignited our cultural upheaval, opening the door to a festive wonderland of sights, sounds, and experiences. This album is the inciting incident that elevated the concert experience with Lollapalooza.

14. **Elliott Smith** - *Either/Or* (1997) - Smith's sheer fragility of emotions is so delicate that there's a real fear if you turned up the volume, it could shatter his voice into a thousand pieces. It's the sincerity in his delivery that keeps you captivated.

15. **The Black Crowes** - *Shake Your Money Maker* (1990) - Caught between the power thrust of metal and angry punch of grunge, The Black Crowes delivered an old school rock record that could shake, rattle, and roll with the best of them.

16. **Weezer** - *Pinkerton* (1996) - It was despised by critics, ignored by radio, but it was cherished by a devoted legion of fans. As the years passed, these fans continued to praise its brilliance with such success that the band (who had broken up) reformed to appease them.

17. **A Tribe Called Quest** - *The Low End Theory* (1991) - After a long day on campus, nothing could be finer than kicking it with friends to the laid-back flow of Q-Tip, Phife Dawg, and the occasional Busta Rhymes cameo. Being angsty all day was tiring; sometimes you just needed some vibes and relaxation.

18. **Jeff Buckley** - *Grace* (1994) - That voice. That damn angelic voice.

19. **Pavement** - *Crooked Rain, Crooked Rain* (1994) - When the museum of indie rock is built, a statue of Pavement will sit on the front steps beckoning all visitors with a snarky smile. *Crooked Rain, Crooked Rain* is the band's perfect storm of sarcastic wit, jangly hooks, and crackerjack songwriting.

20. **Dr. Dre** - *The Chronic* (1992) - Dr. Dre teams up with Snoop Dog for his first album away from N.W.A. *The Chronic* is an immersive theme park ride through L.A. street life, filled with sex, drugs, and violence. And it's worth waiting in line to ride over and over.

21. **DJ Shadow** - *Endtroducing.....* (1996) - This is not a piece of music. This is a piece of art. It's the ripping apart of fragments from every corner of the jukebox and reassembling them like a mad scientist in a mutated, gyrating musical monster.

22. **The Smashing Pumpkins** - *Siamese Dream* (1993) - Billy Corgan's 'mötley cure' from Chicago grabbed the grunge throne with an onslaught of seismic hit after seismic hit.

23. **Beck** - *Midnite Vultures* (1999) - This interplanetary adventure is an interstellar freak-out that reaches for the outer limits of the universe to galaxies far, far away, and back. Ask anyone named Debra...they know.

24. **Radiohead** - *OK Computer* (1997) - A schizophrenic computer giving birth to the age of digital emotions. It's a complicated masterpiece of ones and zeroes that updates as you listen.

25. **The Notorious B.I.G.** - *Ready To Die* (1994) - Straight outta Brooklyn, Biggie's debut album set the blueprint for east coast rap, proving that it didn't take a nation of millions, but one kid with a distinctive voice all his own.

26. **My Bloody Valentine** - *Loveless* (1991) - This shoegazer's paradise is not loveless at all. The music captures the over-churning uncertainty, the uncontrollable stability, the nauseous balance, and the lack of clear thought that encompasses being in love, while at the same time, it's the best feeling you've ever had.

27. **Tori Amos** - *Under The Pink* (1994) - Tori's ability to play the piano with such musical fortitude rivals the complexity of any guitar solo. If a piano could gently weep, Tori would be the one making it cry.

28. **U2** - *Achtung Baby* (1991) - No one thought U2 could follow the epic magnitude and brilliance of their '80s material. Could they? Pay attention, baby, U2 has something even better than the *Joshua Tree*.

29. **Guns N' Roses** - *Use Your Illusion I&II* (1991) - GNR's double album follows their iconic *Appetite For Destruction* by throwing every concept at the wall and seeing what sticks. While not every song earns its keeps, there's an overwhelming amount of superior music that proves why these guys were legends in their own time.

30. **Jay-Z** - *Reasonable Doubt* (1996) - There's no doubt, you can't knock a hustla with this level of bravado. In a decade of hip-hop monuments, Jay-Z emboldened his name on the list with one of hip-hop's all-time finest.

31. **Sleater-Kinney** - *Dig Me Out* (1997) - A venomous attack of blood, sweat, and tears. It's a non-stop, runaway silver bullet train of pure rock n' roll adrenaline.

32. **Lauryn Hill** - *The Miseducation Of Lauryn Hill* (1998) - After she killed us softly with the Fugees, Hill took us back to school with a flawless groove-a-delic soul

ride. This was the only studio album she ever released because honestly, when you get it right the first time, you might as well quit while you're ahead.

33. **Beck** - *Odelay* (1996) - Like a hip-hop remix gone wild in grandpa's guitar barn, Beck's break-out album is a turntable dancing the night away. Beck only knows where it's at.

34. **Green Day** - *Dookie* (1994) - Three kids from Berkeley smoked some pot and made a record.

35. **Live** - *Throwing Copper* (1994) - Live's sophomore effort is a precision performance in songwriting. Each song builds on the one before it, creating an unstoppable momentum that climaxes in a furious uprising of emotional revelation.

36. **Pearl Jam** - *Vs.* (1993) - This outing finds the band stretching the boundaries of their style and sound, setting the stage for a career of experimentation. Still restrained, they deliver an album that rocks just as hard as their debut.

37. **Moby** - *Everything Is Wrong* (1995) - This was one of the first techno albums to establish the genre onto a wide audience. This isn't an album of repetitive throbbing beats; these are strategically crafted songs with musical movements that are orchestral in nature. The album was a sonic leap forward for the genre, opening the door for others to dance their way in.

38. **Portishead** - *Dummy* (1994) - Listening to this album still gives me chills. Beth Gibbons sings like a cold-hearted snake dripping with depressed joy. It's every bit seductive as it is deadly.

39. **Depeche Mode** - *Violator* (1990) - The '80s titans kicked off this decade with their career masterpiece.

40. **Public Enemy** - *Fear of A Black Planet* (1990) - The revolution was not televised, it was pressed to CDs

and spread across our eardrums. Chuck D was a modern-day educator of social change, fighting the power for societal upheaval.

41. **Soundgarden** - *Badmotorfinger* (1991) - Harnessing the dark soul of Sabbath, Chris Cornell's voice never howled fiercer, Thayil's guitar never thrashed louder, Shepherd's bass never throbbed harder, and Cameron's drumming never pounded with such intensity. While future releases were better made for radio stardom, *Badmotorfinger* is made for rocking your ass off.

42. **2Pac** - *Me Against The World* (1995) - This is Tupac at his most sincere, his most honest, his most brilliant. These are songs that don't just make you question the things around you, they make you question yourself.

43. **Built To Spill** - *Perfect From Now On* (1997) - Harvesting their inner crazy horse, the band sounds like Neil Young reborn as a Seattle indie rock band. Except for the fact that Neil Young isn't dead and the band is actually from Boise, Idaho.

44. **Bob Dylan** - *Time Out Of Mind* (1997) - It's a retrospective of life with an acceptance of our future finality. Dylan may be getting old, but he's still better than most of these damn kids.

45. **Pavement** - *Slanted And Enchanted* (1992) - The Stockton boys' debut is a crude, lo-fi, garage rock grinder. It's the album that made indie rock worth listening to.

46. **Fiona Apple** - *Tidal* (1996) - Dripping with heroin chic, you don't have to be a criminal to enjoy this first taste of Apple's dream-like piano boxing. It's a gorgeous ocean of sultry significance.

47. **Alice in Chains** - *Dirt* (1992) - Grunge's elder statesmen leapt out of their box to hit us with an

aptly named album filled with grimy, filth-covered melodies. If there was a bridge between the metalheads of the '80s and the plaid shirt-wearing Gen-Xers, Alice in Chains was manning the toll booth.

48. **Nine Inch Nails** - *The Downward Spiral* (1994) - Trent Reznor has never sounded more disturbed than he does here. You can feel the anxiety, pain, and the hurt as it gets closer.

49. **The Chemical Brothers** - *Exit Planet Dust* (1995) - The Chemical Brothers didn't just show up to the electronic party as a guest; they kicked open the door, knocked down the stereo, and took over with their block rockin' beats.

50. **Sigur Rós** - *Ágætis Byrjun* (1999) - On this breakthrough album, we didn't know anything about them. They were a mystery, an enigma, an ethereal voice in space beckoning us. And we followed it, willingly.

51. **Neutral Milk Hotel** - *In The Aeroplane Over The Sea* (1998) - This album came out of nowhere and embraced us like no other. Then as quickly as it came, the band vanished and that was it. But the band's brevity only emboldens the distraught nature of the music, leaving us with a haunting afterthought of what could have been.

52. **Björk** - *Post* (1995) - The eclectic weirdness of Björk's arthouse, electric ambient jazz isn't just an experiment in big band sentimentality; she delivers her songs with such vocal magnitude, you can envision that this is what Billie Holiday might have sounded like if she was still making music.

53. **Fugazi** - *Repeater* (1990) - You know those obscure rock artists that no one knows except the cool kids

who listen to them in their bedrooms? Fugazi is the band that those obscure artists listen to.

54. **Belle And Sebastian** - *If You're Feeling Sinister* (1996) - Sugary sweet pop songs in their simplest folky form shouldn't resonate with such emotional conscious-ness, but if you're feeling sinister, this is the album that will enlighten your soul.

55. **R.E.M.** - *Out Of Time* (1990) - If you've lost your religion, this is where you could find it.

56. **Orbital** - *In Sides* (1996) - Close your eyes, strap on some headphones and take a psychedelic voyage down the neon-tinted, digital waves into a pulsating electronic wonderland.

57. **Moby** - *Play* (1999) - After opening the doors for electronic music to enter the mainstream, Moby bulldozed the genre forward by drawing on the past. Pulling samples from music's rural roots, he proved that beautiful music is timeless.

58. **Soundgarden** - *Superunknown* (1994) - The album that solidified Cornell and company as rock gods.

59. **Tom Petty** - *Wildflowers* (1994) - Petty's second solo disc finds an aging Petty getting more reflective, sincere, wise, while still wildly clever.

60. **A Tribe Called Quest** - *Midnight Marauders* (1993) - With a mic in their hand, Tribe stirs in some jazz, some vibe, and a dash of Steve Biko, throwing down the conclusion to their funky trifecta that can make even the biggest stiff bug out.

61. **Wilco** - *Summerteeth* (1999) - Wilco's third album is a pinnacle of songwriting from Tweedy. It's an alt-country meets pop masterpiece.

62. **Metallica** - *Metallica (The Black Album)* (1991) - Move over grunge, metal was here first.

63. **The Orb** - *The Orb's Adventures Beyond The Ultraworld* (1991) - Λ triumph in the world of electronica music at a time when electronica didn't know they could even have a triumph.

64. **Sonic Youth** - *Dirty* (1992) - A vital piece of noise rock n' roll from the guitar-driven, New York loving, stuffed animal-f#@king, middle finger waving dirtiest punk band on the planet.

65. **Black Star** - *Mos Def & Talib Kweli Are Black Star* (1998) - Mos Def and Talib Kweli combine forces to activate one of the most flawless rap albums of the decade.

66. **Oasis** - *Definitely Maybe* (1994) - Warring brothers, soccer punks, Beatles rip-off artists; before these united Manchester youths knew they were the best band in the world, they belted out an album of pompous rock decadence.

67. **The Roots** - *Things Fall Apart* (1999) - The most fully realized adrenaline shot to social awareness since Ice Cube told the police to f#@k off. A rebellious heartbeat plays through the album as if the music is alive, fighting for its existence.

68. **Lush** - *Lovelife* (1996) - It's an album of gorgeously addictive shoegaze-influenced, pop songs that get more infectious with every listen.

69. **Temple Of The Dog** - *Temple Of The Dog* (1991) - Pearl Jam and Soundgarden make an album. It's just as great as you think it is.

70. **Morcheeba** - *Big Calm* (1998) - Unlike the sinister atmosphere of their trip hop brethren, *The Big Calm* is a majestic bouquet that embraces you like a warm breeze through a calming meadow under a starry night sky.

71. **Heatmiser** - *Mic City Sons* (1996) - Elliott Smith's previous band before his stellar solo career may find him at his rock star best. This is one of my favorite albums of all time and one of my birthday five.

72. **Cypress Hill** - *Cypress Hill* (1991) - You couldn't find this album anywhere. Stores didn't carry it. You had to find a friend of a friend who had it to make a copy for you. How do I know? Because I had it and I made more cassette copies of this album than any other album all decade.

73. **Outkast** - *Aquemini* (1998) - Before they were apologizing to Ms. Jackson, they were partying in the back of the bus, preparing for the whole world domination.

74. **Faith No More** - *Angel Dust* (1992) - The second album with singer Mike Patton and his operatic vocal range incorporates Patton's freaky antics and John Waters-esque lyrics without compromising the integrity of the music. It's no small victory that they didn't bungle this up, instead they made it sound easy like Sunday morning.

75. **Sebadoh** - *Bakesale* (1994) - When Lou Barlow left Dinosaur Jr. (or was kicked out), it seemed like the bubble had burst on his musical career and he'd be lucky to scrape together a new band. But after years of living all over Sebadoh's 4-track emulsion, Barlow delivered an album that was arguably better than anything he did with his former prehistoric group.

76. **Stone Temple Pilots** - *Purple* (1994) - This is a one-two punch of rock pugilism. It won't just leave your eardrums black and blue but all purple.

77. **Snoop Doggy Dogg** - *Doggystyle* (1993) - Snoop's debut album was the shindiggity that we didn't know we needed. With a refrigerator stocked full of gin

and juice, it was the kind of party you cranked at full volume until the neighbors called in the Marines.

78. **Garbage** - *Version 2.0* (1998) - When singer Shirley Manson commands the stage, I defy anyone not to succumb to her seductive powers.

79. **Uncle Tupelo** - *Anodyne* (1993) - In an era where anger reigned, these guys made country cool again. You didn't have to be mad at the world for people to listen to you; you just had to have something to say.

80. **Primal Scream** - *Screamadelica* (1991) - If a school bus full of hippies traveled across Europe looking for an outdoor festival of Britpop bands, this is the music that would guide their journey.

81. **The Magnetic Fields** - *69 Love Songs* (1999) - A different love song for every conceivable break up out there. Yes, even that one.

82. **Tricky** - *Maxinquaye* (1995) - It's Tricky to trip hop a rhyme that's right on time, it's Tricky, Tricky, Tricky, Tricky.

83. **The Cranberries** - *No Need To Argue* (1994) - Like an Irish siren perched on the edge of the cliffs of Moher beckoning all to hear her howl, Delores O'Riordan and company lure us in with an intimate yet explosive outing that could raise the dead.

84. **Daft Punk** - *Homework* (1997) - What set this apart from their electronic peers was the band's ability to inject an emotionally driven groove into their music. If this album doesn't make you want to get up and dance, then you're dead to me.

85. **Erykah Badu** - *Baduizm* (1997) - This socially conscious exhibit of mystical '70s AM grooves is a sunshine-covered meadow of peace, love, and neo soul.

86. **Ben Harper** - *Fight For Your Mind* (1995) - Harnessing the spirit of Bob Marley, Harper's unique amalgam of styles from reggae to rock to gospel collides in an effort of folk grace.

87. **Sunny Day Real Estate** - *Diary* (1994) - As a rider of one of the early waves of emo, Sunny Day Real Estate's debut is inner turmoil without aggression, angst without anger, and reluctant confidence that established this album as the defining leader of the emo tsunami.

88. **Spiritualized** - *Ladies And Gentlemen We Are Floating In Space* (1997) - The album delivers on everything promised in the dream-like title. It takes you to the very edge of the universe and lets you stretch out, absorb, and become enveloped by the great expanse of space, both literally and figuratively.

89. **Jawbreaker** - *Dear You* (1995) - This album was so detested by Jawbreaker's own fans that the band broke up under the weight of the criticism. Time has been kind to *Dear You*, revealing a scorching teenage revolutionary cry, innovative and influential.

90. **The Cure** - *Wish* (1992) - Their previous album, *Disintegration*, was such a colossal masterpiece, any follow-up would pale in comparison. But *Wish* is a subtle masterpiece in its own way. With bursts of outrage and trauma, this exhilarating flight soars higher and dares harder even if it's not Friday.

91. **Digable Planets** - *Reachin' (A New Refutation Of Time And Space)* (1993) - This lo-fi, jazz-infused rap album is so far ahead of its time, one would need a time-traveling phone booth to go forward into the future just to catch up.

92. **Tom Petty and the Heartbreakers** - *Into The Great Wide Open* (1991) - After the mammoth success of

Petty's solo album *Full Moon Fever*, Petty re-unites with the Heartbreakers for one of the best albums of their career.

93. **The Pharcyde** - *Bizarre Ride II The Pharcyde* (1992) - It's like the coolest kids in high school got together and made the chillest album you'll ever get high to. Don't let it pass you by.

94. **Beastie Boys** - *Ill Communication* (1994) - Listen all y'all...this isn't just a continuation of *Check Your Head* but a graduate-level advance in rhyming. One, two, oh my God, the Beastie Boys are here to set us straight.

95. **R.E.M.** - *Automatic For The People* (1992) - From college rock darlings to arena rock titans, *Automatic For The People* proved that R.E.M. didn't get a raw deal, instead they drove everyone to the moon with a solid set of alternative rock sweetness.

96. **The Get Up Kids** - *Something To Write Home About* (1999) - An emo bolt of lightning. It's an exhilarating collection of rock anthems for the helpless heart.

97. **Dixie Chicks** - *Fly* (1999) - Three women take over the music industry by putting out one of the best country albums since Dolly ran a whorehouse in Texas.

98. **Modest Mouse** - *The Lonesome Crowded West* (1997) - Before becoming one of the biggest bands of the 2000s, Modest Mouse was the little indie band who could.

99. **Travis** - *The Man Who* (1999) - After being trashed by critics for its melodic melancholy, it was the fans who turned the album's notoriety around, giving the band the last laugh.

100. **Ice Cube** - *Amerikkka's Most Wanted* (1990) - Cube's first solo record after busting out of N.W.A. is a fist in

the air in the land of the pissed off.

101. **Swell** - *Too Many Days Without Thinking* (1997) - If grunge was a fine wine that had been aging since the beginning of the decade, this album is the perfection of the aging process. This was my favorite album of 1997.

102. **Jellyfish** - *Bellybutton* (1990) - The joyous evolution of psychedelic rock, twenty-five years in the making.

103. **Bad Religion** - *Stranger Than Fiction* (1994) - With a zoological college professor as your punk rock singer, the album title aptly applies. After ten years of setting the stage for everyone else, these punk icons finally have their own coming-out party.

104. **Elastica** - *Elastica* (1995) - With the rumbling thrust of a drag racer, the album revs to a pressured peak until it hits the song "Stutter" when it explodes with the unburdened velocity of an intergalactic rocket.

105. **Ride** - *Nowhere* (1990) - A swirling storm of guitars, feedback, and Oxford drama, shaken not stirred, served up chilled. The Stone Roses wish their second album sounded this good.

106. **Massive Attack** - *Mezzanine* (1998) - Without Tricky on board, Massive Attack steps aside from the reggae dub and into the glowing pool of symphonic warmth.

107. **Guided By Voices** - *Bee Thousand* (1994) - Intended to be the band's final album, frontman Pollard recorded the songs on a 4-track with the intent of it sounding like the Beatles bootlegs. It has become a beacon for the spirit of musical independence and reinvigorated GBV to keep making music.

108. **Neil Young** - *Harvest Moon* (1992) - Though Young was an inspiration for the angst-fueled Seattle

thunderstorm, this album is the calm after the storm. This album is the peaceful, easy feeling you get sitting around a fire pit watching the sun set on a mountain horizon.

109. **Foo Fighters** - *Foo Fighters* (1995) - The first post-Nirvana release from Dave Grohl is ten times better than any solo album by a drummer ever. Even you, Don Henley.

110. **Porno For Pyros** - *Porno For Pyros* (1993) - Perry Farrell's new band after Jane's Addiction is a weird, wild exploration of Ferrell's transcendent mind.

111. **Dr. Dre** - *2001* (1999) - Dr. Dre owned the decade, from his music in N.W.A. and *The Chronic* to launching the careers of Snoop Dogg and Eminem, and producing major hits for Tupac and Nas. *The Chronic 2001* is Dre's finale to the decade, proving that he still had a little West Coast California love left for us all.

# A TRIBE CALLED QUEST

It was March of 1997. I was on my way to meet my friend in Berkeley for spring break. I had been driving four straight hours from Los Angeles when I pulled into the Fosters Freeze in Los Banos, CA. In the '90s, my road trips had their own musical identity. For a trip to Las Vegas, I listened to an entire Pearl Jam concert from beginning to end; on my trip to San Diego, I listened to Guns N' Roses' *Use Your Illusion* albums back-to-back. That day, it was all four albums by A Tribe Called Quest (their fifth hadn't been released yet). Tribe was smart and savvy, rambunctious and rebellious. They didn't let anything define them, which is why they thrived in an era that rejected definition. Tribe's vibrant relaxed rhythms were the perfect road trip companion. Having just completed my Tribe marathon, and with the remnants of "Stressed Out" still reverbing in my brain, I climbed out of my car, stretched, and hobbled to the take-out window where I ordered a Mountain Dew freeze. Fosters was the only place you could get one, and if you learn anything about me, I love Mtn. Dew. I took my freeze, collapsed on a park bench, and watched the world go by. One of the hazards of '90s life was car break-ins for CDs. Fearing someone might break into my car, I took my CD wallet with me. I must have been lost in the relaxation zone because when I got back to the car to drive onward, I realized I forgot my CD wallet on the bench. I immediately went back, but the wallet was already gone. I drove onto Berkeley having *left my CD wallet in Los Banos.*

## Albums of the '90s:

*People's Instinctive Travels And The Paths Of Rhythm* (1990)
*The Low End Theory* (1991)
*Midnight Marauders* (1993)
*Beats, Rhymes And Life* (1996)
*The Love Movement* (1998)

## The 11 Best Songs By A Tribe Called Quest:

1. **Award Tour** (*Midnight Marauders*)
2. **Can I Kick It?** (*People's Instinctive Travels And The Paths Of Rhythm*)
3. **Scenario** (*The Low End Theory*)
4. **Electric Relaxation** (*Midnight Marauders*)
5. **Steve Biko (Stir It Up)** (*Midnight Marauders*)
6. **Buggin' Out** (*The Low End Theory*)
7. **Oh My God** (*Midnight Marauders*)
8. **I Left My Wallet In El Segundo** (*People's Instinctive Travels And The Paths Of Rhythm*)
9. **Stressed Out** (*Beats Rhymes & Life*)
10. **Like It Like That** (*The Love Movement*)
11. **Bonita Applebum** (*People's Instinctive Travels And The Paths Of Rhythm*)

**Fun Fact:** Jarobi White, one of the founding members of the group, left after the release of their debut album to pursue a career as a professional chef. Since leaving the group, White has been the head chef at multiple critically acclaimed restaurants in Washington D.C., Atlanta, and New York.

# ALICE IN CHAINS

On July 25, 1992, I crowded into the Hollywood Palladium to see an acoustic concert that included Rage Against The Machine, Blind Melon, Tool, and Porno For Pyros. Because none of those bands were well known yet, everyone in the place was there to see the headliner, Alice In Chains. The band had just released their acoustic EP, *Sap*, so they were exclusively playing acoustic. As we watched the opening acts, we saw Maynard from Tool firing a shotgun at the audience, Perry Farrell prancing on stage, and Teri Nunn from Berlin singing songs that didn't take our breath away. Finally, at 2 AM, Alice In Chains graced the stage. Layne's ethereal voice brought a calmed hush to the crowd. They only played two songs, but at 2 AM, that's all they needed to play. As memorable as the acoustic gig was, it was their show at Irvine's Bren Events Center on April 12, 1993, that defied expectations. In the sweaty venue, the band powered through their songs like an industrial factory grinding out no excuses. I was front and center, a mere arm's length away from Layne's raspy howl. Midway through the show, Layne pulled a fan out of the pit and dragged him on stage. There was a gash on this kid's forehead and blood was streaming down his face like a river. Layne took the kid's hand and thrust it into the air and declared, "This guy bled to see Alice In Chains!" This perfectly encapsulates Alice In Chains' live show in a nutshell. It was loud, angry, unpredictable, and there was a good chance you might go home on a stretcher. It's how we loved it and nothing could keep us away.

# Albums of the '90s:

*Facelift* (1990)

*Sap* (1992)

*Dirt* (1992)

*Jar Of Flies* (1994)

*Alice In Chains* (1995)

*MTV Unplugged* (1996)

# The 11 Best Songs By Alice In Chains:

1.  **Would?** (*Dirt*)
2.  **A Little Bitter** (*Last Action Hero* OST)
3.  **Rooster** (*Dirt*)
4.  **Nutshell** (*Jar Of Flies*)
5.  **Love, Hate, Love** (*Facelift*)
6.  **Sea Of Sorrow** (*Facelift*)
7.  **Man in the Box** (*Facelift*)
8.  **Right Turn** (*Sap*)
9.  **Junkhead** (*Dirt*)
10. **Them Bones** (*Dirt*)
11. **Brother** (*Sap*)

**Fun Fact:** The album, *Dirt*, was recorded during the 1992 L.A. Riots. The band has stated that the chaos and violence they witnessed influenced the attitude of their music during those recording sessions.

**Song Note (Would?):** The song is a tribute to Andrew Wood, the lead singer of the Seattle band, Mother Love Bone. Wood died of an overdose in 1990.

# TORI AMOS

I can trace my favorite bands back to the person who introduced me to them.  Some were introduced by friends; others were from Martha Quinn or LA Weekly.  But, if I had a crush on a girl, that girl could get me to listen to anything.  This is how I discovered Tori Amos.  For this book, I am excluding some real names since I'm not in touch with those people anymore.  For the Tori girl, I mean, where would I even look?  Facebook?  Oh wait, there she is.  That was easy.  Wow, she's married and has kids.  Now it would just be weird if I reached out, so I'm just going to call her K.  K and I met at a party and we bonded over music.  A girl could be a serial killer, but if she liked The Cure and Nirvana, I'd give her a chance.  We liked a lot of the same bands, but K loved Tori Amos. I pretended I was a huge fan, which helped me get a date with her.  This meant I better become the biggest Tori Amos fan by date time.  With more motivation than a mosquito's libido, I hurried to Tower Records.  While I was there, I noticed a "special edition" of Tori's album, *Under The Pink*, which included a second disc of B-sides.  I didn't buy it.  On our date, I told K about the special edition album.  She flipped out.  She had to have it.  So, after dinner, we went to Tower and looked for it, but it was already gone.  K thought I was making it up, which soured our pretty good date and was the reason I didn't get a second one.  Though Tori may sound out of place in the musical angst of the '90s, she sang with as much anguish as any goatee-toting singer from Seattle.  At least my downer date made me a Tori fan.

# Albums of the '90s:

*Crucify* (1992)
*Little Earthquakes* (1992)
*Under The Pink* (1994)
*Boys for Pele* (1996)
*From The Choirgirl Hotel* (1998)
*To Venus And Back* (1999)

# The 11 Best Songs By Tori Amos:

1. **Cornflake Girl** (*Under The Pink*)
2. **Crucify** (*Little Earthquakes*)
3. **Precious Things** (*Little Earthquakes*)
4. **God** (*Under The Pink*)
5. **Past The Mission** (*Under The Pink*)
6. **Raspberry Swirl** (*From The Choirgirl Hotel*)
7. **Muhammad My Friend** (*Boys For Pele*)
8. **Glory Of The 80's** (*To Venus And Back*)
9. **Pretty Good Year** (*Under The Pink*)
10. **Hey Jupiter** (*Boys For Pele*)
11. **Caught A Lite Sneeze** (*Boys For Pele*)

**Fun Fact:** Before Tori went solo, she was the lead singer for a glam band called Y Kant Tori Read, which featured future Guns N' Roses drummer, Matt Sorum.

**Song Note (Past The Mission):** This song features guest background vocals by Trent Reznor of Nine Inch Nails.

# AT THE DRIVE-IN

Without the Backstreet Boys, I would have never discovered At The Drive-In. In 1999, it was all about pop music; boy bands with sexy moves and female sirens who were sweet and innocent. Rock was fading. Listeners were looking for something new, an alternative to the alternative, which brought them back to pop. What was scary about the boy band craze was how it spread through older generations. My friends with whom I had endured sweaty mosh pits were turning up the radio to Backstreet Boys, Britney Spears, *NSYNC, and Christina Aguilera. I resisted the lure of their white veneer teeth smiling like beacons to a Stepford wonderland until it was my friend's birthday and she wanted the new Backstreet Boys album. I hated spending money on that crap, but I wanted to be a good friend. In the CD rack next to the Backstreet Boys album was the album *In/Casino/Out* by At The Drive-In. I grabbed the Backstreet Boys and threw it in my basket with the other CDs I was purchasing. Because I was in a rush, I didn't notice I had grabbed At The Drive-In by mistake until I was in the car. Before returning it, I gave it a quick listen. Thirty seconds in, they were my new favorite band. It was a turbulent tornado of disillusioned aggression. Frenetic screams soared over ghostly melodies offering a cosmic atmosphere of psychedelic revolt amidst punk voltage. Dismayed from having to buy the Backstreet Boys, At The Drive-In had just given me hope that there was still some rock rebellion left in a world being swallowed by the pop maelstrom.

## Albums of the '90s:

*Hell Paso* (1994)

*¡Alfaro Vive, Carajo!* (1995)

*Arcobatic Tenement* (1997)

*El Gran Orgo* (1997)

*In/Casino/Out* (1998)

*Vaya* (1999)

## The 11 Best Songs By At The Drive-In:

1. **Chanbara** (*In/Casino/Out*)
2. **Rascuache** (*Vaya*)
3. **Proxima Centauri** (*Vaya*)
4. **Heliotrope** (*Vaya*)
5. **Alpha Centauri** (*In/Casino/Out*)
6. **Speechless** (*El Gran Orgo*)
7. **Pickpocket** (*In/Casino/Out*)
8. **Porfirio Diaz** (*Acrobatic Tenement*)
9. **Transatlantic Foe** (*In/Casino/Out*)
10. **Fahrenheit** (*El Gran Orgo*)
11. **Bradley Smith** (*¡Alfaro Vive, Carajo!*)

**Fun Fact:** The '80s punk band, Bad Brains, named themselves after a lyric from a Ramones song. As big fans of Bad Brains, the band wanted to do the same. Per a suggestion from guitarist Jim Ward, they decided to name the band At The Drive-In, based on a lyric in the Poison song, "Talk Dirty to Me."

# BAD RELIGION

It was a gift to work in radio in the '90s in Los Angeles. Every band came through L.A. to play and I had access to see all of the shows for free. Sometimes, I was lucky enough to get backstage passes. There's nothing cooler for a college kid than to go to a live show and hang out backstage. My most memorable concert experience was seeing Bad Religion in the spring of 1998. A little-known fact: not only was lead singer, Greg Graffin, a professor at UCLA, but he had also been a DJ at our campus radio station. Graffin had a soft spot for our staff and invited our general manager and me to come to their show at the Roxy to watch their soundcheck. With beers in hand, the GM and I watched Bad Religion rip through a blistering mini-seven-song sound check. Bad Religion had just treated us to our own private concert. It gets even better. After the soundcheck, the band invited us to the dressing room where we hung out with them and just chilled until it was time for them to take the stage. To end our night, we still had the full concert to experience. It's one thing to watch the band at our own private show, but to see them transform a packed crowd into a rhythmic pulsating wave of energy is something to experience. Bad Religion could motivate a crowd unlike anyone else. Diving into that crowd, which was bred from pure animal aggression, made you feel like you were a part of the music. While grunge brought mosh pits mainstreams, Bad Religion had already perfected them. In so many ways, this night was stranger than fiction, but at its core, it was just a punk rock show.

# Albums of the '90s:

*Against The Grain* (1990)

*Generator* (1992)

*Recipe For Hate* (1993)

*Stranger Than Fiction* (1994)

*The Gray Race* (1996)

*No Substance* (1998)

# The 11 Best Songs By Bad Religion:

1. **American Jesus** (*Recipe For Hate*)
2. **Better Off Dead** (*Stranger Than Fiction*)
3. **A Walk** (*The Gray Race*)
4. **Stranger Than Fiction** (*Stranger Than Fiction*)
5. **Tiny Voices** (*Stranger Than Fiction*)
6. **In So Many Ways** (*No Substance*)
7. **Punk Rock Song** (*The Gray Race*)
8. **The Handshake** (*Stranger Than Fiction*)
9. **Recipe For Hate** (*Recipe For Hate*)
10. **Anesthesia** (*Against The Grain*)
11. **21st Century (Digital Boy)** (*Against The Grain*)

**Fun Fact:** Pearl Jam's Eddie Vedder sings background vocals on the album, *Recipe For Hate*.

**Song Note (American Jesus):** The song is a response to President George H.W. Bush's comment that the U.S. would win a war in the middle east because they had God on their side.

# BEASTIE BOYS

After their smash debut album, *License To Ill*, the expectations for the Beastie Boys sophomore release were higher than Snoop Dogg at a Cypress Hill concert. When their second album, *Paul's Boutique* came out, no one liked it. Critics hated it. Radio refused to play it. MTV barely touched it. Even though many fans appreciated it, due to the lack of album sales, the Beasties looked to be a one-album wonder. In the spring of 1992, Beastie Boys returned with their third album, *Check Your Head,* and proved everyone wrong. When I first heard Beastie Boys' fuzz-drenched third album, I was uncertain about it. *This is the Beastie Boys?* It took a few listens, but by the end of the week, I was hooked. *This is the Beastie Boys!* I wasn't the only one to embrace the new sound; the affinity for the album spread like peanut butter. *Check Your Head* became the official anthem for every party during my college years. Frat parties blasted it from the rooftops, film school snobs played it while comparing Tarantino to Kubrick, once I even heard it at a cocktail party for the school chancellor. It was our cultural anthem, our mantra, our vibe of life. This album was such an early '90s mainstay, when their follow-up, *Ill Communications*, came out two years later, *Check Your Head* was still the preferred choice. What *Check Your Head* exemplifies is Beastie Boys' ability to evolve and reinvent themselves, to not follow trends but to create them. No longer were they fighting for their right to party, they were the party.

# Albums of the '90s:

*Check Your Head* (1992)

*Ill Communication* (1994)

*Aglio e Olio* (1995)

*The In Sound From The Way Out!* (1996)

*Hello Nasty* (1998)

*Country Mike's Greatest Hits* (1999)

# The 11 Best Songs By Beastie Boys:

1. **Sabotage** (*Ill Communication*)
2. **So What'Cha Want** (*Check Your Head*)
3. **Intergalactic** (*Hello Nasty*)
4. **Gratitude** (*Check Your Head*)
5. **Sure Shot** (*Ill Communication*)
6. **Get It Together** (*Ill Communication*)
7. **Body Movin'** (*Hello Nasty*)
8. **Jimmy James** (*Check Your Head*)
9. **The Negotiation Limerick File** (*Hello Nasty*)
10. **Pass the Mic** (*Check Your Head*)
11. **Finger Lickin' Good** (*Check Your Head*)

**Fun Fact:** In 1999, Beastie Boys recorded a full-length country album, entitled *Country Mike's Greatest Hits*. It was only distributed to friends and family and is incredibly rare to find. (Of course, I have a copy)

# BECK

I always wanted to start my own record label. Except for the lack of contacts, access to distribution, and money, I might have done it. I came close, oddly. While the '80s had the mixtape, the '90s had the burned CD. What sets the burned CD apart is that it sounded like an actual album rather than a cut and paste job. In making my own burned CDs, I felt like I was making official albums. I used to take all the B-sides and non-album tracks from one band and compile them into a fictional album. I would name the albums and even design artwork. I made dozens of these rare track CDs. I made a CD for Nirvana called "Seattle," one for Weezer called "The Orange Album," and one for Nine Inch Nails called "Misunderstood." When it came to Beck, his collection of extra tracks exceeded one CD, forcing me to create three CDs, called "Weird," "Not Weird" and "Really Weird." At the time, Napster had exploded all over our computers with file sharing. I uploaded my fictional albums to Napster's cloud to share. Over time, people found these fake albums and downloaded them. My bootleg albums had slipped into the internet and were being traded. Months later, I was at a friend's party. He was playing my fake Beck album, *Weird*. I asked him where he got it. He smirked and said he got it from his buddy who worked in the music industry, claiming it was an unreleased Beck project. I smiled. I didn't tell him my connection to the album because knowing that I had created a musical entity that was out there as part of the wider musical universe was all the reward I needed.

# Albums of the '90s:

*Golden Feelings* (1993)

*Stereopathetic Soulmanure* (1994)

*Mellow Gold* (1994)

*One Foot In The Grave* (1994)

*Odelay* (1996)

*Mutations* (1998)

*Midnite Vultures* (1999)

# The 11 Best Songs By Beck:

1. **Jack-Ass** (*Odelay*)
2. **Sexx Laws** (*Midnite Vultures*)
3. **Mixed Bizness** (*Midnite Vultures*)
4. **One of These Days** (*Cold Brains* single)
5. **Where It's At** (*Odelay*)
6. **Debra** (*Midnite Vultures*)
7. **Dead Melodies** (*Mutations*)
8. **Asshole** (*One Foot In The Grave*)
9. **Loser** (*Mellow Gold*)
10. **Nicotine & Gravy** (*Midnite Vultures*)
11. **Sissyneck** (*Odelay*)

**Fun Fact:** When Beck signed to Geffen records, he made sure his deal allowed him to work with other record labels where he could release his non-commercial and experimental music.

# BELLE AND SEBASTIAN

Nothing compares to March Madness. In college, collegiate sports are your world. They're a part of you. The players went to class with you, lived in the same dorms, and ate at the same cafeteria as you did. They were your classmates, your friends. Watching your friends come back from an 11-point deficit to upset a ranked team is a completely unique thrill. As a UCLA fan, I grew accustomed to that thrill, but one time I got to experience it through the eyes of another school. During spring break 1997, I went to Berkeley to visit my friend Melissa (the Tribe Called Quest road trip). When I arrived, I learned that our plans for the next day revolved around Cal's basketball game in the 2nd round of the NCAA tournament. Since it was only Cal's second chance to reach the Sweet Sixteen in 37 years, she was not missing it. The night before the game, we caught up, drank cheap wine, and listened to Belle and Sebastian. Being a young adult without a care in the world, Belle and Sebastian's music spoke to this moment in my life. The music had uncertainty, but it also had hope. The next day, I went CD shopping and bought the Belle and Sebastian album with the red cover. I met up with Melissa at halftime to watch the rest of the game. Cal would win the game and reach the Sweet Sixteen, which caused utter jubilation around town. Even though I was from UCLA, I couldn't help but get swept up in the emotion. Seeing other people with a collective smile on their faces was unexpected bliss. Like Belle and Sebastian, college sports speak to youth that the future holds endless possibilities.

## Albums of the '90s:

*Tigermilk* (1996)
*If You're Feeling Sinister* (1996)
*Dog On Wheels* (1997)
*Lazy Line Painter Jane* (1997)
*3...6...9 Seconds Of Light* (1997)
*The Boy With The Arab Strap* (1998)
*This Is Just A Modern Rock Song* (1998)

## The 11 Best Songs By Belle & Sebastian:

1. **If You're Feeling Sinister** (*If You're Feeling Sinister*)
2. **The Boy With The Arab Strap** (*The Boy With The Arab Strap*)
3. **Seeing Other People** (*If You're Feeling Sinister*)
4. **Sleep The Clock Around** (*The Boy With The Arab Strap*)
5. **Get Me Away From Here, I'm Dying** (*If You're Feeling Sinister*)
6. **Like Dylan In The Movies** (*If You're Feeling Sinister*)
7. **Dirty Dream Number Two** (*The Boy With The Arab Strap*)
8. **This Is Just A Modern Rock Song** (*This Is Just A Modern Rock Song*)
9. **A Century Of Fakers** (*3...6...9 Seconds Of Light*)
10. **My Wandering Days Are Over** (*Tigermilk*)
11. **Me And The Major** (*If You're Feeling Sinister*)

**Fun Fact:** Lead singer Stuart Murdoch was diagnosed with Myalgic Encephalomyelitis, commonly known as chronic fatigue syndrome. Stuart used music to cope with his pain by writing songs that led him to form Belle And Sebastian.

# BIKINI KILL

There is little debate that Nirvana and their song, "Smells Like Teen Spirit" had a significant impact on the '90s, but did you know that Bikini Kill is the reason why? In the '90s, Seattle was a beacon for musicians seeking something other than the glossy pop or hairy metal of the '80s. Seattle offered an open-source platform for artists to be creative without adhering to MTV standards. I had friends who moved to the city to join this growing movement, who I visited regularly. I loved Seattle. It was a big city with the feel of a small town. There were no attitudes, no egos, and honestly, no angst. It was a community of acceptance. No matter how weird you were, you always fit in. As much as I loved the city, I was there because of the music. Where did Alice In Chains hang out? Where was Pearl Jam's rehearsal space? And the big one, where was Kurt Cobain's old apartment? Turns out, it wasn't in Seattle but Olympia, an hour south of the city. I still went. While Kurt was living there, he dated Tobi Vail, drummer of Bikini Kill, and often hung out with the band. One night, Bikini Kill singer, Kathleen Hanna wrote "Kurt smells like teen spirit" on his apartment wall. This spontaneous graffiti message written in a drunken haze would inspire Kurt to pen the decade's anthem. Bikini Kill was a pivotal influence in founding riot grrl rock, but it's this creative improvisation that truly changed the world. I stood outside the modest house and appreciated what had happened there. It was the most boring activity I did in Seattle, but it's the one I remember the most.

## Albums of the '90s:

*Revolution Girl Style Now!* (1991)
*Bikini Kill* (1992)
*Pussy Whipped* (1993)
*Yeah Yeah Yeah Yeah* (1993)
*Reject All American* (1996)
*The Singles* (1998)

## The 11 Best Songs By Bikini Kill:

1. **Carnival** (*Revolution Girl Style Now!*)
2. **Rebel Girl** (*Yeah Yeah Yeah Yeah*)
3. **Finale** (*Reject All American*)
4. **This Is Not A Test** (*Revolution Girl Style Now!*)
5. **Demirep** (*The Singles*)
6. **Reject All American** (*Reject All American*)
7. **Magnet** (*Pussy Whipped*)
8. **I Like Fucking** (*The Singles*)
9. **Jigsaw Youth** (*Yeah Yeah Yeah Yeah*)
10. **Jet Ski** (*Reject All American*)
11. **Anti-Pleasure Dissertation** (*The Singles*)

**Fun Fact:** Drummer Tobi Vail started a feminist zine called Jigsaw that focused on promoting girl bands while emphasizing feminist issues. Her zine has since been archived by Harvard university as a resource for research into counterculture.

# BJÖRK

Before YouTube, before TikTok, MTV ruled all. While the music of the '90s defined us, music videos were how we expressed ourselves. We danced the vogue, got jiggy at Al's Diner, and partied like it was 1979. We spoke out in class, our teen spirit erupted during prep rallies, and we overtook our high school hallways with perfectly choreographed flash mobs more than one time. We knew every bump on Sinead O'Connor's head, how big Billie Joe Armstrong's eyes could bulge, and how many push-ups Mark Wahlberg's biceps could do. Bee girls fluttered, waterfalls were chased, silence was enjoyed, and every day was a good day, even in the cold November rain. One artist truly mastered the music video: Björk. Whether Björk was a truck driving maniac in the nightmarish "Army of Me" or a little lost imp in a hellish forest in "Human Behavior," her mischievous elfish persona elevated the ground-breaking imagery in her videos. From the 8-bit dreams of "Hyperballad" to the android uprising in "All Is Full of Love," Björk's videos exposed digital power not just as a bright vision of tomorrow but an omen of our inevitable unraveling. Not every Björk video was ripe with existential terror; "It's Oh So Quiet" is a colorful blast of musical theater that would make Rodgers and Hammerstein bell kick. And "Big Time Sensuality" finds Björk expressing her innocent adorableness as she playfully dances her heart out on the back of a truck. While some MTV videos left us bittersweet or feeling like criminals, Björk's videos were such a ray of light, even Alicia Silverstone stopped cryin'.

## Albums of the '90s:

*Debut* (1993)
*Post* (1995)
*Homogenic* (1997)

## The 11 Best Songs By Björk:

1. **Hyperballad** (*Post*)
2. **Jóga** (*Homogenic*)
3. **Hunter** (*Homogenic*)
4. **Isobel** (*Post*)
5. **Human Behavior** (*Debut*)
6. **Possibly Maybe** (*Post*)
7. **Violently Happy** (*Debut*)
8. **Alarm Call** (*Homogenic*)
9. **Venus As a Boy** (*Debut*)
10. **Unravel** (*Homogenic*)
11. **It's Oh So Quiet** (*Post*)

**Fun Fact:** Film directors Michael Gondry (*Eternal Sunshine of the Spotless Mind*) and Spike Jonze (*Being John Malkovich*), along with fashion designer Alexander McQueen, were some of the people Björk enlisted to direct her videos.

# THE BLACK CROWES

In December 1994, I was a senior at UCLA, and I was heavy into study mode for my upcoming finals week. At about 7 PM on December 10th, my girlfriend called me from a payphone in Hollywood. She told me that she was standing outside the Whisky A Go Go and had two tickets to that night's secret Black Crowes concert. The show was in one hour and I had to come immediately. She left me with the choice of either doing the responsible thing or racing into Hollywood and seeing one of the biggest rock bands in the world in a tiny club that held fewer people than my history lecture halls. I wasn't stupid. I quickly threw on clothes, hopped in my car, and hurried up Sunset Blvd. I literally arrived at the venue within a minute of the doors opening. My girlfriend beamed with the biggest smile when I arrived. After packing into the Whisky, for the next two hours, we stood five feet from the band as they jammed through a tight set of their most iconic songs. The Black Crowes were the only mainstream rock band to survive in a world dominated by grunge rock, gangsta rap, and Axl Rose's ego. They represented the last in a lineage of true-blooded American rock, the groovy, guitar-driven, BBQ-eating, truck-driving, rock 'n' roll that built America. They were like watching Zeppelin, the Eagles, and CCR all rolled into one big fat joint. Seeing them at the Whisky was like being transported back to the golden era of the Sunset Strip when the Byrds swung and Jim Morrison wailed. It is one of the best shows I've ever seen, and I still aced all my finals.

## Albums of the '90s:

*Shake Your Money Maker* (1990)
*The Southern Harmony And Musical Companion* (1992)
*Amorica* (1994)
*Three Snakes And One Charm* (1996)
*By Your Side* (1999)

## The 11 Best Songs By The Black Crowes:

1. **Remedy** (*The Southern Harmony And Musical Companion*)
2. **Jealous Again** (*Shake Your Money Maker*)
3. **Hard To Handle** (*Shake Your Money Maker*)
4. **Wiser Time** (*Amorica*)
5. **Hotel Illness** (*The Southern Harmony And Musical Companion*)
6. **Seeing Things** (*Shake Your Money Maker*)
7. **She Gave Good Sunflower** (*Amorica*)
8. **She Talks To Angels** (*Shake Your Money Maker*)
9. **Sister Luck** (*Shake Your Money Maker*)
10. **Girl From A Pawnshop** (*Three Snakes And One Charm*)
11. **Descending** (*Amorica*)

**Fun Fact:** The cover of their 1994 album *Amorica* showed a close-up of a woman's red, white, and blue bikini bottom with exposed pubic hair. The photo was taken from the cover of the Bicentennial issue of Hustler magazine. The record company airbrushed the cover to get rid of the hair after many stores refused to display it.

# BLIND MELON

In the fall of 1995, I was driving home from my internship at James Cameron's Lightstorm Entertainment. The company had just released its underwhelming film, *Strange Days*. The tepid response to the film wasn't holding the company back as they had already begun prep on their next movie about a gigantic boat. Yes, that movie. I was listening to L.A.'s prominent alternative rock radio station, 106.7 KROQ. KROQ was literally the most important American radio station in the late '80s/early '90s. For every alternative song that would be a hit during that era, KROQ played it first, months before you knew it existed. I was listening to a Blind Melon block when the DJ revealed that singer Shannon Hoon had tragically died of an overdose. What affected me most wasn't the death itself but the lack of compassion for it. Within weeks, Blind Melon was an afterthought, a one-hit-wonder, a '90s footnote. The band's most popular song was a kitschy, twangy ditty known as "No Rain." Its music video featured the infamous Bee Girl, a little girl dressed in a bee costume. As much as the Bee Girl was the band's calling card, she was also their scarlet letter. While "No Rain" was pop radio candy, it by no means represented the rest of the band's Southern rock-inspired Skynyrd-ology. The band had just released their matured album, *Soup*, to lukewarm reviews. Initially a failure, years later, the album would find cult status as an underappreciated '90s gem, leaving us to merely wonder what Blind Melon's future could have sounded like.

# Albums of the '90s:

*Blind Melon* (1992)
*Soup* (1995)
*Nico* (1996)

# The 11 Best Songs By Blind Melon:

1. **Galaxie** (*Soup*)
2. **Change** (*Blind Melon*)
3. **Walk** (*Soup*)
4. **Soul One** (*Nico*)
5. **Deserted** (*Blind Melon*)
6. **Candy Says** (*Change* single B-side)
7. **Mouthful Of Cavities** (*Soup*)
8. **I Wonder** (*Blind Melon*)
9. **Pull** (*Nico*)
10. **Soak The Sin** (*Blind Melon*)
11. **Soup** (*Nico*)

**Fun Fact:** Frontman Shannon Hoon was childhood friends with Axl Rose. Hoon was invited by Guns N' Roses to sing back-up on the song, "Don't Cry," and can be seen performing alongside the band in the song's music video.

# BLUR

It was December 31st, 1999. It wasn't just the end of the decade or the century; it was the end of the millennium. It was the biggest New Year's Eve in a thousand years. I had to do something huge. I decided to meet my friend Elton in London. We planned to celebrate the momentous event by standing along the river Thames, watching the clock on Big Ben hit midnight. We weren't the only ones who had that idea. There were over a million people there who wanted the same experience. For hours, we stood in the pouring rain with people singing and dancing, splashing mud and letting go of a thousand years of inhibitions. There was a small fear circulating that all the computers in the world would instantly crash at midnight, in an event dubbed Y2K. But all those anxieties were erased when the chimes of Big Ben rang with a resounding bellow. The entire city let out a giant roar that lasted all night. In the melee celebration, I was separated from my friends. Alone in London, I found my way to a tent where a DJ was playing club music. I stood by watching the dancing youths when I was approached by a quirky girl in vintage glasses. She told me no one should be alone at the start of a new era and she would stay with me until I found my friends. We talked and talked...and danced. When I finally spotted my friends, I asked her to come with us. She smiled and said she had friends of her own. She gave me a New Year's kiss and headed down the street. She never gave me her name, but I will always remember she was wearing blue jeans and a Blur T-shirt.

# Albums of the '90s:

*Leisure* (1991)

*Modern Life Is Rubbish* (1993)

*Parklife* (1994)

*The Great Escape* (1995)

*Blur* (1997)

*13* (1999)

# The 11 Best Songs By Blur:

1. **Blue Jeans** (*Modern Life Is Rubbish*)
2. **Song 2** (*Blur*)
3. **Coffee And TV** (*13*)
4. **Girls And Boys** (*Parklife*)
5. **Trimm Trabb** (*13*)
6. **Sing** (*Leisure*)
7. **Trouble In The Message Centre** (*Parklife*)
8. **Look Inside America** (*Blur*)
9. **This Is A Low** (*Parklife*)
10. **For Tomorrow** (*Modern Life Is Rubbish*)
11. **Beetlebum** (*Blur*)

**Fun Fact:** Bassist Alex James has become a reputable cheesemaker in his spare time. He has a 200-acre farm in Oxfordshire that produces many kinds of cheese, including one named "Blue Monday" after the New Order song.

# DAVID BOWIE

I didn't listen to David Bowie in the '90s because he was, well, old. Okay, he wasn't that old. At the time I'm writing this book, I am the same age as Bowie was in the '90s. I know I'm not hip, but I also know I'm not old. But in college, Bowie's midlife music didn't relate to me. Or so I thought. One of my roommates was a massive Bowie fan. He claimed that Bowie was the most influential artist to '90s music and spent every day trying to convince me. He pointed to Marilyn Manson's album *Mechanical Animals* (which was an homage to Bowie) and Nirvana's iconic performance of Bowie's "Man Who Sold The World" on *MTV Unplugged* as evidence. He wasn't just an obsessed fan; he was also a collector who owned every Bowie release in every format. Vinyl? Yes. Cassette? Yes? MiniDisc? 8-track? Reel to reel? Yes, yes, yes. Via the UCLA radio station, I had access to promotional material. Bowie wasn't popular among my station staff, so I passed on any radio single or promo we had to him. Until one day, he gave me back a CD. It was Trent Reznor's remix of Bowie's "I'm Afraid Of Americans." My friend demanded I listen to it. It featured both Bowie and Trent screaming in unison like fiendish demon twins. It didn't just sound current; it sounded ahead of the curve. It gave me a reason to revisit Bowie's '90s work, and I discovered my friend was right. Bowie's music was a chameleon, changing with the trends and pushing the boundaries of significance. Bowie deserves his place in '90s culture as much as the artists he influenced.

## Albums of the '90s:

*Black Tie White Noise* (1993)
*The Buddha Of Suburbia* (1993)
*1. Outside* (1995)
*Earthling* (1997)
*Hours* (1999)

## The 11 Best Songs By David Bowie:

1. **Seven** (*Hours*)
2. **Strangers When We Meet** (*The Buddha Of Suburbia*)
3. **Outside** (*1. Outside*)
4. **I'm Deranged** (*1. Outside*)
5. **Dead Against It** (*The Buddha Of Suburbia*)
6. **I'm Afraid Of Americans** (Nine Inch Nails Remix) (*I'm Afraid Of Americans* single B-side)
7. **Jump They Say** (*Black Tie White Noise*)
8. **Untitled No. 1** (*The Buddha Of Suburbia*)
9. **Nite Flights** (*Black Tie White Noise*)
10. **Seven Years In Tibet** (*Earthling*)
11. **Real Cool World** (*Cool World* OST)

**Fun Fact:** To promote the album *Earthling*, Bowie released the song "Telling Lies" as a download from his website. It was the first song ever to be officially released as a downloadable track.

**Song Note (Jump They Say):** The song explores Bowie's feelings when his brother Terry died by suicide in 1985.

# GARTH BROOKS

I was not a Garth Brooks fan. I didn't have anything against him; I just wasn't a fan. Whether I liked him or not, Brooks' music was a part of my college life. I can't think back to a party where someone didn't put on Garth's signature song, "Friends In Low Places." Every single time the song was played, the entire room exploded in a full volume off-key sing-along. To witness a packed apartment of flannel-wearing grunginistas (not sure that's a word) suddenly wrap their arms around each other like a Gen-x cowboy choir, with impromptu Texas accents was something to behold. There's no other song from the decade that invoked such an impulsive karaoke-infected reaction. Garth Brooks dominated the charts until he tested his own limitations. In 1999, Brooks transformed into the fictional rocker Chris Gaines. I was working at Sony Studios when Chris Gaines filmed a live performance at one of the sound stages. Using our studio badges, my co-worker Katie and I snuck into the show. Once in the crowd, we pushed toward the front until we were standing a few feet away from Brooks. I'm sure some fans would have gladly killed Celine Dion to be in my position, so I didn't take it for granted. Watching Brooks thunder across the stage like a midnight cowboy taking his final ride was as rock n' roll as they come. I have far more respect for an artist who is willing to take a risk and fail than one who never takes a risk at all. And though the Chris Gaines experiment flopped, I left the show with nothing but admiration for Brooks, not as a country star but as an artist.

# Albums of the '90s:

*No Fences* (1990)
*Ropin' The Wind* (1991)
*The Chase* (1992)
*In Pieces* (1993)
*Fresh Horses* (1995)
*Sevens* (1997)

# The 11 Best Songs By Garth Brooks:

1. **The Thunder Rolls** (*No Fences*)
2. **The Night I Called the Old Man Out** (*In Pieces*)
3. **That Summer** (*The Chase*)
4. **Face To Face** (*The Chase*)
5. **The Night Will Only Know** (*In Pieces*)
6. **Night Rider's Lament** (*The Chase*)
7. **Victim Of The Game** (*No Fences*)
8. **Burning Bridges** (*Ropin' The Wind*)
9. **Two Of A Kind, Workin' On A Full House** (*No Fences*)
10. **That Ol' Wind** (*Fresh Horses*)
11. **The Beaches Of Cheyenne** (*Fresh Horses*)

**Song Note (The Thunder Rolls):** Brooks originally wrote this song for Tanya Tucker. Tucker recorded the song but never released it. She graciously gave the song back to Brooks so he could record it himself.

# BUILT TO SPILL

Built To Spill was not played on the radio. They were not played on MTV. They didn't headline Lollapalooza. They weren't featured on any magazine covers. They were elusive. The only way to find out about Built To Spill was through word of mouth. And word of mouth about the band spread like Forrest Gump going for a jog. The band had its own mythology. Unless you saw them in concert, you didn't even know what they looked like. In the spring of 1997, they were touring in support of their album, *Perfect From Now On*. I had backstage passes to the show at the Troubadour and was eager to meet singer Doug Martsch. I was already in the VIP area when Martsch arrived. He slid in the room like a Deadhead vagabond, scruffy beard, T-shirt, and sporting a backpack. I tried to pierce the crowd of people surrounding him, but the band had to go on stage and my chance to meet Doug went with it. Or so I thought. The next day, Built To Spill played a free show at UCLA. Because I worked for the radio station, I could stand on the side of the stage to watch the performance. Having just seen them, I was blown away by how this free show was just as good as the Troubadour show. After the band finished, Doug left the stage and walked past me. Then, he stopped. He turned around and looked at me and said, "Weren't you at the show last night?" I stumbled through my words; I think I said yes, but who the hell knows. Doug smiled and said, "Thanks for coming out again," then walked away. We never officially met, but Doug Martsch recognized me, and that is out of site.

# Albums of the '90s:

*Ultimate Alternative Wavers* (1993)
*There's Nothing Wrong With Love* (1994)
*The Normal Years* (1994)
*Perfect From Now On* (1997)
*Keep It Like A Secret* (1999)

# The 11 Best Songs By Built To Spill:

1. **Car** (*There's Nothing Wrong With Love*)
2. **Carry The Zero** (*Keep It Like A Secret*)
3. **Big Dipper** (*There's Nothing Wrong With Love*)
4. **Out Of Site** (*Perfect From Now On*)
5. **Made-Up Dreams** (*Perfect From Now On*)
6. **Else** (*Keep It Like A Secret*)
7. **Broken Chairs** (*Keep It Like A Secret*)
8. **You Were Right** (*Keep It Like A Secret*)
9. **Stab** (*There's Nothing Wrong With Love*)
10. **Nowhere Nothin' Fuckup** (*Ultimate Alternative Wavers*)
11. **Stop The Show** (*Perfect From Now On*)

**Fun Fact:** Built to Spill has found some of their most loyal fans, surprisingly, in the world of skateboarding. Because of that, they license their music for use in skate, snowboard, and surf videos for free.

# CAKE

My favorite story about seeing Cake in concert has nothing to do with Cake. I went with a group of friends to see their show. These jive-talking cowboys dominated the audience like a hyper-focused bull rider fighting for his eight seconds. They charged out of the gates, powered through their songs with such an explosive jolt that the entire audience rocked back on their heels like they were being bucked in the face from the sonic thrusts. We left the show too amped up to go home, so we went to grab a bite at a diner called Swingers. Swingers emerged in the '90s as the rock star-encrusted version of Denny's, a late-night cafe that catered to the denizens of Hollywood. On any given night, you could find yourself a couple of booths away from the Red Hot Chili Peppers, Jakob Dylan, or Beck. On this night, my friends and I sat at an open table next to a couple. Within seconds of sitting down, we noticed that we were sitting next to Simon Le Bon, singer of Duran Duran. My friend sitting next to him was the only one who didn't notice. We tried to quietly inform her, but she didn't believe us. Her response was an inappropriately loud, "That is not Simon Le Bon." Simon was ever charming and admitted he was, in fact, who we thought he was. We spent the rest of the meal talking with him. Simon was so nice he even shared his eggs with us because he said they were the best thing on the menu, going so far as to scrape his food on to our plates to prove it. Truthfully, the eggs were pretty good. Moral of the story, you *can* have your cake and eat Simon Le Bon's eggs, too.

# Albums of the '90s:

*Motorcade Of Generosity* (1994)
*Fashion Nugget* (1996)
*Prolonging The Magic* (1998)

# The 11 Best Songs By Cake:

1. **I Will Survive** (*Fashion Nugget*)
2. **Never There** (*Prolonging The Magic*)
3. **Frank Sinatra** (*Fashion Nugget*)
4. **Let Me Go** (*Prolonging The Magic*)
5. **Friend Is A Four Letter Word** (*Fashion Nugget*)
6. **Rock 'N' Roll Lifestyle** (*Motorcade Of Generosity*)
7. **The Distance** (*Fashion Nugget*)
8. **Never, Never Gonna Give You Up** (*Friend Is A Four Letter Word* single B-side)
9. **Satan Is My Motor** (*Prolonging The Magic*)
10. **Up So Close** (*Motorcade Of Generosity*)
11. **Mexico** (*Prolonging The Magic*)

**Fun Fact:** The band's name Cake comes from the verb cake and not the dessert. According to the band, it is in reference to the moment when something becomes part of your life that you can't get rid of, like gum on the bottom of your shoe.

**Song Note (I Will Survive):** Gloria Gaynor detested Cake's version of her song. She didn't like that they changed the lyrics to make it more profane.

# THE CARDIGANS

I could tell a lot about a person by the CDs they owned, especially the ones they kept in their car. Trust me, I judged. When I would get into someone's car, I would immediately analyze their CDs. If they had Dave Matthews, Spin Doctors, and Seal, they probably listened to a lot of mainstream radio. If they had Pavement, Dinosaur Jr., and the Stone Roses, they were deep in the indie rock scene. Once, I got in a car, and the driver had Pantera, LeAnn Rimes, and Shaggy. I didn't know what to think except I really needed to get out of that car. I was out with a friend one night in Hollywood when we met two girls. After spending some time with them, we split off. My friend drove one girl home while I grabbed a ride with the other one. The first CD I noticed in this girl's car was the Cardigans album, *The First Band On The Moon*. Coincidentally, I had just purchased that album, which immediately instigated an epic discussion about music that could only be finished over Matzo Ball soup at Canter's Deli. It turns out we had identical tastes in music and had been to many of the same concerts. With no desire for our marathon discussion to end, we opted to go back to my place. Then, something terrible happened. On the way home, she changed CDs and put on the 4 Non Blondes, my least favorite band of all time. I knew I could never respect the musical taste of anyone who listened to the 4 Non Blondes. We arrived at my place, I said good-bye, hopped out of her car, and never saw her again. We should have kept listening to the Cardigans.

## Albums of the '90s:

*Emmerdale* (1994)
*Life* (1995)
*First Band On The Moon* (1996)
*The Other Side Of The Moon* (1997)
*Gran Turismo* (1998)

## The 11 Best Songs By The Cardigans:

1. **My Favourite Game** (*Gran Turismo*)
2. **Lovefool** (*First Band On The Moon*)
3. **Erase/Rewind** (*Gran Turismo*)
4. **Fine** (*Life*)
5. **Sick & Tired** (*Emmerdale*)
6. **Daddy's Car** (*Life*)
7. **Never Recover** (*First Band On The Moon*)
8. **Starter** (*Gran Turismo*)
9. **Been It** (*First Band On The Moon*)
10. **Celia Inside** (*Life*)
11. **Your New Cuckoo** (*First Band On The Moon*)

**Fun Fact:** Lead singer Nina Persson had never sung before in her life when she was asked to be the frontwoman of The Cardigans.

**Song Note (My Favourite Game):** The Cardigans are gamers. So much so, that they named their album, *Gran Turismo* after the video game of the same name. This song plays at the opening of *Gran Turismo 2*.

# THE CHEMICAL BROTHERS

It was May 10, 1997. The Chemical Brothers were a mere 15 minutes into their set when the power of their rockin' beats blew the building's main electrical fuse, plunging the entire venue into absolute darkness. The true proving ground of the '90s musical landscape was the ability to put on an amazing live show. When I heard raves about the Chemical Brothers live, I was shocked. There was no way that two guys pushing buttons could be on the same tier as Cobain's scream, Cornell's wailing guitars, or Rage Against The Machine's pure unbridled aggression. I had to know what the hype was all about, so my friend Heba bought us tickets to their LA show at the Shrine Expo. When I saw booths selling glow-in-dark plastic crap, I felt my expectations crumble, fearing rave culture was being commercialized. Once the band arrived on stage, my assumptions turned to dust. The music was an avalanche of vibrations that rained down over my entire body. I danced, and I *don't* dance. It bordered on orgasmic. And just like with anything too exciting, there's a risk of a premature explosion. That's when the Chemical Brothers blew a fuse and the electricity in the entire hall went out. Here's the crazy part, the audience didn't freak out. Instead, they screamed in rhythm, clapping, and stomping. The audience was keeping the music going. The lights eventually came back on, and without losing a beat, the band dropped right back into the song. I left that night completely convinced. Who knew pushing buttons could be so out of control?

## Albums of the '90s:

*My Mercury Mouth* (1994)

*Exit Planet Dust* (1995)

*Dig Your Own Hole* (1997)

*Surrender* (1999)

## The 11 Best Songs By The Chemical Brothers:

1. **Leave Home** (*Exit Planet Dust*)
2. **In Dust We Trust** (*Exit Planet Dust*)
3. **Loops Of Fury** (*Wipeout 2097* OST)
4. **Out of Control** (*Surrender*)
5. **Block Rockin' Beats** (*Dig Your Own Hole*)
6. **One Too Many Mornings** (*Exit Planet Dust*)
7. **If You Kling To Me I'll Klong To You** (*My Mercury Mouth*)
8. **Got Glint?** (*Surrender*)
9. **Life Is Sweet** (*Exit Planet Dust*)
10. **Music: Response** (*Surrender*)
11. **The Private Psychedelic Reel** (*Dig Your Own Hole*)

**Fun Fact:** Though they are not brothers, they originally called themselves the Dust Brothers after the American producing team. The real Dust Brothers didn't appreciate the homage and asked them to change their name. They chose Chemical Brothers after their song, "Chemical Beats."

**Song Note (Out of Control):** The song was co-written by New Order's Bernard Sumner, who also provides guest vocals alongside Primal Scream's Bobby Gillespie.

# THE CRANBERRIES

When the Cranberries' debut album was released, I was in the thick of my hard rock phase. The Cranberries' hit song "Linger" was, well, let's face it...*girlie*. Even though I adored many female rockers, I was still young and very insecure. Let me explain. Remember, the context of time changes the meaning of a word. While the term "girlie" in the 2020s reeks of toxicity, that's not exactly what it meant back then. Nor was it a stab at feminism. It was about insecurity. The greatest blow to a man's ego is to feel like he's not a "man," that he's not mature. The term *girlie* wasn't an insult accusing someone of being "like a woman," it's accusing that person of being like a child, of being immature. For a guy, your ego is more fragile than a papier-mâché eggshell, so putting that ego on the line for a soft rock Irish folk band...it felt like a gamble. It wasn't until the Cranberries put out their grizzly battle cry called "Zombie" that I did an about-face. As ass-backward as this was, it was the Cranberries that helped tear down the stigma that floated around female-led rock bands. Singer Delores O'Riordan's voice dominated like a Gothic valkyrie blaring an ear-splitting battle cry as she shredded through a Norse war field beheading her enemies. As the Cranberries popularity continued to grow, I realized that listening to female rock bands wasn't girlie at all. Women had just as much pent up anger and frustrations as men. Listening to the Cranberries didn't make me girlie; it was thinking that it did that was the real sign of immaturity.

## Albums of the '90s:

*Everybody Else Is Doing It, So Why Can't We?* (1992)
*No Need To Argue* (1994)
*To The Faithful Departed* (1996)
*Bury The Hatchet* (1999)

## The 11 Best Songs By The Cranberries:

1. **Zombie** (*No Need To Argue*)
2. **Promises** (*Bury The Hatchet*)
3. **Animal Instinct** (*Bury The Hatchet*)
4. **I Can't Be With You** (*No Need To Argue*)
5. **Dreams** (*Everybody Else Is Doing It, So Why Can't We?*)
6. **Ode To My Family** (*No Need To Argue*)
7. **Forever Yellow Skies** (*To The Faithful Departed*)
8. **Ridiculous Thoughts** (*No Need To Argue*)
9. **How** (*Everybody Else Is Doing It, So Why Can't We?*)
10. **I Just Shot John Lennon** (*To The Faithful Departed*)
11. **Delilah** (*Bury The Hatchet*)

**Fun Fact:** The album cover for *Bury The Hatchet* is by Storm Thorgerson, who has produced iconic album covers for Led Zeppelin's *House Of The Holy* and Pink Floyd's *Dark Side Of The Moon.*

**Song Note (Zombie):** The song is in reference to an IRA (Irish Republican Army) bombing that killed two children.

# CYPRESS HILL

I had a dilemma. I was hosting my first dorm party and I wanted to make an impression on my new friends but I needed Cypress Hill to do that. In 1991, the wicked crunch of Cypress Hill's hip-hop fiesta serenaded our world. Rooted in proud Latino culture, Cypress Hill was gritty, tumultuous, and filled with phuncky energy. They came from a few steps over the wrong side of the tracks, which was just enough that you felt like you were doing something wrong, but inclusive enough that you felt like you belonged. Cypress Hill wasn't family-friendly like Paula Abdul dancing with a cartoon kat. They were too raunchy for radio and too edgy for MTV. If you walked into a record store, the "hot release" rack was filled with Mariah Carey, Natalie Cole, and Garth Brooks. Cypress Hill was not on the rack, and in most stores, they weren't on any rack at all. This happened to me. I told my friends I had the album and would be playing it at the party. But that was a lie. I didn't have it. I naively thought I could buy it the day of. Only, when I went to Westwood to purchase it, no store carried it. I panicked. I could try Tower Records on Sunset, which was notorious for having every album ever released but I didn't have a car. So, I had to take a city bus there. Thankfully, my luck changed. Due to its popularity, Tower Records had a stash of Cypress Hill CDs behind the counter. I made my purchase and hurried home. That night, my party was so insane the dorm monitors shut it down, which in college terms means it was "hella fly." I owe it all to Cypress Hill.

## Albums of the '90s:

*Cypress Hill* (1991)

*Black Sunday* (1993)

*Cypress Hill: Temples Of Boom* (1995)

*Cypress Hill IV* (1998)

## The 11 Best Songs By Cypress Hill:

1.  **How I Could Just Kill A Man** (*Cypress Hill*)
2.  **Insane In The Brain** (*Black Sunday*)
3.  **Hand On The Pump** (*Cypress Hill*)
4.  **The Funky Cypress Hill Shit** (*Cypress Hill*)
5.  **Break 'Em Off Some** (*Black Sunday*)
6.  **Hole In The Head** (*Cypress Hill*)
7.  **Boom Biddy Bye Bye** (*Cypress Hill III: Temples Of Boom*)
8.  **When The Shit Goes Down** (*Black Sunday*)
9.  **Clash of The Titans/Dust** (*Cypress Hill IV*)
10. **The Phuncky Feel One** (*Cypress Hill*)
11. **Psycobetabuckdown** (*Cypress Hill*)

**Fun Fact:** During their 1993 performance on Saturday Night Live, the band smoked marijuana on stage then proceeded to trash their instruments. Because of this, they have been banned from performing on the show ever again.

**Fun Fact 2:** Cypress Hill is the first Latino Rap Group to go platinum in album sales.

# DE LA SOUL

In the early '90s, even though a few rap songs had broken into the mainstream, rap as a whole was still thought of as a fringe music genre destined to die at any minute. As a college kid, if you told me rap music was temporary, I would have slapped you upside your head. As much as Nirvana and Pearl Jam defined our generation, Dr. Dre and Snoop Dogg were just as relevant and influential. It wasn't unusual to hear a mix where "Smells Like Teen Spirit" went into "Nuthin' But A 'G' Thang" and everybody at the party knew the lyrics to both songs. This was the glory of the *Judgement Night* soundtrack. On this groundbreaking soundtrack, a rock artist and a rap artist collaborated on each song. Like Edie Brickell with a crystal ball reading our generation's mind, this soundtrack was ahead of its time. Pearl Jam teamed up with Cypress Hill, Mudhoney played with Sir-Mix-A-Lot, and Faith No More jammed with the Boo-Yaa T.R.I.B.E. The best track came from the combo of De La Soul and Teenage Fanclub mixed with an infectious sample of Tom Petty's "Free Fallin'." What made this song stand out from the herd was how seamless the music flowed together, like the two artists had been breaking it down for years. It sounded like a De La Soul song, it sounded like a Teenage Fanclub song, hell, it even sounded like a Tom Petty song. It represented the future direction where music was headed. And, even though I think the soundtrack is one of the best of the decade, I've still never seen the movie.

## Albums of the '90s:

*De La Soul Is Dead* (1991)
*Buhloone Mindstate* (1993)
*Clearlake Auditorium* (1994)
*Stakes Is High* (1996)

## The 11 Best Songs By De La Soul:

1. **Ego Trippin' (Part Two)** (*Buhloone Mindstate*)
2. **A Roller Skating Jam Named "Saturdays"** (*De La Soul Is Dead*)
3. **Millie Pulled A Pistol On Santa** (*De La Soul Is Dead*)
4. **Keepin' The Faith** (*De La Soul Is Dead*)
5. **Itzsoweezee (HOT)** (*Stakes Is High*)
6. **My Brother's A Basehead** (*De La Soul Is Dead*)
7. **Breakadawn** (*Buhloone Mindstate*)
8. **4 More** (*Stakes Is High*)
9. **Ring Ring Ring (Ha Ha Hey)** (*De La Soul Is Dead*)
10. **I Am I Be** (*Buhloone Mindstate*)
11. **Stakes Is High** (*Stakes Is High*)

**Fun Fact:** De la Soul is part of the Native Tongues collective, which features like-minded rap groups that focus on positive, Afrocentric lyrics and jazz-inspired beats. Other Native Tongue artists include A Tribe Called Quest, The Jungle Brothers, Queen Latifah, Monie Love, and Black Sheep.

# DEPECHE MODE

It was my first concert. My friends were concert first-timers, too, and it showed. Wearing board shorts, pastel surf shirts, and flip-flops, we arrived to see Depeche Mode at the Shoreline Amphitheatre. We quickly realized that we were more out of place than Pat Boone singing heavy metal songs. We looked like idiots. We looked like those kids who only liked the band because of that "one song" on the radio. But it wasn't true. I had every album. I knew every song. If I wanted others to know my DM devotion, I had to prove it. Overcome with an urge of assimilation, my friends and I hit the merch table and purchased Depeche Mode shirts (I still have mine). We tossed our surf shirts in the nearest trash bin and headed inside the venue. This tour took place in the summer of 1990. I was about to enter my senior year of high school. I was obsessed with Depeche Mode's recently released album, *Violator*. I listened to it on repeat. I bought every CD single. I knew every B-side and remix. This show was a required pilgrimage to my DM credibility, even if it meant asking my dad to drive me to San Francisco. I had him drop us off about a quarter of a mile down the road because the only thing more embarrassing than wearing surf shirts to a Depeche Mode concert was having your dad drop you off at a Depeche Mode concert. All my high school insecurities evaporated the moment the band took the stage. They were the sweetest perfection. Being my first live show, Depeche Mode did not let me down and set the ultra-high standard for every concert I would see after that.

## Albums of the '90s:

*Violator* (1990)

*Songs of Faith And Devotion* (1993)

*Ultra* (1997)

## The 11 Best Songs By Depeche Mode:

1. **Enjoy The Silence** (*Violator*)
2. **It's No Good** (*Ultra*)
3. **Policy Of Truth** (*Violator*)
4. **Halo** (*Violator*)
5. **Sea Of Sin** (*World In My Eyes* single B-side)
6. **My Joy** (*Walking In My Shoes* single B-side)
7. **World In My Eyes** (*Violator*)
8. **Useless** (*Ultra*)
9. **Mercy In You** (*Songs Of Faith And Devotion*)
10. **Barrel Of A Gun** (*Ultra*)
11. **In Your Room** (*Songs Of Faith And Devotion*)

**Personal Note:** I had backstage passes to the Sex Pistols reunion concert at Universal Amphitheatre in 1996. After the show, I was waiting for the valet to retrieve my car. Dave Gahan of Depeche Mode was waiting in the valet line next to me. Even though I turned in my valet ticket before him, Dave got his car first. It's all good.

# BOB DYLAN

Living in Los Angeles, there is always a magnetic draw to Las Vegas, which is only a four-hour drive away. While the allure of going to Vegas was always better in concept than it ever was in execution, that never stopped anyone. In May of 1995, my parents called me and said that they would be in Las Vegas to see Bob Dylan and had two extra tickets to the show. Free Bob Dylan concert? Before I could finish the phone call, I had my bags packed. Dylan was playing at the Joint, a brand-new venue at the Hard Rock Hotel. My parents had upgraded their tickets from standing room only to actual seats, giving me and my friend the original tickets. The standing room only tickets were actual designated spots. My friend and I were ushered through a strategically positioned crowd and were placed against the back wall. We were warned not to leave our spots for any reason. Even though the show started on this odd note, once Dylan took the stage, I tried to enjoy the show, but Dylan wasn't any help. His singing was mumbled and his guitar playing was adequate. Being my first time seeing Dylan, I was disappointed. Two years later, a heart infection would hospitalize Dylan, nearly killing him. This near-death episode gave Dylan a rebirth, inspiring him to record *Time Out Of Mind*, his best album in years. I would see Dylan on this tour, and it was like seeing a more vibrant, confident version of himself. He had evolved. Witnessing Dylan's transformation was the most Dylanesque experience coming from an artist whose career was defined by reinvention.

## Albums of the '90s:

*Under The Red Sky* (1990)
*Good As I've Been To You* (1992)
*World Gone Wrong* (1993)
*Time Out Of Mind* (1997)

## The 11 Best Songs By Bob Dylan:

1. **Dignity** (*Greatest Hits 3*)
2. **Love Sick** (*Time Out Of Mind*)
3. **Not Dark Yet** (*Time Out Of Mind*)
4. **Trying to Get To Heaven** (*Time Out Of Mind*)
5. **Born In Time** (*Under The Red Sky*)
6. **Blackjack Davey** (*Good As I Been To You*)
7. **You Belong To Me** (*Natural Born Killers* OST)
8. **Jack-A-Roe** (*World Gone Wrong*)
9. **T.V. Talkin' Song** (*Under The Red Sky*)
10. **Diamond Joe** (*Good As I Been To You*)
11. **Highlands** (*Time Out Of Mind*)

**Fun Fact:** Before the release of *Good As I've Been To You*, Dylan recorded a full album of traditional songs with multi-instrumentalist David Bromberg. Dylan wasn't happy with the results and abandoned the sessions. The album remains unreleased to this day.

**Song Note (Highlands):** When released, it was the longest song in Bob Dylan's catalog at 16 minutes and 31 seconds.

# ELECTRONIC

New Order was my favorite band in high school. I had a *Low Life* T-shirt that I wore religiously. One day when I was wearing the shirt, a friend asked me what I thought of Electronic, the new band by New Order singer Bernard Sumner. I was speechless. I didn't know he had a new band. To make it worse, it featured Johnny Marr of the Smiths on guitar, another of my favorite bands. I was embarrassed. I had to right this wrong. No place in town was selling their CD. My only chance to find it was to drive to Fresno, which was about sixty miles away. I had just received my driver's license, so my parents didn't let me drive anywhere farther than school. Driving to Fresno was out of the question...but only if they knew about it. My swim practice was two hours long. Driving to swim practice was ten minutes each way. That gave me two hours and twenty minutes to drive to Fresno, find the CD, and get home. I took a chance, ditched swim practice, and raced up to Fresno. I found the CD in the first store, bought it, and jumped right back into the car. As I was driving home, listening to Electronic's late-night vivid metro dance grooves, I noticed I was low on gas. Having spent all my money, I didn't have enough cash to fill up the tank. I had to guts it. I didn't even look at the road; I only stared at the fuel arrow, dipping below the E. I pulled into my driveway, drifting on fumes just in time for dinner. The next morning my mom noticed the fuel gauge. I thought I was busted, but all she said was, "make sure you fill-up the tank next time." She didn't know. I had gotten away with it.

## Albums of the '90s:

*Electronic* (1991)
*Raise The Pressure* (1996)
*Twisted Tenderness* (1999)

## The 11 Best Songs By Electronic:

1. **For You** (*Raise The Pressure*)
2. **Tighten Up** (*Electronic*)
3. **Second Nature** (*Raise The Pressure*)
4. **Disappointed** (*Cool World* OST)
5. **Vivid** (*Twisted Tenderness*)
6. **Dark Angel** (*Raise The Pressure*)
7. **Imitation Of Life** (*Forbidden City* single B-side)
8. **Late At Night** (*Twisted Tenderness*)
9. **Twisted Tenderness** (*Twisted Tenderness*)
10. **Get The Message** (*Electronic*)
11. **Gangster** (*Electronic*)

**Fun Fact:** Originally, Bernard Sumner of New Order set out to record a solo album. When he enlisted Johnny Marr of the Smiths for musical assistance, they opted to form a new band, which became Electronic.

**Fun Fact 2:** On each album, Sumner and Marr recruit a rotating set of artists to fill out the band. The first album featured Chris Lowe and Neil Tennant of the Pet Shop Boys. The second album featured Karl Bartos of Kraftwerk, along with Danny Saber and Ged Lynch from Black Grape. The third album featured Jimi Goodwin from the Doves.

# ELECTRONICA

I was in a record shop on Melrose boulevard when a guy burst through the door like a fugitive, frantic, man on a mission. He plowed his way to the front counter and blurted out to the clerk, "I'm looking for this song, but I don't remember the name of the song or the name of the band." Even though that's all he said, the clerk did not hesitate and calmly replied, "Is it 'Kernkraft 400' by Zombie Nation?" The customer's eye grew wide like the moon as he ecstatically screamed, "Yes!" How the clerk had any idea what song this guy was looking for I will never know, but this is how electronica music existed during the decade. There was no radio station dedicated to electronic music, there was no show on MTV, no magazines were writing about it. It existed only from the fingertips of a DJ at an after-midnight rave or passed along by word of mouth. If you heard a song and you fell in love with it, it became a game of throwing darts at the wall in the dark, hoping you knew someone who knew a guy who knew a guy who could enlighten you on how to find it. I attended dozens of raves, but I discovered my favorite songs via friends. My next-door neighbor, Ali, used to wake me up at 2 in the morning to play me the newest remix by Moby or the latest 12-inch record by some kid out of Manchester. Electronica was a mystery, like a cryptic code that was constantly changing. There is no specific sound that is electronica; instead, it's an umbrella term for a diverse set of genres that all embraced the digital revolution. Electronica wasn't just a type of music; it was a mindset. It was a way of looking at life. It was the new counterculture that built its own world underneath the existing one. It was ours and everyone was welcome, but it wasn't for everyone. It was music that didn't have boundaries, standards, or deliberate structure. It was hard for some people to grasp, but those who did appreciate it loved the ingenuity that it could be anything we wanted it to be. It was a magical place separate from society with its own music, its own stars, and its own rules. The following list is as vast as the genre itself. I pulled some of the most important, popular, and influential tracks from that era. I selected songs from as many subgenres as possible, including techno, trance, house, trip hop, ambient, drum and bass, synth and IDM, among others. These are songs that had a huge impact on the culture, the genre, and most importantly, on me.

# The 111 Best Electronica Songs:

1. **Everytime You Touch Me** - Moby (*Everything Is Wrong*)
2. **Around The World** - Daft Punk (*Homework*)
3. **Halcyon + On + On** - Orbital (*Orbital 2*)
4. **Unfinished Symphony** - Massive Attack (*Blue Lines*)
5. **Block Rockin' Beats** - The Chemical Brothers (*Dig Your Own Hole*)
6. **Kernkraft 400** - Zombie Nation (*Leichenschmaus*)
7. **Children** - Robert Miles (*Dreamland*)
8. **Sandstorm** - Darude (*Before The Storm*)
9. **Red Alert** - Basement Jaxx (*Remedy*)

10. **Sour Times** - Portishead (*Dummy*)
11. **Born Slippy** - Underworld (*Trainspotting* OST)
12. **Lebanese Blonde** - Thievery Corporation (*The Mirror Conspiracy*)
13. **Breathe** - The Prodigy (*The Fat of The Land*)
14. **Better Off Alone** - Alice DJ (*Who Needs Guitars Anyway?*)
15. **Music Sounds Better With You** - Stardust (Non-album single)
16. **Midnight In A Perfect World** - DJ Shadow (*Entroducing...*)
17. **Little Fluffy Clouds** - The Orb (*The Orb's Adventures Beyond The Ultraworld*)
18. **The Launch** - DJ Jean (Non-album single)
19. **Blues Skies** - BT with Tori Amos (*Ima*)
20. **Move (You Make Me Feel So Good)** - Moby (*Move* EP)
21. **Teardrop** - Massive Attack (*Mezzanine*)
22. **Hyperballad** - Bjork (*Post*)
23. **Da Funk** - Daft Punk (*Homework*)
24. **6 Underground** - Sneaker Pimps (*Becoming X*)
25. **What Can You Do For Me** - Utah Saints (*Utah Saints*)
26. **Sing It Back** - Moloko (*I Am Not A Doctor*)
27. **Busy Child** - The Crystal Method (*Vegas*)
28. **The Rockafeller Skank** - Fatboy Slim (*You've Come A Long Way, Baby*)
29. **Windowlicker** - Aphex Twin (Non-album single)
30. **The Box Parts 1 & 2** - Orbital (*In Sides*)
31. **Sexy Boy** - Air (*Moon Safari*)
32. **Don't Stop** - ATB (*Movin' Melodies*)
33. **The Bomb! (These Sounds Fall Into My Mind)** - The Bucketheads (*All In The Mind*)

34. **You Don't Know Me** - Armand Van Helden (*2 Future 4 U*)
35. **Toxygene** - The Orb (*Orblivion*)
36. **Trigger Hippie** - Morcheeba (*Who Can You Trust?*)
37. **2Wicky** - Hooverphonic (*A New Stereophonic Sound Spectacular*)
38. **Leave Home** - The Chemical Brothers (*Exit Planet Dust*)
39. **Bodyrock** - Moby (*Play*)
40. **Rabbit In Your Headlights** - UNKLE and Thom Yorke (*Psyence Fiction*)
41. **Firestarter -** The Prodigy (*The Fat Of The Land*)
42. **Saltwater** - Chicane (*Behind The Sun*)
43. **Never Gonna Come Back Down** - BT (*Movement In Still Life*)
44. **Out Of Space** - The Prodigy (*Experience*)
45. **Going Out Of My Head** - Fatboy Slim (*Better Living Through Chemistry*)
46. **You're Not Alone** - Olive (*Extra Virgin*)
47. **What Is Love** - Haddaway (*The Album*)
48. **Far Out** - Sonz Of A Loop Da Loop Era (*Far Out* Non-album single)
49. **James Brown Is Dead** - L.A. Style (*L.A. Style*)
50. **9 PM (Til I Come)** - ATB (*Movin' Melodies*)
51. **Glory Box** - Portishead (*Dummy*)
52. **Go** - Moby (*Moby*)
53. **Right Here, Right Now** - Fatboy Slim (*You've Come A Long Way, Baby*)
54. **Polynomial-C** - Aphex Twin (*Xylen Tube* EP)
55. **It's A Fine Day** - Opus III (*Mind Fruit*)
56. **Why Does My Heart Feel So Bad?** - Moby (*Play*)
57. **Roygbiv** - Boards Of Canada (*Music Has The Right To Children*)

58. **Papua New Guinea** - The Future Sound Of London (*Accelerator*)
59. **Big Time Sensuality** - Bjork (*Debut*)
60. **Comin' Back** - The Crystal Method (*Vegas*)
61. **Forbidden Fruit** - Paul Van Dyk (*Seven Ways*)
62. **Missing (Todd Terry Remix)** - Everything But The Girl (*Amplified Heart*)
63. **Dusted** - Leftfield (*Rhythm And Stealth*)
64. **Turn Around** - Phats & Small (*Now Phats What I Small Music*)
65. **Don't Call Me Baby** - Madison Avenue (*The Polyester Embassy*)
66. **Feeling So Real** - Moby (*Everything Is Wrong*)
67. **Angel** - Goldie (*Timeless*)
68. **Get Get Down** - Paul Johnson (*The Groove I Have*)
69. **Rhythm Is A Dancer** - Snap! (*The Madman's Return*)
70. **I'm Alive** - Stretch & Vern (Non-album single)
71. **Ultra Freaky Orange** - Neotropic (*Ultra Freaky Orange* EP)
72. **Brown Paper Bag** - Roni Size/Reprazent (*New Forms*)
73. **Bike** - Autechre (*Incunabula*)
74. **Cream** - Blank & Jones (*In Da Mix*)
75. **Single** - Everything But The Girl (*Walking Wounded*)
76. **Alberto Balsalm** - Aphex Twin (*...I Care Because You Do*)
77. **Don't Go** - Awesome 3 (Non-album single)
78. **Are You There?** - Wink (*Hearhear*)
79. **Le Voie Le Soleil** - Patrick Prins (*Movin' Melodies*)
80. **Out of Control** - Chemical Brothers (*Surrender*)
81. **Encore Une Fois** - Sash! (*It's My Life*)
82. **Sweet Harmony** - Liquid (*Liquid* EP)

83. **Overcome** - Tricky (*Maxinquaye*)
84. **Hasty Boom Alert** - U-ziq (*Lunatic Harness*)
85. **Safe From Harm** - Massive Attack (*Blue Lines*)
86. **Song For Lindy** - Fatboy Slim (*Better Living Through Chemistry*)
87. **Don't Laugh** - Winx/Josh Wink (Non-album single)
88. **Rhythm of the Night** - Corona (*Rhythm Of The Night*)
89. **Needin' U** - David Morales Presents The Face (Non-album Single)
90. **Belfast** - Orbital (*Orbital*)
91. **Something Good** - Utah Saints (*Utah Saints*)
92. **Let Forever Be** - Chemical Brothers (*Surrender*)
93. **A Magical Moment** - Paul Van Dyk (*45 RPM*)
94. **Dreaming** - BT (*Movement In Still Life*)
95. **Inner City Life** - Goldie (*Timeless*)
96. **Trip Like I Do** - The Crystal Method (*Vegas*)
97. **Perpetual Dawn** - The Orb (*The Orb's Adventures Beyond The Ultraworld*)
98. **Blue (Da Ba Dee)** - Eiffel 65 (*Europop*)
99. **Praise You** - Fatboy Slim (*You've Come A Long Way, Baby*)
100. **Xtal** - Aphex Twin (*Selected Ambient Works 85-92*)
101. **Protection** - Massive Attack (*Protection*)
102. **Discós Revenge** - Gusto (Non-album single)
103. **Music Takes You** - Blame (Non-album single)
104. **Obsession** - Ultra-Sonic (*Tekno Junkies '92–'94*)
105. **Plasticine** - Plastikman (*Sheet One*)
106. **Flat Beat** - Mr. Oizo (*Analog Worms Attack*)
107. **Sparkles** - Tiësto (*Magik Four: A New Adventure*)
108. **Deep Inside** - Hardrive (*Deep Inside* EP)
109. **Camargue** - CJ Bolland (*The 4th Sign*)

110. **Flash** - Green Velvet (Non-album single)
111. **Higher State Of Consciousness** - Wink (Non-album single)

**Fun Fact/Personal Note:**  In the music video for Fatboy Slim's "Praise You," the fictional Torrance Community Dance Group executes a very poorly choreographed dance routine in front of a movie theater in Westwood Village.  While I was in college, I worked at that movie theater.

# FAITH NO MORE

I was on a road trip with three friends to the Bay Area, when from out of nowhere, my friend who was driving screamed, "I know what *IT* is! It's a frosty frozen treat from San Francisco." No one in the car had any idea what he was babbling about, which caused us to erupt in an explosion of laughter. It was a good ten minutes later when we all managed to calm down, so he could explain. The IT he was referring to was the IT mentioned in the Faith No More song, "Epic." The song is about IT. Though there are tons of allusions to what IT might be, IT is never clearly defined. My friend thought he had figured it out; he thought IT was a reference to the ice cream sandwich sold in the freezer section of convenience stores in the Bay area. Faith No More singer, Mike Patton, has hinted that IT might be sex or drugs, but he has never in any way inferred that he's hocking dessert items. When "Epic" went to radio in 1990, its aggressive guitars and furious energy caused it to be labeled a heavy metal song. Faith No More was not a heavy metal band. Their music had metal elements in it, but it also had funk, punk, and R&B (no seriously). "Epic" became a phenomenon because of its music video, which had a life of its own due to a controversial final segment, featuring a goldfish, flopping around outside its bowl, gasping for air. That flopping piscine became a social meme. It was more famous than half the bands on MTV. I may never know what IT is, but every time I hear the song, I still think of the ice cream sandwich from San Francisco.

## Albums of the '90s:

*Live At The Brixton Academy* (1991)
*Angel Dust* (1992)
*King For A Day...Fool For A Lifetime* (1995)
*Album Of The Year* (1997)

## The 11 Best Songs By Faith No More:

1. **Midlife Crisis** (*Angel Dust*)
2. **Digging The Grave** (*King For A Day*)
3. **The Cowboy Song** (*Live At Brixton Academy*)
4. **Be Aggressive** (*Angel Dust*)
5. **Perfect Crime** (*Bill & Ted's Bogus Journey* OST)
6. **King For A Day** (*King For A Day*)
7. **Land Of Sunshine** (*Angel Dust*)
8. **Kindergarten** (*Angel Dust*)
9. **Helpless** (*Album Of The Year*)
10. **Evidence** (*King For A Day*)
11. **Easy** (*Angel Dust*)

**Fun Fact:** Mike Patton has the greatest vocal range of any known pop singer, which traverses six octaves from Eb1 to E7. His range is slightly better than Corey Taylor of Slipknot, Axl Rose of Guns N' Roses, and Mariah Carey of herself.

**Fun Fact 2:** In high school, Faith No More drummer Mike Bordin was in a band with fellow Faith No More guitarist Jim Martin and future Metallica bassist Cliff Burton. Their band placed 4th in the 1979 Hayward "Battle of the Bands."

# FISHBONE

As glam rock waned on the Los Angeles Sunset Strip, a new crop of bands emerged. In the late '80s in L.A., four bands became the visionaries of the city. They were Jane's Addiction, Red Hot Chili Peppers, Thelonious Monster, and Fishbone. Despite the Chili Peppers and Jane's Addiction having mainstream acclaim, on the street level, in L.A., it was all about Fishbone. Fishbone were the kings of L.A. Everyone in the band was a master musician, exceeding the proficiency of the average hair metal rocker. They were adored by the fans and idolized by their peers. When you have Perry Ferrell and Anthony Kiedis looking up to your musical prowess, you have achieved something most people only fantasize about. They were Los Angeles' house band. They were the band that Angelenos expected to show up to start the party or shut the place down. They expressed the jubilant soul that lurked inside Angelenos' hearts. Everyone wanted to be like them. They were so adored, Orange County bands like Sublime and No Doubt would drive up to see Fishbone play just for motivation. This was the infectious influence that Fishbone had. Their explosive stage performance was a funky tornado that sucked you up, spun you around, and spit you out, like an e-ticket roller coaster with a broken seat belt. Fishbone was the living embodiment of our city. Though they had some minor radio hits, it never translated to a bigger audience. Fishbone will always be the teacher, the mentor, the inspiration, but without them, '90s radio would have sounded very different.

## Albums of the '90s:

*Set The Booty Up Right* (1990)
*The Reality Of My Surroundings* (1991)
*Give A Monkey A Brain And He'll Swear He's The Center Of The Universe* (1993)
*Chim Chim's Badass Revenge* (1996)

## The 11 Best Songs By Fishbone:

1. **Everyday Sunshine** (*The Reality Of My Surroundings*)
2. **Unyielding Conditioning** (*Give A Monkey A Brain*)
3. **In The Name of Swing** (*Set The Booty Up Right*)
4. **Lemon Meringue** (*Give A Monkey A Brain*)
5. **No Fear** (*Give A Monkey A Brain*)
6. **Hide Behind My Glasses** (*Set The Booty Up Right*)
7. **Sunless Saturday** (*The Reality Of My Surroundings*)
8. **Housework** (*The Reality Of My Surroundings*)
9. **Those Days Are Gone** (*The Reality Of My Surroundings*)
10. **Nutt Megalomaniac** (*Give A Monkey A Brain*)
11. **Alcoholic** (*Chim Chim's Badass Revenge*)

**Personal Note:** Frontman Angelo Moore used to hang out at UCLA's coffee house. I found this out during my freshman year at school when I held the door open for him. As a thank you, he flashed me the biggest smile I'd ever seen.

# THE FLAMING LIPS

I was on my back, laying head-to-head with my friends, staring at the ceiling, fully immersed in an album unlike I had ever heard. We were listening to The Flaming Lips album, *Zaireeka*, a Timothy Leary drenched magical musical experiment. There had never been an album like it and there hasn't been one since. *Zaireeka* was comprised of four separate compact discs that were meant to be played on four separate CD players simultaneously. The tracks from each CD player would come together like an audio-Voltron and form a complete song. Since the album needed four stereos, with users pressing "play" at the exact same time, it created a situation where every time that you listened to it, it would be slightly different because users would never push play at the same precise moment, creating minor differences even if by hundredths of a second. The Flaming Lips had created a way for the listener to be an active part of the music. As I lay there, letting the reverb drip over me, I realized that this album wasn't just an experiment, it was a product of our era. It was a product of the existence of the compact disc. At no other time would a major label (Warner Bros) even consider releasing something this daring. It was because our generation embraced the weird. We dared to see how far we could push boundaries, then celebrated every attempt. This is how I came to be lying on the floor, surrounded by friends, all anxiously waiting to have our collective minds blown. The Flaming Lips may have been flying their freak flag since the '80s, but they are a true product of the '90s.

## Albums of the '90s:

*In A Priest Driven Ambulance* (1990)
*Hit To Death In The Future Head* (1992)
*Transmissions From The Satellite Heart* (1993)
*Clouds Taste Metallic* (1995)
*Zaireeka* (1997)
*The Soft Bulletin* (1999)

## The 11 Best Songs By The Flaming Lips:

1. **Feelin' Yourself Disintegrate** (*The Soft Bulletin*)
2. **What Is The Light?** (*The Soft Bulletin*)
3. **Turn It On** (*Transmissions From The Satellite Heart*)
4. **When You Smile** (*Clouds Taste Metallic*)
5. **Waitin' For A Superman** (*The Soft Bulletin*)
6. **Race For The Prize** (*The Soft Bulletin*)
7. **Psychiatric Expectations** (*Clouds Taste Metallic*)
8. **Talkin' 'Bout The Smiling Deathporn Immortality Blues (Everyone Wants To Live Forever)** (*Hit To Death In The Future Head*)
9. **Gingerale Afternoon (The Astrology Of A Saturday)** (*Hit To Death In The Future Head*)
10. **A Machine In India** (*Zaireeka*)
11. **Buggin'** (Mokram Mix) (*The Soft Bulletin*)

**Fun Fact:** Warner Bros. signed the band to a record deal after their A&R executive attended a show in Oklahoma where the band's pyrotechnics caught the building on fire and almost burned down the venue.

# FOO FIGHTERS

Being a UCLA basketball fan was my obsession. In 1995, my Bruins were the number one team in the country, and nothing could pull me away from watching their games, even a top-secret concert. "I have a surprise for you," my girlfriend said when she called me. She was going to a show that night and had an extra ticket. "It's the drummer from Nirvana's new band," she blurted out. *The drummer from Nirvana?* Dave Grohl? Yes, I loved Nirvana. But Nirvana was Kurt Cobain, not Grohl. Does Dave Grohl think he's good enough to have his own band? Krist Novoselic, maybe...but Grohl? There's never been a rock drummer to have his own successful band except maybe Don Henley, Phil Collins, Ringo Starr...okay, nevermind. It was a week before March Madness, so I didn't go to the show. My girl came over later that night. She brought me a cassette of Foo Fighters' yet-to-be-released debut album. Within the first few seconds of the lead-off track, "This Is A Call" I knew I had made a mistake. I had said "no" to one of the first Foo Fighters concerts ever. I wasn't going to make the same mistake twice. So, when Foo Fighters opened for Mike Watt's tour, where Dave Grohl and Eddie Vedder filled in as his backing band, I was there. I don't think anyone could have predicted that Nirvana's drummer would front another iconic rock band of the '90s, especially me. I may have missed their first show, but at least the UCLA Bruins basketball team won the national championship.

# Albums of the '90s:

*Foo Fighters* (1995)
*The Colour And The Shape* (1997)
*There Is Nothing Left To Lose* (1999)

# The 11 Best Songs By Foo Fighters:

1. **I'll Stick Around** (*Foo Fighters*)
2. **Learn To Fly** (*There Is Nothing Left To Lose*)
3. **Everlong** (*The Colour And The Shape*)
4. **New Way Home** (*The Colour And The Shape*)
5. **This Is A Call** (*Foo Fighters*)
6. **Headwires** (*There Is Nothing Left To Lose*)
7. **For All the Cows** (*Foo Fighters*)
8. **Monkey Wrench** (*The Colour And The Shape*)
9. **Breakout** (*There Is Nothing Left To Lose*)
10. **Alone + Easy Target** (*Foo Fighters*)
11. **Baker Street** (*My Hero* single B-Side)

**Fun Fact:** Even though Dave Grohl was the drummer in his previous two bands, Scream and Nirvana, both bands let Grohl sing lead vocals on at least one song. In Scream, Dave sang lead on the song "Gods Look Down" and while in Nirvana, Dave sang lead on the B-side "Marigold."

**Song Note (I'll Stick Around):** The song is about Courtney Love and all the animosity that Grohl had for her during the post-Nirvana years.

# FUGAZI

In high school, I was a great swimmer. I was on the varsity swim team all four years. During my senior year, my club team was invited to compete in an international swim competition in Holland. I was one of only 30 Americans invited to participate. As I discussed earlier, my road trips always had a musical component to them; plane flights weren't any different. Since flights to Europe took much longer, listening to only one band could get tedious, but I still wanted a theme. Since I would be far away from home, I decided to bring music recommended by my friends, all of it new to me. Loaded with a backpack full of mixtapes, I discovered many good albums on this trip: *Cloudcuckooland* by The Lightning Seeds, *Bellybutton* by Jellyfish, and *The Cactus Album* by 3rd Bass. The best suggestion was Fugazi's *Repeater*. From my very first listen, I was in on it. Even though frontmen Guy Picciotto and Ian McKaye were born out of the punk world, Fugazi wasn't punk. It wasn't rock, either. It was its own sound. It was like musical mayhem with a melody. If chaos made a pop song, it would sound like this. It was wild and untamed while emitting beauty in its caustic passion. It became my go-to cassette during the trip, and I played it before every race to motivate me. That motivation propelled me to the finals in the 100-meter butterfly while our relay team placed third (in the world), making me quite the minor threat.

# Albums of the '90s:

*Repeater* (1990)

*Steady Diet Of Nothing* (1991)

*In On The Kill Taker* (1993)

*Red Medicine* (1995)

*End Hits* (1998)

*Instrument Soundtrack* (1999)

# The 11 Best Songs By Fugazi:

1. **Merchandise** (*Repeater*)
2. **Repeater** (*Repeater*)
3. **Caustic Acrostic** (*End Hits*)
4. **Public Witness Program** (*In On The Kill Taker*)
5. **Blueprint** (*Repeater*)
6. **Five Corporations** (*End Hits*)
7. **Turnover** (*Repeater*)
8. **Great Cop** (*In On The Kill Taker*)
9. **Sieve-Fisted Find** (*Repeater*)
10. **KYEO** (*Steady Diet Of Nothing*)
11. **Bed For The Scraping** (*Red Medicine*)

**Personal Note:** On an episode of the CBS drama *Family Law*, one of the characters was a rebellious teenager who needed to have a punk rock tattoo. I was working on the show at the time and convinced the producers to give her a Fugazi tattoo.

# G. LOVE & SPECIAL SAUCE

At the end of the 1998 school year, G. Love & Special Sauce had the most played song at the UCLA radio station, but it wasn't that easy to get there. When their debut album was released in 1994, I was still a bottom-rung DJ. I had recently discovered G. Love on of all things, "Friday Night Videos," which was like the fast-food version of MTV. I tried to convince the managers to play some of their songs like "Baby's Got Sauce" or "This Ain't Living." But the band's blues-inspired, busker attitude didn't fit into the 4AD-worshipping, shoegazer mentality at the station. It wasn't until I became GM that I was finally able to give G. Love his sauce. I brought a new philosophy to our station. No more obscure indie rock sludge; I wanted to play songs with hooks but not songs being played on radio. Playing songs that were on the radio was counter-productive. We were never going to beat KROQ playing the same songs as KROQ. We needed to use the same philosophy; just be different. So, I picked the most radio-friendly jingles that weren't being played on the radio. Instead of The Cardigans "Lovefool," we played "Never Recover." Instead of Radiohead's "Paranoid Android," we played "Electioneering." Instead of Third Eyed Blind's "Semi-Charmed Life," we played any other band. When I received G. Love's third album, *Yeah, It's That Easy,* I chose "You Shall See" for our rotation. Even though the label wanted me to play a different track, my choice was a hit. The staff loved it. Our audience requested it. And, it became the year's most-played song.

## Albums of the '90s:

*G. Love And Special Sauce* (1994)
*Coast To Coast Motel* (1995)
*Yeah, It's That Easy* (1997)
*Philadelphonic* (1999)

## The 11 Best Songs By G. Love & Special Sauce:

1. **This Ain't Living** (*G. Love And Special Sauce*)
2. **You Shall See** (*Yeah, It's That Easy*)
3. **Baby's Got Sauce** (*G. Love And Special Sauce*)
4. **The Things That I Used To Do** (*G. Love And Special Sauce*)
5. **Rodeo Clowns** (*Philadelphonic*)
6. **Stepping Stones** (*Yeah, It's That Easy*)
7. **Dreamin'** (*Philadelphonic*)
8. **I-76** (*Yeah, It's That Easy*)
9. **Kiss and Tell** (*Coast To Coast Motel*)
10. **Numbers** (*Philadelphonic*)
11. **Cold Beverage** (*G. Love And Special Sauce*)

**Song Note (Rodeo Clowns):**   The song is written by Jack Johnson and features him as a guest on vocals and guitar. This is the first official song released by Jack Johnson.

# GANG STARR

During an interview with Mike Tyson on *The Arsenio Hall Show*, Arsenio said he thought that Tyson should be one of the Jacksons because he swung like Reggie but talked like Michael. Pissed, Tyson leapt out of his seat and tried to pummel Arsenio. *The Arsenio Hall Show* wasn't just a show; it was an event. It was the coolest talk show on television. Arsenio had guests that the networks wouldn't even consider because they were too controversial, like Tupac Shakur (that's right, Tupac was too controversial). From Bill Clinton jamming on the saxophone to Vanilla Ice being accused of appropriating black culture, it was like watching a high stakes spin of controversy roulette every night. For the entire run of the show, in an era without internet, if you missed it, you missed it. When the show finally came to an end, Arsenio planned a major musical finale to end all finales. He invited the sickest rappers of the day to perform the most epic rap cypher ever to be put on tape. From A Tribe Called Quest to MC Lyte to KRS-One, each MC handed the mic off to one another in a show of mass solidarity. When Gang Starr's Guru stepped up, everything stopped. All the background noise faded away to give the spotlight to his lyrical appeal. Guru's presence went galaxies beyond being a rapper. He was a poet, a storyteller, a leader. He had a boldness that emanated through his words. Giving Guru national exposure in his show's final episode was one last trailblazing moment for Arsenio.

## Albums of the '90s:

*Step Into The Arena* (1991)
*Daily Operation* (1992)
*Hard To Earn* (1994)
*Moment of Truth* (1998)

## The 11 Best Songs By Gang Starr:

1. **Work** (*Moment Of Truth*)
2. **Code of The Streets** (*Hard To Earn*)
3. **Mass Appeal** (*Hard To Earn*)
4. **Just To Get A Rep** (*Step Into The Arena*)
5. **As I Read My S-A** (*Step Into The Arena*)
6. **Check The Technique** (*Step Into The Arena*)
7. **Ex-Girl To Next Girl** (*Daily Operation*)
8. **Execution of A Chump** (*Step Into The Arena*)
9. **Blowin' Up The Spot** (*Hard To Earn*)
10. **Jazz Thing** (*Mo' Better Blues* OST)
11. **She Knows What She Wants** (*Moment of Truth*)

**Fun Fact:** Rapper Guru created a side project called Jazzmatazz, which combined rap production over live jazz musicians. Some of the jazz artists recruited for the project included Donald Byrd, Branford Marsalis, Roy Ayers, and Herbie Hancock, alongside guest vocals from Jamiroquai, Isaac Hayes, Erykah Badu, and Chaka Khan.

# GARBAGE

In the early days of the internet, new websites would pop up daily and open the doors to technology we never thought possible. Those websites were rudimentary, text-driven HTML, with little visual range. I spent a lot of time on websites for bands, which at the time, only featured tour dates, discographies, biographies, and pictures. I devoured the discography pages for one reason. The '90s gave birth to the cult of the CD single, and the cult of the CD single cared about B-sides. A CD single typically featured the newest hit song by your favorite band with bonus tracks usually not featured on the album. I collected these CD singles for the non-album tracks, which were live tracks, covers, remixes, or an unreleased song. On the internet, I could find lists of all the B-sides on every CD single. I discovered numerous songs that I never even knew existed. After purchasing the CD single for Garbage's "Queer," which had two unreleased tracks, I checked the internet to see what other rare tracks Garbage had on their singles. After a few clicks, I found a treasure trove. I discovered a web page with MPEG-2 sound files (precursor to the MP3) for every Garbage B-side. Each song took a few minutes to download, but by the end of the night, I had my first digital collection of songs. CD singles cost as much as $15 each. To collect all the CD singles for an album could cost over $100. I had just acquired all the Garbage B-sides for free. It was an omen to the future of music. Who better than the tech-driven, digital emotions of Garbage to introduce me to what that future would become?

## Albums of the '90s:

*Garbage* (1995)
*Version 2.0* (1998)

**Note:** Though Garbage only released two albums during the decade, they released 12 singles to radio with over sixty B-sides, consisting of remixes, alternate versions, and unreleased tracks. This list reflects the best of those B-sides.

## The 11 Best B-Sides By Garbage:

1. **Soldier Through This** (*You Look So Fine* single)
2. **Special** (Rickidy Raw R&B Mix) (*When I Grow Up* single)
3. **Can't Seem To Make You Mine** (*When I Grow Up* single)
4. **Girl Don't Come** (*Only Happy When It Rains* single)
5. **Deadwood** (*I Think I'm Paranoid* single)
6. **Thirteen** (*Push It* single)
7. **#1 Crush** (Original Mix) (*Vow* single)
8. **Medication - acoustic** (*Special* single)
9. **Sleep** (*Only Happy When It Rains* single)
10. **Trip My Wire** (*Queer* single)
11. **You Look So Fine** (Fun Lovin' Criminals Remix) (*You Look So Fine* Single)

**Fun Fact:** Before forming Garbage, drummer Butch Vig had had a successful career in the music industry as a producer. Some of the albums that he produced include Sonic Youth's *Dirty*, Smashing Pumpkins' *Siamese Dream*, and Nirvana's *Nevermind*.

# THE GET UP KIDS

It was the late '90s when I discovered The Get Up Kids. Though they are technically emo, they embody the spirit of grunge, the animalistic passion to break out and run. The momentum of their guitars propelled their songs forward like a roller coaster blasting out of the gates. When they did decide to slow down, they became sincere and introspective, communicating on an empathetic level. They filled a void to compensate for the airwaves being overrun by a boy band insurgency. It was glorious to hear that rock and roll was still alive somewhere. I was completely infatuated with the band. If there was a school dance, I would have asked them to it. I needed to spread their glory to everyone I knew. Technology was still rather primitive in the late '90s. I made the incredibly stupid mistake of trying to email a Get Up Kids song to my friend. What I didn't realize was the song file was too large for the work servers. The song file was so large that it crashed the servers of a major film studio. Yes, I crashed the entire network of a major web-slinging studio because I tried to email a Get Up Kids song. Luckily, I didn't get in trouble for it, mainly because they had no idea that I was the culprit. This was the beginning of sharing song files, something that would eventually decimate music purchasing. As the '90s came to an end, you had to look harder to find good music. When you discovered a new rock band, the yearning to share it with friends perpetuated a culture into digital music that would eventually take over.

# Albums of the '90s:

*Four Minute Mile* (1997)

*Woodson* (1997)

*Red Letter Day* (1999)

*Something To Write Home About* (1999)

## The 11 Best Songs By The Get Up Kids:

1. **Mass Pike** (*Red Letter Day*)
2. **Holiday** (*Something To Write Home About*)
3. **Out Of Reach** (*Something To Write Home About*)
4. **Central Standard Time** (7-inch split with The Anniversary)
5. **Action & Action** (*Something To Write Home About*)
6. **Don't Hate Me** (*Four Minute Mile*)
7. **No Love** (*Four Minute Mile*)
8. **Ten Minutes** (*Something To Write Home About*)
9. **Forgive And Forget** (*Red Letter Day*)
10. **Valentine** (*Something To Write Home About*)
11. **On With The Show** (*I <3 Metal* compilation)

**Fun Fact:** The Get Up Kids used all their savings to produce their first 7-inch record "Shorty/The Breathing Method." They hired a Mike Mogis in Lincoln, Nebraska to produce it for them for $600. A couple of years later, Mike would go on to join the band Bright Eyes.

# GREEN DAY

Lollapalooza dictated culture. Originally, it was a traveling carnival, featuring around ten of the most relevant musical acts of the year, who had been hand-selected as representatives for each facet of music to headline the main stage, while on the side stage, a slew of up-and-coming artists would rotate from city to city. In 1994, Green Day was booked as the main stage's opening act. I had never seen Green Day and I wanted to make it in time for their set. I had been to previous Lollapaloozas and no one showed up on time. If you got there when the doors opened, you'd be sitting in a big grassy field by yourself. Green Day was different. We planned to get to the show an hour before Green Day's set, giving us plenty of time to get in and get settled. But when we arrived, the line of cars for the parking lot at Cal State Dominguez Hills stretched back for miles, evident of Green Day's popularity. It took us over an hour to get into the parking lot. When we finally made it to the main gates, we could already hear Green Day's three-chord sonic punches. We hauled ass to catch a glimpse of their set. When we got to the main stage, the field was packed with pogoing youths bouncing to the jackhammering rendition of the song, "She." I shoved my way through the crowd, fighting to get to the front. I made it to the pit the moment Green Day played their final chords and walked off. I may have only seen Green Day play half of a song that day (I would see them again another time), but in the end, though it was like pulling teeth to get there, it was a blast.

## Albums of the '90s:

*1,039/Smooth* (1990)

*Slappy* (1990)

*1,000 Hours* (1990)

*Kerplunk* (1991)

*Dookie* (1994)

*Insomniac* (1995)

*Nimrod* (1997)

## The 11 Best Songs By Green Day:

1. **Basket Case** (*Dookie*)
2. **One Of My Lies** (*Kerplunk!*)
3. **Scattered** (*Nimrod*)
4. **Burnout** (*Dookie*)
5. **She** (*Dookie*)
6. **Welcome To Paradise** (*Kerplunk!/Dookie*)
7. **Going To Pasalacqua** (*39/Smooth*)
8. **Uptight** (*Nimrod*)
9. **Christie Road** (*Kerplunk!*)
10. **Paper Lanterns** (*Slappy*)
11. **Brain Stew** (*Insomniac*)

**Fun Fact:** The original version of Lollapalooza only existed for seven summers. The first Lollapalooza line-up in the summer of 1991 featured only nine acts with Jane's Addiction as the main headliner. Green Day played during the fourth summer line-up but skipped one of the dates to play at Woodstock 1994.

# GUNS N' ROSES

It was September 16th, 1991. It was a Monday night. There was nothing special about this Monday except that at midnight, when it became Tuesday, September 17th, 1991; *Use Your Illusion*, the colossal follow-up to Guns N' Roses' iconic debut album, *Appetite For Destruction*, would finally be released. *Use Your Illusion* wasn't just an album. It was two albums. It was two and a half hours of brand-new music from the biggest rock band in the world and the band that had defined my high school existence. The new album was going on sale at midnight. The anticipation for the *Use Your Illusion* albums was as big as anything had been in my lifetime. GN'R fans across the country lined up outside their favorite record store so they could buy the GN'R albums the minute they were released. It was the first time in history that fans lined up to buy music at midnight. It wouldn't be the last. This activity was so successful, Monday midnight music sales became a weekly occurrence. I lived in a small town, so my line was short. I only waited for a few minutes, but I read in bigger cities that people waited as long as six hours. As soon as I made my purchase, I hurried home where I stayed up until 3 AM listening to both albums all the way through. I thought *Use Your Illusion* would be the album that defined my college years. In retrospect, it wasn't. It was the swan song of my high school years. It was the final album of my teenage self. I didn't stay up late that night to hear the future; I did it to hold onto the last moments of my youth for as long as I could.

## Albums of the '90s:

*Use Your Illusion I* (1991)
*Use Your Illusion II* (1991)
*The Spaghetti Incident?* (1993)

## The 11 Best Songs By Guns N' Roses:

1. **Civil War** (*Use Your Illusion II*)
2. **Estranged** (*Use Your Illusion II*)
3. **Coma** (*Use Your Illusion I*)
4. **You Could Be Mine** (*Use Your Illusion II*)
5. **Locomotive** (*Use Your Illusion II*)
6. **November Rain** (*Use Your Illusion I*)
7. **Pretty Tied Up** (*Use Your Illusion II*)
8. **Right Next Door To Hell** (*Use Your Illusion I*)
9. **Ain't It Fun** (*The Spaghetti Incident?*)
10. **Don't Cry** (*Use Your Illusion I*)
11. **Oh My God** (*End Of Days* OST)

**Fun Fact:** During his hiatus from the band, bassist Duff McKagan took economics classes at Seattle University. With his newfound expertise as a financial advisor, he was hired by Playboy magazine to write a financial column for them.

**Song Note (Civil War):** This is the last song recorded and released to feature original drummer, Steven Adler. It is also the only song on the *Use Your Illusion* albums where he is credited to have played.

# BEN HARPER

Ben Harper was the best guitarist of the '90s. I'm not being biased; I saw all the great guitarists from the decade play live: Chris Cornell, Jim Martin, James Hetfield, Dimebag, Dave Navarro, Tom Morello, Slash, even Jack White. Ben Harper was better than all of them. In college radio, even though went dark during the summer, the labels still sent us new music. In summer 1997, when Harper released his album, *The Will To Live,* instead of leaving the CD on a shelf for three months, I did the responsible thing and brought it home. Instantly, it landed in my heavy rotation. Harper was playing at the Palace and it became my must-see show of the summer. Harper started the show, playing solo with just his voice and guitar. He silenced the room. Even the most self-absorbed Hollywood hipster was mesmerized. Then, he took it to the next level. Harper laid his electric guitar across his lap and went to town. It was like he was channeling Muddy Waters' soul as he ripped through a 25-minute blues solo. It was like he was having a Patrick Swayze *Ghost*-like experience through his guitar. If he had only played that solo and nothing else, it still would have been one of the best live shows I had seen. After the show, my friend and I sat in silence for about 10-minutes before my friend mumbled, "Wow. Ben Harper just ruined concerts for me." He was right. An artist might write a great song or come up with a great riff but none of that matters until you're on stage. You have to be able to stand on your own or, in Ben Harper's case, sit on your own.

## Albums of the '90s:

*Welcome To The Cruel World* (1994)

*Fight For Your Mind* (1995)

*The Will To Live* (1997)

*Burn To Shine* (1999)

## The 11 Best Songs By Ben Harper:

1. **Another Lonely Day** (*Fight For Your Mind*)
2. **Burn One Down** (*Fight For Your Mind*)
3. **Glory and Consequence** (*The Will To Live*)
4. **Oppression** (*Fight For Your Mind*)
5. **Jah Work** (*The Will To Live*)
6. **Excuse Me Mr.** (*Fight For Your Mind*)
7. **Burn To Shine** (*Burn To Shine*)
8. **Don't Take That Attitude To Your Grave** (*Welcome To The Cruel World*)
9. **The Will To Live** (*The Will To Live*)
10. **Welcome To The Cruel World** (*Welcome To The Cruel World*)
11. **Mama's Got A Girlfriend Now** (*Welcome To The Cruel World*)

**Fun Fact:** Ben comes from a musical family. His grandmother used to play with Pete Seeger and Woody Guthrie. His grandparents also owned a music store, where Harper worked when he was a teen.

# HEATMISER

In a decade filled with iconic rock music, it was an obscure indie band that stole my heart and delivered my favorite album. Introducing, Heatmiser's *Mic City Sons*. The album is a post-grunge triumph. The emotional range traverses across a landscape of desolate loneliness, desire, and pain. It erupts in confidence as much as it collapses in on itself. It exudes a cascade of emotions built on inner turmoil. With two lead vocalists, there's a duality that permeates throughout the songs like a subtext battling for primetime exposure. Heatmiser's tenure was temporary and the band would break up following the release of this album. The band members carried on with their own musical efforts. Bassist Sam Coomes formed Quasi with his wife Janet Weiss of Sleater-Kinney. Guitarist/singer Neil Gust formed the band No. 2, to critical success. Tony Lash moved into producing Death Cab For Cutie albums. And singer/guitarist Elliott Smith, would have an influential solo career. It's hard to say where Heatmiser's legacy fits. While many critics call them the launching pad to Elliott Smith's career, to me, they were so much more. I have listened to *Mic City Sons* more than any other album from this decade. More than *Check Your Head*, *Ten*, *In Utero*...all of them. What connected me to that album was its sincerity. It embodied all the angst from the music that came before it, by bottling it in a tight package, harnessing its wrath to deliver a concise and accessible feeling. *Mic City Sons* is more than an album; it has been my therapist, my escape, and my best friend.

## Albums of the '90s:

*Dead Air* (1993)
*Cop And Speeder* (1994)
*Yellow No 5* (1994)
*Mic City Sons* (1996)

## The 11 Best Songs By Heatmiser:

1. **Pop In G** (*Mic City Sons*)
2. **Half Right** (*Mic City Sons*)
3. **Antonio Carlos Jobim** (*Cop And Speeder*)
4. **Cruel Reminder** (*Mic City Sons*)
5. **Plainclothes Man** (*Mic City Sons*)
6. **Flame!** (*Cop And Speeder*)
7. **Trap Door** (*Cop And Speeder*)
8. **See You Later** (*Mic City Sons*)
9. **Blackout** (*Dead Air*)
10. **Get Lucky** (*Mic City Sons*)
11. **Cannibal** (*Dead Air*)

**Fun Fact:** After their break up, all four members of Heatmiser reunited one last time on the No. 2 song, "Never Felt Better" in some capacity. The song was released as a demo bonus track in 2015.

**Personal Note:** Every year on my birthday, I listen to my five favorite albums of all time. Since its release, *Mic City Sons* has been included as one of my birthday five.

# HELMET

I saw a lot of great shows at the Troubadour: Sleater-Kinney, Built To Spill, and Cibo Matto, among others. It was also the venue where I had the most surreal concert experience. I had progressively become a Helmet fan with each release. They straddled the line between metal and grunge, wavering with seamless execution. The band was touring for their newest album, *Aftertaste*. I had acquired VIP passes, which meant I could go upstairs and sit in a private room and watch the show through a plate glass window. Only, the VIP room was packed. It was hard enough to reach the bar, let alone getting a peek at the show. Because of the large crowd, I was asked to leave the upstairs area because it was for executives only. Executives? It was an indie metal concert. How many executives of anything want to see an indie metal concert? Knowing how bad I wanted to see the show, the concerned label rep looked to find another place for me. She put me in the only available spot left, which happened to be *on the stage*. I was standing on the corner of the stage for the entire show. For 90 blistering minutes, I leaned against the band's speaker as the feverish guitar stampede vibrated through every part of my body. I was standing so close to lead singer Page Hamilton; I could conceivably reach out and pat him on the back if I dared. I watched Hamilton bulldoze through a tremendous set of glorious noise. I could see the reverb of every fret. I could see the sweat on his forehead. In some strange way, it felt like I was a part of the band that night, that I was part of the show. It was exactly what I wanted.

## Albums of the '90s:

*Strap It On* (1990)

*Meantime* (1992)

*Betty* (1994)

*Born Annoying* (1995)

*Aftertaste* (1997)

## The 11 Best Songs By Helmet:

1. **Unsung** (*Meantime*)
2. **Driving Nowhere** (*Aftertaste*)
3. **Exactly What You Wanted** (*Aftertaste*)
4. **Milquetoast** (*Betty*)
5. **Pure** (*Aftertaste*)
6. **Speechless** (*Betty*)
7. **Blacktop** (*Strap It On*)
8. **Wilma's Rainbow** (*Betty*)
9. **In The Meantime** (*Meantime*)
10. **Street Crab** (*Aftertaste*)
11. **Like I Care** (*Aftertaste*)

**Fun Fact:**  Frontman Page Hamilton originally attended the Manhattan School of Music to study jazz guitar.

**Fun Fact 2:**  Hamilton was one of the guitarists in the guitar orchestra that recorded the score for the 1995 Michael Mann film, *Heat*.

# ICE CUBE

Ice Cube's "It Was A Good Day" felt real.  It felt so real that fans have tried to figure out what day the song could have occurred.  Fans researched which days the Lakers beat the Supersonics (who no longer exist) and compared that to the days when Los Angeles had no smog and beepers were available.  Though Cube has never revealed a specific date, the fans have determined that song took place on January 20, 1992.  At this point, the song had transcended into mythology.  It is a crisp snapshot of inner-city life with an undertone of humanity that everyone can relate to.  It's the exhilaration in the minor victories of life; from dominating a pick-up game of basketball or watching your favorite team win.  With its laid-back, slow groove, it was acceptable to be played anywhere.  I can prove it.  I was visiting my hometown of Visalia, CA.  It's a small town that might have been the last town in America to embrace rap music.  I was in the mall, sipping on my Orange Julius looking at Nintendo games in Sears when I heard it.  The music playing over the loudspeakers changed from whatever country song was breakin' achy hearts into Ice Cube's masterpiece. The mellow roll of the Isley Brothers sample, "Footsteps In The Dark," enveloped the store with a wickedly smooth rhythm.  My first thought was, "Damn, Sears is the shit."  I wasn't the only one who thought this.  As I glanced across the counter, I saw a middle-aged woman, rocking the sky-high mom hair, not only groovin' out but singing along.  Even she knew Ice Cube was a pimp and loved him for it.

## Albums of the '90s:

*AmeriKKKa's Most Wanted* (1990)

*Death Certificate* (1991)

*The Predator* (1992)

*Lethal Injection* (1993)

*War & Peace Vol. 1 (The War Disc)* (1998)

## The 11 Best Songs By Ice Cube:

1. **The Nigga Ya Love To Hate** (*AmeriKKKa's Most Wanted*)
2. **Jackin' For Beats** (*Kill At Will*)
3. **When Will They Shoot?** (*The Predator*)
4. **Gangsta's Fairytale** (*AmeriKKKa's Most Wanted*)
5. **It Was A Good Day** (*The Predator*)
6. **No Vaseline** (*Death Certificate*)
7. **Wicked** (*The Predator*)
8. **Dead Homiez** (*Kill At Will*)
9. **Endangered Species (Tales From The Darkside)** (*Kill At Will*)
10. **Bop Gun (One Nation)** (*Lethal Injection*)
11. **Check Yo Self** (*The Predator*)

**Fun Fact:** After starring in the film *Boyz N The Hood*, by director John Singleton, it was John who suggested that Ice Cube try screenwriting. Ice Cube's first screenplay was the comedy hit film *Friday*.

# JAWBREAKER

Jawbreaker's *Dear You* was supposed to be the next big thing. It was supposed to be the next *Dookie*...the next *Smash*...the next *Nevermind*. Sadly, it wasn't. Not everything in this book is about the greats. Some are the "almost were" or the "never was." Working in radio, I watched many indie bands pay their dues before breaking into the mainstream. The more I witnessed it, the better I became at picking out the bands that would breakout. Bush, The Wallflowers, Jimmy Eat World, Korn, Incubus, I called all of them. I'm not bragging, but I called them. There were plenty of great bands that broke out that I didn't call, as well as plenty of crappy bands who made it that I never thought would. I'm looking at you, Creed. I was positive Jawbreaker was poised for stardom. They had the sound. They had the angst. They could write hooks catchier than a curly tail grub. I was so confident that Jawbreaker would save our generation that I didn't expect what happened next. The fans detested the glossy sound of their new album, *Dear You*, and turned on them. Literally! During concerts, the fans would actually turn their backs to the band when they played the new songs. It was too much for any band to withstand. Because of the criticism and lack of radio traction, the band broke up. It was unfun to see them crash. Ironically, for Jawbreaker, years later, *Dear You*, the album that broke them up, would find an audience, become influential, and be considered one of the seminal punk albums of the decade. How's that for revenge therapy?

## Albums of the '90s:

*Unfun* (1990)

*Bivouac* (1992)

*24 Hour Revenge Therapy* (1994)

*Dear You* (1995)

*Live 4/30/96* (1999)

## The 11 Best Songs By Jawbreaker:

1. **Chemistry** (*Dear You*)
2. **Accident Prone** (*Dear You*)
3. **The Boat Dreams From The Hill** (*24 Hour Revenge Therapy*)
4. **Save Your Generation** (*Dear You*)
5. **Boxcar** (*24 Hour Revenge Therapy*)
6. **Sluttering (May 4th)** (*Dear You*)
7. **Want** (*Unfun*)
8. **West Bay Invitational** (*24 Hour Revenge Therapy*)
9. **Do You Still Hate Me?** (*24 Hour Revenge Therapy*)
10. **Shield Your Eyes** (*Bivouac*)
11. **Kiss The Bottle** (*Music For The Proletariat* compilation)

**Fun Fact:** One reason that fans originally disliked *Dear You* was because of the change in singer Blake Schwarzenbach's voice on the album. Fans blamed the production, but in actuality, it was due to throat surgery that Blake had to remove polyps.

# JAY-Z

I changed hip-hop. Yes, me personally. And it's because of Jay-Z's album, *Reasonable Doubt*. My hip-hop director at the UCLA radio station used to say *Reasonable Doubt* was better than Nas' *Illmatic*. To understand the gravity of that statement, you have to understand the boldness of its claim. Before *Illmatic*, rap embodied the brashness of self. Hip-hop was based on bravado. The strength of a rapper came from within, from their confidence, the authority in their words. Then, Nas changed the game. His album *Illmatic* was so introspective with its inner-city narratives, it elevated rap and repaved the road that hip-hop would travel. Two years later came *Reasonable Doubt*. Jay-Z's album took the essence of what came before him, threw it in a mix, and created an album that was the blueprint for the future. Rap always showed off its swagger, but Jay-Z was the first to embrace it as a lifestyle. Jay-Z wasn't a gangsta, he was a hustla. While many rappers defined themselves by how much money they spent, Jay-Z defined himself by how much money he could make. Even though he came from a hard knock Brooklyn life, Jay-Z proved that you could still have street cred in a business suit. After listening to *Reasonable Doubt*, I created the Sunday School, an entire day of hip-hop at UCLA's radio station. We were the first college station in the country to do it, and it was our most popular day of the week. The following year, hundreds of college radio stations copied our format. Is *Reasonable Doubt* better than *Illmatic*? That question is irrelevant since the answer is up to you.

## Albums of the '90s:

*Reasonable Doubt* (1996)
*In My Lifetime, Vol. 1* (1997)
*Vol. 2...Hard Knock Life* (1998)
*Vol. 3...Life And Times of S. Carter* (1999)

## The 11 Best Songs By Jay-Z:

1. **Dead Presidents II** (*Reasonable Doubt*)
2. **Brooklyn's Finest** (*Reasonable Doubt*)
3. **The City Is Mine** (*In My Lifetime, Vol. 1*)
4. **Hard Knock Life (Ghetto Anthem)** (*Vol. 2...Hard Knock Life*)
5. **Politics As Usual** (*Reasonable Doubt*)
6. **D'Evils** (*Reasonable Doubt*)
7. **A Week Ago** (*Vol. 2...Hard Knock Life*)
8. **Ain't No Nigga** (*Reasonable Doubt*)
9. **Who You Wit II** (*In My Lifetime, Vol. 1*)
10. **Can't Knock the Hustle** (*Reasonable Doubt*)
11. **Big Pimpin'** (*Vol. 3...Life And Times of S. Carter*)

**Fun Fact:** Jay-Z holds the record for most chart-topping albums by a solo artist with his eleven #1 albums on the Billboard 200. The previous record belonged to Elvis Presley with ten #1 albums.

**Fun Fact 2:** Jay-Z, Busta Rhymes, and Notorious B.I.G. all attended high school together.

# THE JESUS LIZARD

There's nothing nice about the Jesus Lizard. There's nothing pop. Nothing rock. Nothing radio friendly. I don't even think they like radios. They are crass, crude, ugly, grotesque, out of line, disgusting creatures, whose music sounds like they just don't give a flying fig to chords, structure, or anything resembling a song. Somehow the band's guttural howl all comes together in a beleaguered celebration to the end of common decency. This is the type of music a demonic grave digger would listen to while burying his latest victim who is still alive. At shows, their frenzied tantrums thump to a level not suitable for younger viewers. I don't know that for a fact because I've never seen them live. Being in radio, I could go to any concert I wanted, but I couldn't go to every concert I wanted. Some nights, I had to work. On the night of the Jesus Lizard show, I was stuck working the world premiere for *Extreme Measures*. I met up with my friends after the show for a drink, only they weren't drinking. They said the Jesus Lizard show was so intense; it felt like Tarantino's gimp had brutally pulverized them into submission. With the furious mosh pit, the cascading cacophony of noise, and the inexorable attack on their eardrums, when they left the show, it felt like they were being let out of prison. As exhausting as the show was, it was a life-altering experience. They loved every minute of it. And I gave up seeing that for Gene Hackman. For all the great bands I was lucky to see live, the Jesus Lizard will always be the one that got away.

# Albums of the '90s:

*Head* (1990)

*Goat* (1991)

*Liar* (1992)

*Lash* (1993)

*Down* (1994)

*Shot* (1996)

*Blue* (1998)

# The 11 Best Songs By The Jesus Lizard:

1. **Puss** (*Liar*)
2. **Countless Backs Of Sad Losers** (*Down*)
3. **Then Comes Dudley** (*Goat*)
4. **Thumbscrews** (*Shot*)
5. **Gladiator** (*Liar*)
6. **Thumper** (*Shot*)
7. **Horse** (*Down*)
8. **Blue Shot** (*Shot*)
9. **Glamorous** (*Lash*)
10. **Nub** (*Goat*)
11. **Skull Of A German** (*Shot*)

**Fun Fact:** When he failed out of college, frontman David Yow turned to music as a back-up career.

**Song Note (Puss):** After touring together, The Jesus Lizard and Nirvana released a dual 7-inch vinyl single. The Jesus Lizard's "Puss" was the A-side, and Nirvana's "Oh, The Guilt" was the B-side.

# KORN

"I have seen the future of metal" the UCLA radio program director declared. The program director was a huge metal head. He wasn't just a Metallica-loving, Maiden-worshipping metalhead; he loved it all. He loved Russian industrial metal, Scandinavian death metal, and German speed metal. So when he made that statement, it came with a lot of weight. He had seen Korn play the night before and was still rattled by the spectacle. Outside of Metallica's *Black* album, metal had been on hiatus since the Seattle invasion. To hear that metal might be making a comeback, I was skeptical. I had mixed reactions after listening to Korn's debut album. They were messed up. What the hell was the singer doing? He wasn't screaming, he wasn't yelling, it was like he was shouting devilish incantations. As much as I knew Bill Clinton felt our pain, I knew Korn's singer, Jonathan Davis, was a lunatic. Rumors about his unchecked aggression varied from him being a dark Lord to being an unmedicated schizophrenic. No matter what his inner turmoil was, he delivered an animalistic shriek that shattered all expectations. Korn comes straight out of Bakersfield, which could make anyone want to scream their lungs out. So the next time I was headed back to the Central Valley with a friend, I introduced him to Korn. He lasted three songs before turning off the stereo. He wasn't a fan. In later releases, Korn would reach for pop radio riffs, but their debut album remains an explosive hell-mouth that truly did usher in a nü metal revolution.

## Albums of the '90s:

*Korn* (1994)
*Life Is Peachy* (1996)
*Follow The Leader* (1998)
*Issues* (1999)

## The 11 Best Songs By Korn:

1. **Got The Life** (*Follow The Leader*)
2. **Falling Away From Me** (*Issues*)
3. **Blind** (*Korn*)
4. **Shoots And Ladders** (*Korn*)
5. **Make Me Bad** (*Issues*)
6. **Good God** (*Life Is Peachy*)
7. **A.D.I.D.A.S.** (*Life Is Peachy*)
8. **Clown** (*Korn*)
9. **Freak On A Leash** (*Follow The Leader*)
10. **Let's Get This Party Started** (*Issues*)
11. **No Place To Hide** (*Life Is Peachy*)

**Fun Fact:** Lead singer Jonathan Davis was learning to be a mortician when he was hired to sing for the band. His time being a mortician left Davis with a fear of automobiles.

**Song Note (Shoots And Ladders):** The lyrics delve into the topic of how nursery rhymes can actually have darker meanings. The song references nursery rhymes such as "Ring Around the Rosie," "London Bridge" and "This Old Man."

# LIVE

One afternoon, in the spring of 1994, I arrived at the UCLA radio station to a venomous argument over what was better, Pearl Jam's *Vs.* or Live's *Throwing Copper*. Radio station geeks can get pretty riled up over music if you disagree. The station had been spinning *Throwing Copper* for about a week, and we were playing every song. *Throwing Copper* was a DJ's dream as each song was incredibly radio-friendly with its own unique personality from the fired-up aggression of "Stage" to the sprawling landscapes of "Pillar of Davidson" to the radio jangle of "All Over You" to falling placentas in "Lighting Crashes." *Throwing Copper* was a gigantic leap in songwriting from their debut, *Mental Jewelry*. I remember our GM proclaiming, "Pearl Jam wishes they could have made an album this good." I disagree and believe that both albums are spectacular. Both bands were dealing with widespread popularity and used that platform to experiment with their sound, trying new melodies with more diversity. While college radio geeks can really argue about any song, there was a point to be made. Coming on the heels of Cobain's death, there was a void. There was a need for music that was tangent and relevant. Ed Kowalczyk's Pennsylvania drawl made alt rock relatable, singing about struggling waitresses and shit towns. *Throwing Copper* would dominate the radio and MTV on its way to outselling Pearl Jam. At that moment in time, it didn't matter whether you preferred *Vs.* or *Throwing Copper;* because it was Live that dominated.

# Albums of the '90s:

*Mental Jewelry* (1991)
*Throwing Copper* (1994)
*Secret Samadhi* (1997)
*The Distance To Here* (1999)

# The 11 Best Songs By Live:

1. **White, Discussion** (*Throwing Copper*)
2. **I Alone** (*Throwing Copper*)
3. **Operation Spirit** (*Mental Jewelry*)
4. **Lakini's Juice** (*Secret Samadhi*)
5. **Pillar Of Davidson** (*Throwing Copper*)
6. **Heropsychodreamer** (*Secret Samadhi*)
7. **Sparkle** (*The Distance To Here*)
8. **Pain Lies On The Riverside** (*Mental Jewelry*)
9. **Waitress** (*Throwing Copper*)
10. **Waterboy** (*Mental Jewelry*)
11. **Lightning Crashes** (*Throwing Copper*)

**Fun Fact:** The lyrics from the album, *Mental Jewelry*, are based on the teachings of the Indian philosopher; Jiddu Krishnamurti, who preached for a revolution via the nature of the mind and meditation.

**Song Note (I Alone):** The song lyrics tell the story of Luke 8:22-25 from the Bible when Jesus calms a storm while at sea with his disciples.

# MARY LOU LORD

Walking distance from UCLA was Rhino Records, the '90s king of L.A.'s Westside music scene. Whatever indie release you were looking for, there's a good chance that Rhino had at least two in stock. From a staff that knew the trending Sub Pop 7-inches to a clientele that worshipped 4AD, and a music selection that delved into the deep corners of jazz, blues, and soul, a visit to Rhino Records was like a trip through a musical Candyland. Rhino held live shows with artists like Lou Barlow, Juliana Hatfield, Soundgarden, and even Nirvana. The best show I saw at Rhino was Mary Lou Lord. During a midday shopping frenzy, Lord jammed through a blissfully intimate set. Even though she played a full concert in Hollywood that night, this Rhino show was so pure and simple, it exceeded the big show in every way. At a concert, you already have the audience's attention; at Rhino, you had to earn it. Armed with only an acoustic guitar and her busker-fueled personality, Lord had the place captivated. I watched shoppers literally stop searching through Swedish metal imports just to watch Lord perform. Lord's talent was her charm and it was enchanting. She had a fragile complexity, a vulnerable innocence like she was opening up the door to all her emotional secrets begging us to like her despite her flaws. She's the kind of girl that Ethan Hawke would have followed around Europe just to hear her sing. Though pop radio traction evaded her, Lord will always be the bridesmaid you should have married and the best '90s artist you've never heard.

# Albums of the '90s:

*Real* (1992)

*TSWL* (1993)

*Mary Lou Lord* (1995)

*Martian Saints!* (1997)

*Mind the Gap* (1997)

*Got No Shadow* (1998)

*Pace of Change* (1998)

*Lights Are Changing* (1998)

# The 11 Best Songs By Mary Lou Lord:

1. **Western Union Desperate** (*Got No Shadow*)
2. **His Indie World** (*Lights Are Changing*)
3. **I Figured You Out** (*Martian Saints!*)
4. **Some Jingle Jangle Morning** (*Mary Lou Lord*)
5. **His Lamest Flame** (*Got No Shadow*)
6. **Lights Are Changing** (*Lights Are Changing*)
7. **Sunspot Stopwatch** (*Martian Saints!*)
8. **On The Avenue** (*Pace Of Change*)
9. **Two Boats** (*Got No Shadow*)
10. **The Bridge** (*Lights Are Changing*)
11. **Martian Saints!** (*Martian Saints!*)

**Fun Fact:** The song "I Figured You Out" was written by Elliott Smith, who tried to throw out the song because it sounded too much like the Eagles. Lord rescued it and recorded it herself.

# LUSH

In the early days of the internet, I took a class at UCLA to learn HTML. With that skill, I landed a job programming for a web company at Universal Studios. I was hired to help program an internet-based, first-person game inspired by *Jurassic Park: The Ride.* It was the first browser-based game of its kind. I can't take a lot of credit for it. All I did was program the HTML frame to set the game in the browser, but I did program the heck out of that frame. To deliver the game, it took long hours, late nights, and the most eclectic assortment of music. In the programming room, you might hear the industrial thunder of KMFDM or NIN. In the writer's room, it was Pavement or anything from Matador records. In the graphics room, it was a mixed bag of classic rock, heavy metal, and Neil Diamond. Yeah, you read that right. Late at night, while chugging my 11th Mtn. Dew, there was one band that I would inevitably play to save me from my nagging sleep deprivation: Lush. I loved Lush. Singer Miki Berenyi's snarky, hellbent delivery was belted out with such playful disdain; it was every bit seductive as it was mesmerizing, igniting a compelling attraction. Their music had a dreamy urgency that was stimulating and calming, creating its own wistful atmosphere. Blaring the cosmic melodies of *Split* through my headphones was like being transported to a heavenly bliss, where I could drown out my distracting world. I wouldn't say Lush was the reason that I made all my deadlines, but I wouldn't have succeeded without them.

## Albums of the '90s:

*Gala* (1990)
*Spooky* (1992)
*Split* (1994)
*Lovelife* (1996)
*Topolino* (1997)

## The 11 Best Songs By Lush:

1. **Ladykillers** (*Lovelife*)
2. **Hypocrite** (*Split*)
3. **Light From A Dead Star** (*Split*)
4. **For Love** (*Spooky*)
5. **Ciao!** (*Lovelife*)
6. **Heavenly Nobodies** (*Lovelife*)
7. **Kiss Chase** (*Split*)
8. **When I Die** (*Split*)
9. **Ex** (*Topolino*)
10. **Lovelife** (*Split*)
11. **Untogether** (*Spooky*)

**Fun Fact:** Iconic photographer Annie Liebowitz was a huge fan of the band's style. She wanted to photograph them as the "look of the '90s," which could be used for ad campaigns. Lush turned down her offer to concentrate on their music.

**Personal Note:** When attending the Lollapalooza festival in 1992, Lush was the first band I watched. This was how I discovered them.

# MADONNA

"You have to see this movie. It has the best opening scene ever." That was what my friend told me about the newest indie movie, *Reservoir Dogs*. I didn't know it at the time, but that film would be my introduction to the world of Quentin Tarantino, who would have an incredible influence over my growth in film. The movie was playing in Westwood, so I went to see it. I assumed the opening scene would be some bullet-ridden action sequence, but it wasn't. It was seven guys, having a conversation about the meaning of Madonna's song, "Like A Virgin." Though there was no violence in the first scene, it was the most action-packed scene I had ever seen. It was Tarantino's dialogue that was the non-stop action. The characters shot out rapid-fire lines of dialogue like bullets, hitting targets left and right. These hard-nosed bank robbers weren't discussing criminal acts; they were discussing pop music. This scene tore down every convention and reinvented an entire genre of film in five minutes. During the '90s, Madonna was an '80s icon adrift in a sea of plaid. When she teamed with William Orbit to produce the album *Ray Of Light*, it was a multi-platinum seller, receiving six Grammy nominations, including Album of the Year. They called it a comeback, but Madonna was inescapable during the decade. From being a pop culture reference in Tarantino's dialogue to her X-rated *Sex* book to her film *Truth Or Dare* to her musical *Evita*, she was always relevant. Madonna reinvented herself with every new trip around the sun and always remained a material girl.

## Albums of the '90s:

*I'm Breathless* (1990)
*Erotica* (1992)
*Bedtime Stories* (1994)
*Evita* (1996)
*Ray Of Light* (1998)

## The 11 Best Songs By Madonna:

1. **Vogue** (*I'm Breathless*)
2. **Nothing Really Matters** (*Ray Of Light*)
3. **Frozen** (*Ray Of Light*)
4. **Deeper And Deeper** (*Erotica*)
5. **Drowned World/Substitute For Love** (*Ray Of Light*)
6. **Skin** (*Ray Of Light*)
7. **Rescue Me** (*Immaculate Collection*)
8. **Ray Of Light** (*Ray Of Light*)
9. **Secret** (*Bedtime Stories*)
10. **I'll Remember** (*With Honors* OST)
11. **Thief Of Hearts** (*Erotica*)

**Fun Fact:** In 1992, Madonna released her book entitled *Sex*, filled with explicit matter, including nude pictures of herself. Even though it was priced at $50, the book was so popular it sold out everywhere. The publisher had to order reprints within 48 hours of it being released. The book topped the best sellers list and is still the fastest-selling coffee table book of all time. There was one person who was not a fan of the book; her then-boyfriend Vanilla Ice. After the book's release, Vanilla Ice broke up with Madonna.

# THE MAGNETIC FIELDS

A couple of days after Christmas 1999, I was spending the music gift card that I had received during the holidays. At the counter, the cashier was pricing a stack of CDs. On the top of the pile was The Magnetic Fields *69 Love Songs*. This massive three-disc set is comprised of 69 songs about, you guessed it, love. The album sounded pretentious, but the cashier proclaimed it was his favorite album of the year and in the running for his favorite album of the decade. He said the album wasn't an album about love; it was a satire about love songs. This intrigued me. Did frontman Stephen Merritt have a dark heart to create a mocking tribute to the hopeless romantics? Was he some jaded lover spitting a diatribe of sarcasm? I had to know, so I bought it. The first listen, I was unimpressed. I don't think I even made it past disc one. I shoved it away and moved on. Over the years, I'd revisit the album, growing fonder with repeat listens. Even though Merritt has claimed these songs have no real romantic value, I find that hard to believe. As a writer myself, nothing I do is without meaning. If Merritt took the time to compose the prose, then he deliberately created that sentiment. Maybe by ignoring his feelings, Merritt tapped into his intuitive emotive tissue, where his subconscious was speaking through his cynicism. *69 Love Songs* joins multiple genres together in an interwoven blanket of endearment. With so many diverse styles, the album appeals to a range of people experiencing romance in a multitude of ways. *69 Love Songs* isn't a satire; it's a statement.

# The 11 Best Songs From The Magnetic Fields *69 Love Songs*:

1. **All My Little Words** (*Volume 1*)
2. **Busby Berkeley Dreams** (*Volume 3*)
3. **No One Will Ever Love You** (*Volume 2*)
4. **I Don't Want To Get Over You** (*Volume 1*)
5. **The Book Of Love** (*Volume 1*)
6. **How To Say Goodbye** (*Volume 3*)
7. **Epitaph For My Heart** (*Volume 2*)
8. **Meaningless** (*Volume 3*)
9. **I Think I Need A New Heart** (*Volume 1*)
10. **I Can't Touch You Anymore** (*Volume 3*)
11. **A Chicken With Its Head Cut Off** (*Volume 1*)

**Fun Fact:** Originally, *69 Love Songs* was conceived to have 100 songs in total. Frontman Stephen Merritt opted to lower the number to 69 because he liked the idea of separating the albums into three CDs of 23 songs each. This is not the only time that Merritt has attempted such a vast musical undertaking. In 2017, when Merritt turned 50, he released the album, *50 Song Memoir*, which featured 50 songs on five albums with each song representing a year of his life. A few years later, Merritt released the album, *Quickies*, featuring 28 songs of abbreviated lengths with the shortest being a mere 17 seconds long.

# MASSIVE ATTACK

My first post-college job was working for the TV show *Friends*. Yes, that *Friends*. Specifically, I worked for the production company (Bright, Kaufman, Crane), who also made *Veronica's Closet* and *Jesse*. I primarily worked nights for *Jesse* as a night P.A. (while I spent Friday nights on the *Friends* set). As a night P.A., when the writers finished a new draft of a script, it was my job to drive copies around town and deliver them to the actors, so that they could read the new draft in the morning. My job was spent driving all over Los Angeles in the wee hours of the night like a roving grifter looking to score. It got lonely. Every week, I'd pick up new CDs to have fresh music to listen to. One album stood out: *Mezzanine* by Massive Attack. Even with its chilled-out vibes and low energy growl, it was stimulating like a kinetic puff of mystic air. It was my safe from sleep album. When I felt myself nodding off, I would quickly switch to *Mezzanine* and instantly be brought back to life. It didn't make sense. It was mellow, it was relaxed. *Mezzanine* didn't have the energy of rock. It played like a beautiful soundtrack to the night horizon. When I would glide down over Mulholland, it wasn't Tom Petty that serenaded me, it was the dizzy groove of "Black Milk," the pulsating evolution of "Angel," and Elizabeth Fraser's angelic siren on "Teardrop." Winding through the canyons of Beverly, I felt immersed in the surroundings, like the music was part of the landscape. *Mezzanine* isn't my favorite Massive Attack album, but it did save my sanity for one summer.

# Albums of the '90s:

*Blue Lines* (1991)
*Protection* (1994)
*Mezzanine* (1998)

# The 11 Best Songs By Massive Attack:

1. **Unfinished Sympathy** (*Blue Lines*)
2. **Teardrop** (*Mezzanine*)
3. **Safe From Harm** (*Blue Lines*)
4. **Protection** (*Protection*)
5. **Blue Lines** (*Blue Lines*)
6. **Black Milk** (*Mezzanine*)
7. **Man Next Door** (*Mezzanine*)
8. **Karmacoma** (*Protection*)
9. **Angel** (*Mezzanine*)
10. **Lately** (*Blue Lines*)
11. **Euro Child** (*Protection*)

**Fun Fact:** In 1991, the group briefly shortened their name to "Massive" for the release of their single, "Unfinished Sympathy." This was done to avoid any controversy with the ongoing Persian Gulf War.

**Song Note (Teardrop):** Vocalist Elisabeth Fraser was recording this song with the band when she learned about the death of her friend, Jeff Buckley. The emotion in the song is an homage to him.

# METALLICA

Before social media, popular music was the closest thing we had to viral sensations. The life-influencing obsession over MTV videos was on display in MTV's animated show, *Beavis and Butthead*. Beavis and Butthead were two idiotic teenagers, who obsessed about chicks, metal music, and setting things on fire while commenting on which music videos ruled, and which ones sucked. Somehow, these moron's musical tastes became society's gold standard. It's true. Their badge of approval was so powerful, it could make or break an artist's career. Just ask Winger. After Beavis and Butthead mercilessly mocked them, radio stations dropped the band from their playlists, and concert ticket sales dried up faster than a Bob Dole celebration dinner. Beavis and Butthead's favorite two bands were plastered right on the front of their T-shirts: AC/DC and Metallica. In the days before DVDs and digital libraries, the only way to own something was to record it off the TV onto a VHS tape. I had been recording *Beavis and Butthead* episodes all summer at a friend's house since I didn't have cable at home. But my presence became a nuisance as I spent one evening recording episodes while my friend was trying to have a date. After that, I had to compensate him. I found a Metallica shirt for him, exactly like the one Beavis wore on the show. It worked until...my tape was stolen during one of his parties. My friend felt so bad, he gave me the shirt back. I loved that shirt. I wore it all decade until I shared it with a friend because he showed me how to use Napster.

## Albums of the '90s:

*Metallica (The Black Album)* (1991)
*Load* (1996)
*Reload* (1997)
*Garage Inc.* (1998)

## The 11 Best Songs By Metallica:

1. **Bleeding Me** (*Load*)
2. **The Outlaw Torn** (*Load*)
3. **Enter Sandman** (*Black*)
4. **The Struggle Within** (*Black*)
5. **Don't Tread On Me** (*Black*)
6. **Wasting My Hate** (*Load*)
7. **Fuel** (*Re-Load*)
8. **The Unforgiven** (*Black*)
9. **Die, Die My Darling** (*Garage Inc.*)
10. **Fixxxer** (*Re-Load*)
11. **Holier Than Thou** (*Black*)

**Fun Fact:** Metallica's album *Load* is 78 minutes and 59 seconds long, the exact length of a full CD. They had to shorten the song "The Outlaw Torn" by a full minute so the whole album could fit on the CD.

**Fun Fact 2:** Metallica is the only band to perform on all seven continents.

# MOBY

In the early days of L.A. rave culture, Moby was a ghost. Every rave I attended, it was rumored that Moby was going to show up and spin. Whether the rave was in an airport hangar, a warehouse, or even a grocery store, the myth of Moby always hung in the air. I went to one rave on a private yacht anchored off the shore of Marina Del Rey. The only way to get to the rave was to pay a large man with a gun 50 bucks to motor you out there in his speed boat. After a nauseating boat trip to the yacht, we were welcomed to a seafaring fantasy. Tables full of drugs, any drugs, all drugs, all free. Snack tables with candy. Clothing optional. It was a party designed from Lewis Carroll's curious psyche. Pure fantasy. Like all previous raves, it was a "sure thing" that Moby would be there. I had never seen Moby. I had only heard rumblings about his epic performances. He was the pied piper of this blossoming underground electronic scene. Finally, at 3 AM, a small man wrapped in a black hoodie climbed onto the DJ platform. The crowd went bonkers. The small man raised one fist in the air, eliciting a cauldron of screams. Then, the music exploded all around us. A kinetic frenzy of digital waves washed over us like a warm bath. It was electric heaven but only lasted three songs as the man dropped out of sight and was gone. I never saw his face and I always wondered if that really was Moby. Was the myth of Moby that powerful that the mere thought of him was all the audience needed? If so, it only goes to show why Moby is the most pivotal hero of why electronic music exists today.

# Albums of the '90s:

*Moby* (1992)
*Early Underground* (1993)
*Ambient* (1993)
*Move* (1993)
*Everything Is Wrong* (1995)
*Animal Rights* (1996)
*I Like To Score* (1997)
*Play* (1999)

# The 11 Best Songs By Moby:

1. **Everytime You Touch Me** (*Everything Is Wrong*)
2. **Move (You Make Me Feel So Good)** (*Move*)
3. **Why Does My Heart Feel So Bad?** (*Play*)
4. **Natural Blues** (*Play*)
5. **Bodyrock** (*Play*)
6. **Go** (*Moby*)
7. **Feeling So Real** (*Everything Is Wrong*)
8. **When It's Cold I'd Like To Die** (*Everything Is Wrong*)
9. **Porcelain** (*Play*)
10. **God Moving Over The Face Of The Waters** (*Everything Is Wrong*)
11. **Thousand** (*Next Is The E*)

**Song Note (Thousand):** This song holds the Guinness World Record for the song with the most beats-per-minute (BPM). Like its title suggests, the song has over a thousand beats per minute, topping out at 1,015 bpm.

# MODEST MOUSE

When Modest Mouse first played live, audiences started the concerning custom of shouting "Built To Spill" at shows, insinuating that Modest Mouse was a knock-off of said band. It was even believed if you shouted "Built To Spill" loud enough, lead singer Isaac Brock would leap off the stage and fight whoever said it. I always thought it was just a rumor until I saw them play a show at club Moguls in L.A. in 1997. Mogul's was basically a big room in the back of a bar with a stack of metal risers where you could sit and watch bands or pygmy football teams, whoever they could book. Tonight, the club had around 100 flannel-wearing hipsters in it. Modest Mouse took the stage to tepid cheers. They were barely one song into the set when some jackass decided to put the "Built To Spill" rumor to the test. Brock immediately threw down his guitar and leapt into the crowd, fists flying. I was too far in the back to see the fight. I thought for sure that was the end of the show, but as soon as the perpetrator was escorted from the club, Brock returned to the stage and busted right back into their set as if this was all part of the plan. I absolutely loved it, because honestly, I feel like the jackass deserved it. If someone tells you not to stick your hand in a shark's mouth because he'll bite it off, then you go and stick your hand in the shark's mouth, you don't blame the shark when you now have a hook for a hand. Modest Mouse would bite back on their critics and eventually breakthrough into radio stardom in the 2000s. But in the '90s, they were at their introspective lonesome best.

## Albums of the '90s:

*This Is A Long Drive For Someone With Nothing To Think About* (1996)
*Interstate 8* (1996)
*The Lonesome Crowded West* (1997)
*The Fruit That Ate Itself* (1997)
*Night On The Sun* (1999)

## The 11 Best Songs By Modest Mouse:

1. **Trailer Trash** (*The Lonesome Crowded West*)
2. **Breakthrough** (*This Is A Long Drive For Someone*)
3. **Doin' The Cockroach** (*The Lonesome Crowded West*)
4. **Custom Concern** (*This Is A Long Drive For Someone*)
5. **Heart Cooks Brain** (*The Lonesome Crowded West*)
6. **Polar Opposites** (*The Lonesome Crowded West*)
7. **Sunspots In The House Of The Late Scapegoat** (*The Fruit That Ate Itself*)
8. **All Night Diner** (*Interstate 8*)
9. **Teeth Like God's Shoeshine** (*The Lonesome Crowded West*)
10. **Out Of Gas** (*The Lonesome Crowded West*)
11. **Whenever You Breathe Out, I Breathe In** (*Broke* single)

**Fun Fact:** In the Supreme Court case of *MGM vs. Grokster*, Modest Mouse is mentioned in the legal documents. Supreme Court Justice, David Souter, wrote "Users seeking Top 40 songs, for example, or the latest release by Modest Mouse..."[1] in reference to civilians downloading songs.

---

[1] *MGM v. Grokster*, 545 U.S. 913, 919, 926 (2005)

# MORRISSEY

In the fall of 1991, I stopped in to use the bathroom at Pauley Pavilion, UCLA's iconic basketball court, on the way home from campus. As I was washing up, I noticed movement in the stall behind me. A friend of mine was hiding in the stall because there was a Morrissey concert at Pauley Pavilion that night, and he didn't have tickets. He planned to hide in the stall for eight hours in hopes of evading security and sneaking into the show. You cannot just be a Morrissey fan. Appreciating Morrissey takes a certain type of devotion. Listening to Morrissey doesn't signify what kind of music you like; it signifies what kind of person you are. Think about it. If I told you I was a Morrissey fan, you could picture my exact look in your head, from the frumpy black clothes to the slicked-back hair. My friend was planning to spend eight hours cramped inside a bathroom stall to see Moz. To him, it showed his dedication. Morrissey was a romantic. The lovelorn lost souls worshipped him. They would do anything Moz asked. That night, that happened. Halfway through the show, Moz, unbeknownst to security, invited the crowd to join him on stage. He may have been speaking glibly, but his fans took him seriously. The entire audience rushed the stage, knocking over chairs, breaking down barriers, and causing Morrissey to be hurried off. The show was canceled as a riot ensued. At first, I was mad at seeing an abbreviated set, but now, in retrospect, I appreciate witnessing the pure power of Morrissey in a historic musical moment of pandemonium.

# Albums of the '90s:

*Kill Uncle* (1991)

*Your Arsenal* (1992)

*Vauxhall and I* (1994)

*Southpaw Grammar* (1995)

*Maladjusted* (1997)

# The 11 Best Songs By Morrissey:

1. **Tomorrow** (*Your Arsenal*)
2. **We Hate It When Our Friends Become Successful** (*Your Arsenal*)
3. **Why Don't You Find Out For Yourself** (*Vauxhall And I*)
4. **The National Front Disco** (*Your Arsenal*)
5. **November Spawned A Monster** (*November Spawned A Monster* single)
6. **Seasick, Yet Still Docked** (*Your Arsenal*)
7. **Sing Your Life** (*Kill Uncle*)
8. **You're Gonna Need Someone On Your Side** (*Your Arsenal*)
9. **The Boy Racer** (*Southpaw Grammar*)
10. **Alma Matters** (*Maladjusted*)
11. **He Knows I'd Love To See Him** (*November Spawned A Monster* single B-side)

**Fun Fact:** Before joining the Smiths, Morrissey was a published novelist and had a series of short books released. The subjects included the New York Dolls and James Dean.

# SET-BREAK / I HATE MOVIE SOUNDTRACKS

In the late '90s, some friends and I started a website called I Hate Everything. Now, we really didn't hate everything; the site was satire, parody. We told funny stories about random things that would happen to us. Some of them were true, while others were exaggerated for effect. We were very upfront that this was all in good fun. One of my articles was entitled, "I Hate Trader Joe's." I really didn't hate Trader Joe's; truthfully, I love it. My article was more of a back-handed compliment to the company that they were so good at providing fun pre-packaged meals that they took all the creative power away from me doing it myself. They were too good. It was a joke. Unfortunately, our audience never really bought into the concept of the site. We received tons of hate emails about our posts. Too many readers thought we were being serious. I even received a death threat because I gave a Tiffany album a bad review (even though I gave every album a bad review). There were a few positive emails. One of the most glowing reviews we ever received came two years after we stopped updating the site. Someone had gone through the entire site, read every post, and sent a long email praising our comedic talents and wondering if we were ever going to re-launch the site. It gave me momentary hope that maybe we had a future, but when thinking about it, one positive email isn't exactly the groundswell we needed.

I Hate Everything dot com ran for about a year and stayed online for another three years until I finally stopped paying the hosting fees. Before its demise, I had created a list of possible future posts. One post was about the movie soundtracks that flooded the marketplace during the '90s. I was annoyed that every movie had to have a soundtrack that accompanied it; most of them were nothing more than cash grabs. While I never actually wrote the post back then, I always wanted to. So, here is why I hated movie soundtracks during the '90s (all the while, loving them at the same time).

\*　　　　\*　　　　\*

Movie soundtracks in the '90s mostly sucked. Every movie that came out during the decade had to have a soundtrack attached to it. I'm not talking about the film's score, which was meticulously orchestrated by a professional film composer. I'm referring to the soundtrack, an album of pop songs that usually had little or no connection to the movie and was only released to make money off the film's name. This trend didn't happen overnight.

In the '80s, films like *Footloose, Pretty In Pink,* and *Fast Times At Ridgemont High* all had fun soundtracks that captured the time and place of the film. Each film specifically dealt with teen culture, and the music on the soundtrack was a sonic snapshot of the music of the times. On top of that, the music from these soundtracks was imperative to the storytelling in the film.

The '90s were no different. There were plenty of great soundtracks that accurately synced with their films. You had films like *Wedding Singer, Dazed And Confused, Forrest Gump,* and *Boogie Nights* which all dealt with a specific historical era and the music was an audio sample of that era. The soundtracks to *Boogie Nights* and *Dazed And Confused* were so popular that they even spawned sequels. It wasn't just nostalgic soundtracks that had credibility. The soundtrack to *Trainspotting* featured mostly original music that sonically painted their movie's world in the way the filmmakers wanted the audience to experience it. The music was integral to the storytelling. *Trainspotting* was another film whose soundtrack was so popular that it spawned a second disc of music. *Pulp Fiction, Go, Velvet Goldmine*, even *Sister Act* were other integral soundtracks that had music that directly affected the films' stories. These soundtracks were well-received because of their authenticity. They re-inserted you into the atmosphere of their films.

There were noteworthy soundtracks across all genres. We had hip-hop soundtracks to films like *Higher Learning, Belly*, and *Street Fighter*; R&B soundtracks for *Waiting to Exhale, Boomerang*, and Whitney Houston's *The Bodyguard*. Country music had *Hope Floats* and *The Thing Called Love*. Some studios attempted to be daring and predict future trends. The *Judgment Night* soundtrack included rock bands and rap artists recording songs together, like Living Colour with Run-DMC, Pearl Jam with Cypress Hill, and Slayer with Ice-T. The *Spawn* soundtrack featured rock bands combining forces with electronic artists, like The Crystal Method with Filter, Marilyn Manson with the Sneaker Pimps, and Orbital with Metallica.

While these soundtracks were notable (and the exceptions to the crappy ones), the soundtrack that had the biggest influence on the genre was from the Cameron Crowe film, *Singles*. *Singles* followed a group of young adults coming of age, dating, and enjoying life in Seattle. If you haven't been keeping track, Seattle had a huge impact on this decade's music. *Singles* not only highlighted the culture but included popular Seattle rock bands in the film and on the soundtrack. Only the film wasn't a big hit. It wasn't a flop, either. It made a middling 18 million, which was 10 million less than the Sylvester Stallone picture, *Stop Or My Mom Will Shoot*. *Singles* barely broke even and ranked 66th in the box office that year. *Singles* wasn't a total failure, largely due to the success of the soundtrack, which sold over 2 million copies. At $10 a disc (and I'm low-balling it) that's 20 million in sales. That means the soundtrack made more money than the movie. The success of the *Singles* soundtrack is because it included new songs from the biggest rock bands in the world, like Smashing Pumpkins, Soundgarden, Alice In Chains, and Pearl Jam. Those bands drove the album sales and proved a very important point, the soundtrack could bail out the box office. Once the studios realized this, the flood gates opened.

Moving forward, studios would pack their soundtracks with trending bands, whether they fit with the movie or not. The idea was reasonable. The movie could drive soundtrack sales, *and* if the soundtrack had popular music, it could drive box office sales. Many flailing movies benefited from this tactic like *Hackers* and *The Saint*. But the film that benefited the most was *Empire Records*. This movie made an extremely low box office gross, coming in at $150,000. That's awful by any standard. The soundtrack was packed with trending bands like the Gin Blossoms, Better Than Ezra, The Cranberries, and Cracker, and went on to sell over 2 million copies. That means the soundtrack made 100 times more money than the movie. This was the moment that the soundtrack became more important than the film.

Soundtracks were no longer symbiotic properties. They were marketing tools; compilations, packed with songs by popular bands, put together by marketing teams to boost sales. At a certain point, you could tell that the marketing department no longer even cared whether the music fit with the movies. Take the *Batman Forever* soundtrack. While the first *Batman* film in 1989 received a full album of newly composed Prince songs, it still felt authentic. Once director Tim Burton left the franchise, the marketing team swooped in and created a highly listenable jukebox compilation of songs by popular bands that had no affiliation with the tone, story, or plot of the movie. With new songs by Seal, U2, The Offspring, Method Man, Massive Attack, PJ Harvey, and Sunny Day Real Estate, you could tell this was put together by someone who knew music. The *Batman Forever* soundtrack is the best-compiled soundtrack of the decade that has absolutely nothing to do with the film. Though the studio may have forced the filmmakers to insert some of these songs in the background of the scenes, there is no connection between the music and the storytelling. Listening to the soundtrack in no way reminds me of the movie.

While *Batman Forever* was at least a good compilation of songs, others couldn't even do that. Rage Against The Machine on the *Godzilla* soundtrack was the biggest head slap moment of the decade. The most anti-establishment band being featured on a big-budget studio film soundtrack illustrated that the industry had full-on lost their minds. The marketing teams were so detached from the music and focused on the analytics, they didn't even realize that Rage's song was lyrically trashing big studio films like *Godzilla*. Despite Rage putting out a pretty good song on an otherwise mediocre soundtrack, the inclusion was laughable. While this might not seem like this is a big deal, it actually had a profound and detrimental effect on the music industry.

When the marketing teams no longer cared what people wanted to hear and started making soundtracks as promotional vehicles for their lesser-known bands, it had a devastating ripple effect. These lesser-known bands were lesser-known for a reason. They weren't as impactful or as important as many of the artists driving the mainstream. Because these bands went on to affect the culture, you could feel the quality of mainstream music take a huge nosedive. It was one thing that studios felt this incessant need to make a soundtrack as a mere cash grab but when that music started to influence culture, it turned ugly.

When Our Lady Peace, Days of the New, Tonic, Duncan Shiek, Audioweb, Dishwalla, Oleander, or Placebo are your album highlights, you've completely lost touch with what is trending. Instead, you're trying to get the audience to listen to what you want them to hear. Yeah, yeah, I hear you. You like some of the songs from the bands I listed. That's fine. I'm not saying these bands are terrible (maybe some are); I'm pointing out that the quality of the bands pales in comparison to the precision that earlier soundtracks had utilizing influential bands that were symbiotic with the film content. Let's go back to the *Singles* soundtrack. Those bands weren't just popular; they also existed in the world of the movie. They were as much a part of that film as the actors were, and honestly, possibly more. *Singles* had two songs by Pearl Jam. *10 Things I Hate About You* had two songs by Letters to Cleo. Letters to Cleo! Really? That's your big album draw? This is a movie about teenage culture and the music is supposed to mirror that. Letters To Cleo had a couple of decent songs but they're not driving any teenage rebellion; they're album filler. When your soundtracks become more filler than hits, the filler songs become the hits. These filler songs are what audiences hear, so these are the songs they let define them. And when average songs define your world, your bar for music quality is severely lowered.

The downfall of the soundtrack occurred because the studios took advantage of the situation and ruined it. I hated soundtracks because they were used as a tool to manipulate me as a buyer. This was a time before the internet. I couldn't go online and buy the one song I wanted from the soundtrack. I had no choice but to buy the whole thing. I bought the *Coneheads* soundtrack just for the new song, "Soul To Squeeze" by Red Hot Chili Peppers. I bought the *I Know What You Did Last Summer* soundtrack just for the Offspring song "D.U.I.." I bought the *Basketball Diaries* soundtrack for the Soundgarden song "Blind Dogs." I hadn't seen any of these movies and I had very little interest in the other songs on the soundtracks, but I bought them anyway. I have boxes of CD soundtracks from movies I've never seen with songs that I've listened to once. It was infuriating.

The biggest heartbreak is the soundtrack quality opened with such hope. The *Singles* soundtrack stood above the rest. It drew a line in the sand that all soundtracks should aspire to be. Along with the soundtracks that I listed above, others exhibited this cinematic spirit where the music and the movie were creatively linked; films like *Good Will Hunting*, *He Got Game*, *Lost Highway*, *Rushmore*, and *That Thing You Do!* But for every inspired *Romeo + Juliet* soundtrack, you had five times as many dreadful *Barb Wire* soundtracks. And, even the worst of them, unfortunately, always had one song you wanted.

# MUDHONEY

I caught Salmonella from Eddie Vedder's favorite restaurant when visiting Seattle. I don't know if it really was his favorite restaurant, that's just what I heard. I visited Seattle a lot when I was in college. I loved the city; if it weren't for the film industry, I would have moved there. Even after catching this horrible stomach bug, I still went back. Gloomy and rainy, Seattle became the go-to destination for '90s culture. As was mentioned in the previous chapter, Seattle culture was best reflected in the Cameron Crowe film, *Singles*. *Singles* was a look at the dating battlefield for Gen-Xers, who were redefining typical gender roles that had been in existence for hundreds of years. Dating became more challenging but also more exciting. *Singles* captured that. The film also captured that moment in music by including local music heroes like Soundgarden, Screaming Trees, Alice In Chains, and Pearl Jam. The only grunge band that didn't make the cut was Nirvana. Instead of including Nirvana, Crowe opted to go with Mudhoney, who was the biggest thing in Seattle at the time. Truth is, the birth of the grunge came from the band Mudhoney. They were worshipped in Seattle as supersonic kings. Mudhoney was faster, darker, and more ferocious than anyone else. They were the standard you played up to. It was a no-brainer that they should be on the soundtrack. *Singles* was and still is an experience. If you want to travel back in time to the '90s, find a Blockbuster, rent the movie *Singles*, and sit back and experience it. Just don't forget to rewind the tape.

# Albums of the '90s:

*Superfuzz Bigmuff Plus Early Singles* (1990)
*Every Good Boy Deserves Fudge* (1991)
*Piece Of Cake* (1992)
*Five Dollar Bob Mock Cooter Stew* (1993)
*My Brother The Cow* (1995)
*Tomorrow Hit Today* (1998)

# The 11 Best Songs By Mudhoney:

1.  **Suck You Dry** (*Piece Of Cake*)
2.  **Thorn** (*Every Good Boy Deserves Fudge*)
3.  **No End In Sight** (*Piece Of Cake*)
4.  **Deception Pass** (*Five Dollar Bob Mock Cooter Stew*)
5.  **Into The Drink** (*Every Good Boy Deserves Fudge*)
6.  **Overblown** (*Singles* OST)
7.  **Ghost** (*Tomorrow Hit Today*)
8.  **Blinding Sun** (*Piece of Cake*)
9.  **F.D.K.** (*My Brother The Cow*)
10. **Broken Hands** (*Every Good Boy Deserves Fudge*)
11. **Oblivion / {Symbol for Infinity}** (*Tomorrow Hit Today*)

**Song Note (Overblown):** The band was given $20,000 from the movie studio to record the song for the *Singles* soundtrack. The band recorded it for a mere $165 and pocketed the rest of the money.

# NAS

In my day, I used to get eight CDs for a penny. A penny! I'm not exaggerating; in the '90s, you really could get eight CDs for a penny from mail-order music clubs. Clubs like BMG and Columbia House sent out CD catalogues of major releases every month. They offered new customers eight CDs for a penny to join their service. All you had to do was pay for shipping and purchase a few of their CDs at full price ($20) over the next year. Even though their prices were high, if you counted in your free CDs, it averaged out to about $8 each. Not a bad deal. But here's how they got you. Each month, the services offered a featured album and it was *your* responsibility to mail in and tell them you didn't want it. If you forgot, they sent it to you and billed you for it. This happened to me with Nas. One day, I came home to find Nas' *It Was Written* sitting in my mail-box. Annoyed with myself for forgetting to send in my mailer and now stuck with the CD, I gave it a listen. Best mistake I ever made. While some rappers dropped knowledge, Nas was dropping an entire library. His confident flow had such cultural articulation, I felt like I was listening to the hip-hop Bob Dylan. He had the same insightful storytelling, trying to make sense of the world. I called my friend Melissa to share my Nas state of mind. She laughed at my tardiness to the Nas game, "Just wait until you hear *Illmatic*." Though CD clubs introduced me to Nas, I wasn't going to spend $20 and wait four weeks to get *Illmatic* from them. I went to Tower and bought it that day. I've been listening to it ever since.

# Albums of the '90s:

*Illmatic* (1994)
*It Was Written* (1996)
*I Am...* (1999)
*Nastradamus* (1999)

# The 11 Best Songs By Nas:

1. **The World Is Yours** (*Illmatic*)
2. **N.Y. State Of Mind** (*Illmatic*)
3. **The Message** (*It Was Written*)
4. **If I Ruled The World (Imagine That)** (*It Was Written*)
5. **It Ain't Hard To Tell** (*Illmatic*)
6. **Nas Is Like** (*I Am...*)
7. **Memory Lane (Sittin' In Da Park)** (*Illmatic*)
8. **Life We Choose** (*Nastradamus*)
9. **One Love** (*Illmatic*)
10. **New World (***Nastradamus***)**
11. **Life's A Bitch** (*Illmatic*)

**Fun Fact:** Nas' father is acclaimed jazz musician Olu Dara. Dara is a skilled cornetist, guitarist, and singer, who has played as a sideman on dozens of jazz albums through-out his career. Dara even contributed by playing the trumpet on Nas' album, *Illmatic*.

**Song Note (If I Ruled The World):** The song features background vocals by then-unknown singer, Lauryn Hill. Though it was an uncredited cameo, Hill's distinctive voice was easily recognized by her fans.

# NINE INCH NAILS

As a screenwriting student at UCLA's film school, my classes were regulated to writing scripts that would never get made and classes studying films that had already been made. I did take one class where I made a 2-minute short on 16-millimeter film. As part of the MTV generation, I wanted to make a music video. But to what song? Typically, a director picks the song first, then shoots material to pair with it. I knew what I wanted to shoot, but I didn't know what the footage would look like and wanted the song to match it. So, I shot the video first. It was a black and white piece about how emotions in a relationship are similar to the emotions from addiction. When I screened the footage, my teacher didn't think I could make it into something cohesive. My friend Anh suggested that I had been listening to too much Nine Inch Nails. Indirectly, he inspired me. I needed a Nine Inch Nails song. Most of NIN's material featured aggressive clashing of guitars, the outcry of primal urges, and the unabashed dissatisfaction of corporate pigs. But they had one song with soul-bearing introspection. It was called "Hurt." It was dark, brooding, and the perfect choice. I spent the next few weeks with a film splicer, cutting my raw footage to match with the song. At our screening, my teacher was blown away, claiming it was the best short film ever to be made in her class. She gave me an A-plus. I tried to submit it to the end of the year director's film showcase but was rejected because I was a screenwriting student. I guess it was something I could never have.

# Albums of the '90s:

*Broken* (1992)
*Fixed* (1992)
*The Downward Spiral* (1994)
*Further Down The Spiral* (1995)
*Quake* (1996)
*The Fragile* (1999)

# The 11 Best Songs By Nine Inch Nails:

1. **The Perfect Drug** (*Lost Highway* OST)
2. **We're In This Together** (*The Fragile*)
3. **Wish** (*Broken*)
4. **Hurt** (*The Downward Spiral*)
5. **Ruiner** (*The Downward Spiral*)
6. **Piggy** (*The Downward Spiral*)
7. **Closer** (*The Downward Spiral*)
8. **Dead Souls** (*The Crow* OST)
9. **Into The Void** (*The Fragile*)
10. **Burn** (*Natural Born Killers* OST)
11. **Suck** (*Broken*)

**Fun Fact:** Nine Inch Nails composed all the in-game music for the computer game, *Quake*. *Quake* was a new game from the creators of the immensely popular game *Doom*.

**Fun Fact 2:** *The Downward Spiral* was recorded in the mansion where the infamous Manson murders took place. Reznor claims he didn't know this until after he moved in.

171

# NIRVANA

In the fall of 1992, the MTV Video Music Awards came to Pauley Pavilion at UCLA. In an attempt to create a rock show vibe, MTV opened up the pit to UCLA students in an attempt to capture that *teen spirit*. MTV was our scripture and having tickets to the VMAs was cooler than having Super Bowl tickets, Oscar® tickets, and Wonka's Golden ticket...combined. I waited all night for my tickets and found myself sitting front and center. I had better seats than Van Halen! The event was surreal. Pearl Jam ripped through a powerhouse version of "Jeremy," Red Hot Chili Peppers and Ice-T brought the party with "Give It Away," and Guns N' Roses united with Elton John for their epic rocker ballad, "November Rain." One performance would live on in infamy...Nirvana. The band immediately gave the middle finger to the sensors and played the opening bars to their new song "Rape Me" before launching into a scream-fest rendition of "Lithium." All the while, students were flinging themselves off the stage into the mosh pit. It was beautiful chaos until Krist Novoselic hurled his bass guitar into the air and attempted to catch it. He failed miserably as the guitar slammed into his head, busting open his forehead and sending him to the hospital for stitches. As Krist stumbled away, Kurt ended the song by destroying his equipment while Dave Grohl gave Axl Rose a mocking salutation. This was the only time I saw Nirvana play live, but no other performance perfectly captures the pure carnal antagonism that exemplifies everything the band was and will ever be.

# Albums of the '90s:

*Nevermind* (1991)

*Hormoaning* (1992)

*Incesticide* (1992)

*In Utero* (1993)

*MTV Unplugged* (1994)

*From The Muddy Banks Of The Wishkah* (1996)

# The 11 Best Songs By Nirvana:

1. **Smells Like Teen Spirit** (*Nevermind*)
2. **Lithium** (*Nevermind*)
3. **Aneurysm** (*Incesticide/Hormoaning*)
4. **Pennyroyal Tea** (*In Utero*)
5. **Lounge Act** (*Nevermind*)
6. **Sappy** aka **Verse Chorus Verse** (*No Alternative*)
7. **Heart-Shaped Box** (*In Utero*)
8. **In Bloom** (*Nevermind*)
9. **All Apologies** (*In Utero*)
10. **Come As You Are** (*Nevermind*)
11. **Sliver** (*Incesticide*)

**Fun Fact:** Quentin Tarantino offered Kurt Cobain the role of the drug dealer in *Pulp Fiction* (which would be played by Eric Stoltz). Even though Cobain turned down the role, the band still thanked Tarantino in the liner notes for their album, *In Utero*.

# THE NOTORIOUS B.I.G.

I am a non-confrontational person. Except for one time in college when I came close to getting into a fight because I told someone at a party that I thought Biggie Smalls (aka Notorious B.I.G.) was the most overrated rapper in the game. If I had told this guy that I had posted naked pictures of his mom on a giant billboard, it would have elicited less of a violent reaction. The guy took it so personally, I thought he was going to 187 me. The truth is, I was wrong. Biggie and Tupac were pawns in the east coast vs. west coast hip-hop feud. It was basically a turf war over radio exposure and who deserved it more. If you were in the hip-hop community, you had to take sides. Being a white college kid, I felt like I needed to choose. Born and raised on the West Coast, I chose Tupac. It was really one of the dumber things I did because the only reason I was even taking a side was because I thought it made me cool. When both Biggie and Tupac were gunned down, the whole thing seemed trivial and lame. Why did we need to pick? Can you imagine killing someone because they liked Nirvana over Pearl Jam? The Offspring over Green Day? Backstreet Boys over *Nsync? It was moronic. After Biggie's death, I revisited his music and became a fan. Part of me is disappointed that I didn't get into a fight over it. The fight would have been legendary. It would have been a story students told their grandkids; two dumbass white kids getting in a fight over rap music. I'm just happy no one had cell phones back then to document my stupidity.

## Albums of the '90s:

*Ready To Die* (1994)
*Life After Death* (1997)
*Born Again* (1999)

## The 11 Best Songs By The Notorious B.I.G.:

1. **Juicy** (*Ready To Die*)
2. **Hypnotize** (*Life After Death*)
3. **Mo Money Mo Problems** (*Life After Death*)
4. **Everyday Struggle** (*Ready To Die*)
5. **Ten Crack Commandments** (*Life After Death*)
6. **Suicidal Thoughts** (*Ready To Die*)
7. **Going Back To Cali** (*Life After Death*)
8. **Party and Bullshit** (*Who's The Man?* OST)
9. **Who Shot Ya?** (*Ready To Die*)
10. **Notorious B.I.G.** (*Born Again*)
11. **Warning** (*Ready To Die*)

**Fun Fact:** Before Tupac Shakur signed to Death Row Records and became a rival, Biggie and Tupac were friends. They would travel together, and Biggie would often stay at Tupac's home when visiting the West Coast.

# OASIS

"These guys are real rock stars!" my friend declared as he barged into my apartment, pulling out Oasis' new CD, *Be Here Now*, from his yellow Tower Records bag. He ejected whatever CD was playing on my stereo, replaced it with Oasis, and cranked the opening song, "D'You Know What I Mean?" "Listen to the glorious scope," my friend exclaimed. "We are witnessing rock and roll icons in their prime." During the decade, there was a perception championed by Oasis fans that the band was the next Beatles. No one thought this more than the band themselves. Oasis bought into their own myth more than anyone, and it tore them apart as a band. I wasn't an Oasis fan until I watched their performance on *MTV Unplugged*. There was a fight between the brothers, Liam and Noel Gallagher, over who was the true leader of the band. The fight was so bad that Liam refused to sing and went up to the balcony where he heckled the band as they performed without him. Noel filled in on vocals and, honestly, did a fantastic job. Watching Noel's more grounded approach, I was able to appreciate the songwriting on a different level. I liked the show so much that I recorded it on VHS, then I connected my cassette player to it and duped the audio onto a cassette. It sounded grainy, but I loved it because it meant that I had music that you couldn't get anywhere else. My friend was right; witnessing the MTV performance was like witnessing a moment in rock history, made by a band who willed themselves into being rock legends.

## Albums of the '90s:

*Definitely Maybe* (1994)
*(What's The Story) Morning Glory?* (1995)
*Be Here Now* (1997)
*Some Might Say* (1998)

## The 11 Best Songs By Oasis:

1. **Live Forever** (*Definitely Maybe*)
2. **Wonderwall** (*(What's The Story) Morning Glory?*)
3. **Supersonic** (*Definitely Maybe*)
4. **Don't Look Back In Anger** (*(What's The Story) Morning Glory?*)
5. **Whatever** (*Whatever* Non-album single)
6. **Acquiesce** (*Some Might Say* single B-side)
7. **Rockin' Chair** (*Roll With It* single B-side)
8. **Slide Away** (*Definitely Maybe*)
9. **Don't Go Away** (*Be Here Now*)
10. **Morning Glory** (*(What's The Story) Morning Glory?*)
11. **Hello** (*(What's The Story) Morning Glory?*)

**Fun Fact:** A record-breaking 250,000 people attended the Oasis concert at Knebworth in England on August 9, 1996.

**Song Note (Wonderwall):** The song was named after George Harrison's solo album, *Wonderwall Music*, an instrumental soundtrack to the 1968 movie, *Wonderwall*.

# THE OFFSPRING

"I don't know why people like us; we suck." Singer Dexter Holland said this to me when I met him backstage at the Hollywood Palladium in 1997. Though Holland was being facetious, this was a prevailing sentiment about the band since they found their self-esteem. In the mid-90s, a new punk revolution had emerged. Bands like Bad Religion, Green Day, Pennywise, AFI, Rancid, NOFX, and The Offspring took control of the airwaves. The criticisms came fast and hard. Most of the new punk bands were considered "not punk" like their '70s/'80s predecessors but instead, watered-down rip-offs. While Green Day was batting away comparisons to the Clash, The Offspring faced a completely different battle. Most people thought The Offspring just flat out sucked. Their guitar playing was elementary, their songwriting was kitschy, and Dexter Holland couldn't carry a tune if it came with handles. While most of this is true, this is actually what makes The Offspring great. Despite all the technical elements holding them back, The Offspring would write some of the catchiest songs of the entire decade. And the fact that they weren't musical progenies is what made those songs so likeable. They were ordinary guys who just didn't give a flying f*@k. I loved the Offspring, and when they came to L.A., I made sure to get backstage passes. Meeting Dexter was a thrill but hearing his humility in the face of stardom, and having a sense of humor about it, made me realize that they appreciated their success as much as I appreciated meeting them. The Offspring were alright.

## Albums of the '90s:

*Ignition* (1992)

*Smash* (1994)

*Ixnay On The Hombre* (1997)

*Amèricana* (1998)

# The 11 Best Songs By The Offspring:

1. **The Kids Aren't Alright** (*Americana*)
2. **Self-Esteem** (*Smash*)
3. **Gone Away** (*Ixnay On The Hombre*)
4. **Forever And A Day** (*Ignition*)
5. **All I Want** (*Ixnay On The Hombre*)
6. **Bad Habit** (*Smash*)
7. **Smash It Up** (*Batman Forever* OST)
8. **Session** (*Ignition*)
9. **Have You Ever** (*Americana*)
10. **The Meaning Of Life** (*Ixnay On The Hombre*)
11. **Dirty Magic** (*Ignition*)

**Fun Fact:** Singer Dexter Holland always viewed The Offspring as a hobby and never expected them to be as popular as they became. As a fallback, Holland attended USC grad school where he eventually received a Ph.D. in molecular biology.

# ORBITAL

In the fall of 1996, UCLA's radio station went through a major reconstruction. The mixing boards were ripped out, equipment unassembled. Everything was dismantled and laid in boxes in the middle of the room. Before I could re-open the station that year, I had to rebuild it from scratch. I hired an engineer friend for the tech assembly to get the equipment working. I reached out to any ex-DJs who were still in school. I collected a ragtag group of music nerds, and altogether, we re-launched the station. This meant we had to re-launch the content, too. The hard rock wail of my undergrad years was fading away. Guitars were being swapped out for keyboards as music was transitioning to electronica. This was an entire genre of music, completely designated for drug-induced youth who wanted to get high and dance until their brains turned to mush. It was new. It was fresh. I wanted it. We created a whole night dedicated to the genre with rotating DJs. To promote our night sessions, we played electronica songs during our daytime rotation. It was Orbital's song "The Box" that became the flagship song for the promotion. It was played by every DJ and the audiences loved it. Our electronica night became the most popular program our station had ever had in its existence. What Orbital ushered in was a new era of music. For me, it was an even bigger symbol of the two stages of my college career. The analog grunge movement that shaped my undergraduate years was gone, and now, it was replaced with electronic raves of the wide-open digital future.

# Albums of the '90s:

*Orbital* (1991)

*Orbital 2* (1993)

*Snivilisation* (1994)

*In Sides* (1996)

*Middle Of Nowhere* (1999)

# The 11 Best Songs By Orbital:

1. **Halcyon + On + On** (*Orbital 2*)
2. **The Box, Parts 1 & 2** (*In Sides*)
3. **Lush 3-1/Lush 3-2** (*Orbital 2*)
4. **The Girl With The Sun In Her Head** (*In Sides*)
5. **Way Out -->** (*Middle Of Nowhere*)
6. **Forever** (*Snivilisation*)
7. **Belfast** (*Orbital*)
8. **Out There Somewhere, Parts 1 & 2** (*In Sides*)
9. **Impact (The Earth Is Burning)** (*Orbital 2*)
10. **Know Where To Run** (*Middle Of Nowhere*)
11. **Science Fiction** (*Snivilisation*)

**Song Note (Halcyon + On + On):** This is considered to be the band's most popular live song. During the live performance, Orbital typically plays a remix version that incorporates clips from Belinda Carlisle's "Heaven Is A Place On Earth" and Bon Jovi's "You Give Love A Bad Name." It is technically considered the first-ever mash-up.

# OUTKAST

I was working in a TV writer's room in the summer of 1998 when the whole office stopped to watch President Clinton admit he had an affair with a White House intern. Watching the most esteemed person in the country, if not the world, humiliate himself on national television was a hard thing to see. My boss stared at the screen and said, "This is so embarrassing." It was. For Clinton, for his family, for the country, and everyone involved. During Clinton's subsequent impeachment, Outkast dropped their single, "Rosa Parks." The title was a symbolic gesture to the civil rights activist who had refused to give up her seat on a segregated bus in 1955. Everyone loved Outkast's party-rific stomp fest, except one person: the real Rosa Parks, who filed a lawsuit against Outkast for misappropriation of her name. Again, my office went into full spectator mode. Again, it was surreal. And again, my boss, after reading an article about the lawsuit, furrowed his brow and said, "This is so embarrassing." What these two incidents have in common is that they are examples of the idealism we place on our role models. Until then, I looked up to politicians, activists, even singers as infallible perfections, but it was this moment that made me realize they were nothing more than human beings. This is what made Outkast so likeable. They owned up to their flaws, letting the whole wide world know their secrets. By delivering their skeletons with an uninhibited euphoria, everyone could relate to it, even the U.S. President, who had to apologize a trillion times.

# Albums of the '90s:

*Southernplayalisticadillacmuzik* (1994)
*ATLiens* (1996)
*Aquemini* (1998)

# The 11 Best Songs By Outkast:

1. **Rosa Parks** (*Aquemini*)
2. **ATLiens** (*ATLiens*)
3. **Aquemini** (*Aquemini*)
4. **Southernplayalisticadillacmuzik** (*Southernplayalistica dillacmuzik*)
5. **Player's Ball** (*Southernplayalisticadillacmuzik*)
6. **Wheelz of Steel** (*ATLiens*)
7. **Jazzy Belle** (*ATLiens*)
8. **Ain't No Thang** (*Southernplayalisticadillacmuzik*)
9. **Two Dope Boyz (In A Cadillac)** (*ATLiens*)
10. **Phobia** (*Higher Learning* OST)
11. **Synthesizer** (*Aquemini*)

**Fun Fact:** *Aquemini* is the combination of the zodiac signs belonging to Andre 3000 (Gemini) and Big Boi (Aquarius).

**Song Note (Rosa Parks):** Even though the song is named after the civil rights icon, the song actually has nothing to do with her; she is not even mentioned in the lyrics. The song is about the entertainment industry and how it unfairly treats minorities.

# PAVEMENT

I was at a spring break party in my hometown in 1997. My group of friends congregated in a backyard, huddled around a portable stereo, and listened to Pavement's new album, *Brighten The Corners*. My hometown friends were devout Pavement worshippers. They argued over who had the most bootlegs or who saw them perform live the most. How rabid could they get? As the beer ran out, the party attendees headed back inside until all that was left was myself and a girl I had never met. I tried to make small talk asking the girl her thoughts on the new album. I made the huge mistake of telling her I liked it. Her caustic reaction was a resounding, "It sucks. I'm a real Pavement fan. I only like their first two albums." Then, she stormed inside, leaving me alone with only the broken croon of Stephen Malkmus to keep me company. I already had multiple discussions around the merits of Pavement's new album. The tightly wound and refined sound turned off many diehard fans who preferred their Pavement unrefined and sketchy as hell. When I walked inside, I discovered this girl had told everyone that I insulted her taste in music because I liked the new album. Let me repeat that; it was insulting to *her* because I liked the album. She demanded that I leave the party, or she would. I was leaving anyway, but this is the type of ire that brews inside the heart of a Pavement fan. The mere suggestion that *Brighten The Corners* might be as good as their first two albums was enough to get me kicked out of a party. Hell hath no fury like a scorned Pavement fan.

# Albums of the '90s:

*Slanted And Enchanted* (1992)

*Watery, Domestic* (1992)

*Crooked Rain, Crooked Rain* (1994)

*Wowee Zowee* (1995)

*Brighten The Corners* (1997)

*Terror Twilight* (1999)

# The 11 Best Songs By Pavement:

1. **Range Life** (*Crooked Rain, Crooked Rain*)
2. **In The Mouth of A Desert** (*Slanted And Enchanted*)
3. **Elevate Me Later** (*Crooked Rain, Crooked Rain*)
4. **Trigger Cut** (*Slanted And Enchanted*)
5. **Unfair** (*Crooked Rain, Crooked Rain*)
6. **Grounded** (*Wowee Zowee*)
7. **Stop Breathin'** (*Crooked Rain, Crooked Rain*)
8. **Stereo** (*Brighten The Corners*)
9. **Here** (*Slanted And Enchanted*)
10. **Westie Can Drum** (*Stereo* single B-Side)
11. **Type Slowly** (*Brighten The Corners*)

**Fun Fact:** With multiple labels vying to sign Pavement for their first album, Stephen Malkmus chose Matador records for the sole reason that they had a fax machine.

# PEARL JAM

I was sitting in class in the fall of 1993 when a friend walked in, sat next to me, and slammed down the newest Time magazine. On the cover was the screeching face of Eddie Vedder. I stared at the cover in shock. Pearl Jam was my band, my generation. It had been less than a week since they released their sophomore album, *Vs.* Yet, this moment, the moment that Pearl Jam took the cover of Time magazine, represented everything. It was my generation storming up to the podium, grabbing the mic, and showing the boomers how it's done. History has since proclaimed that Nirvana was the biggest band of the '90s, but in 1993, Pearl Jam was bigger. Pearl Jam stood for us. Pearl Jam fought against Ticketmaster for gouging customers with insanely high service charges on concert tickets. How high? My tickets for Faith No More were $20 each, but with service charges and additional fees, it was over $40. Pearl Jam boycotted playing at all Ticketmaster venues, which kept them from performing in L.A. Instead, they played in Indio about two hours away. Pearl Jam sold out the 50,000 plus capacity venue. Meanwhile, Nirvana couldn't even sell out the 25,000-seat Forum in Los Angeles. Everyone I knew went to Pearl Jam. I couldn't find one person to go see Nirvana with me. Pearl Jam were the rebels, fighting against the conglomerates for the people. They were our leaders. Our idols. They deserved the cover of Time magazine because they represented everything our culture was and everything we were fighting for.

# Albums of the '90s:

*Ten* (1991)
*Vs.* (1993)
*Vitalogy* (1994)
*No Code* (1996)
*Yield* (1998)

# The 11 Best Songs By Pearl Jam:

1. **Black** (*Ten*)
2. **Animal** (*Vs.*)
3. **Porch** (*Ten*)
4. **Not For You** (*Vitalogy*)
5. **Rearviewmirror** (*Vs.*)
6. **Corduroy** (*Vitalogy*)
7. **I Got Id** (*Merkin Ball*)
8. **Alive** (*Ten*)
9. **State Of Love And Trust** (*Singles* OST)
10. **Do The Evolution** (*Yield*)
11. **Jeremy** (*Ten*)

**Fun Fact:** Gossard, Vedder, and McCready appeared in the 1992 movie *Singles* as members of the band Citizen Dick with Matt Dillon playing their lead singer. Citizen Dick recorded one song, "Touch Me, I'm Dick," which wasn't officially released until 2015.

**Song Note (Do The Evolution):** The animated music video for this song was drawn by comic book legend, Todd MacFarlane who is the creator of the comic book, Spawn.

# TOM PETTY

Growing up a Star Wars fan, I always knew the franchise wasn't three films, it was meant to be nine films. After the release of *Jedi* in 1983, George Lucas took a hiatus. The hope of more Star Wars films dissolved. Then in 1996, Lucas announced he was producing the prequel trilogy; we were getting more Star Wars films. On May 19th, 1999, the first of the new films (*The Phantom Menace*) would be released. I had tickets to the show, but I needed to line up outside the theater in advance to get a good seat. I thought five hours was enough, but when I arrived at 2:30 PM for the 7:30 PM show, the line was already wrapped around the block. Some people had been waiting an entire month to get a good seat (this is true). I had no choice but to go to the end of the line and wait. At least, I had CDs to listen to, including Tom Petty's new album, *Echo*. After a string of incredible '90s albums from Petty, my expectations were high. Too high. *Echo* didn't have the same presence his previous albums did. *Echo* was more subdued, more lonesome, less wild, less wide open. I was underwhelmed. I prayed Star Wars wouldn't let me down, too. Sadly, it did. Star Wars tried too hard to outdo its former self and it lost track of its humanity that made it loveable in the first place. Petty wasn't trying to outdo himself. *Echo* was different because Petty was different, older, wiser, which translated to his measured reflection on life. I was just too young to grasp it. As I grew older, I learned to appreciate the mature perception of *Echo*. While the Star Wars prequels; just seem more childish.

# Albums of the '90s:

*Into The Great Wide Open* (1991)
*Wildflowers* (1994)
*Playback* (1996)
*She's The One* OST (1996)
*Echo* (1999)

# The 11 Best Songs By Tom Petty:

1. **Learning To Fly** (*Into The Great Wide Open*)
2. **Crawling Back To You** (*Wildflowers*)
3. **Wildflowers** (*Wildflowers*)
4. **Out In The Cold** (*Into The Great Wide Open*)
5. **Waiting For Tonight** (*Playback/Nobody's Children*)
6. **Walls (Circus)** (*She's The One* OST)
7. **King's Highway** (*Into The Great Wide Open*)
8. **Grew Up Fast** (*She's The One* OST)
9. **Mary Jane's Last Dance** (*Greatest Hits*)
10. **Two Gunslingers** (*Into The Great Wide Open*)
11. **Echo** (*Echo*)

**Fun Fact:** Petty had a supporting role in Kevin Costner's post-apocalyptic film, *The Postman*. Petty played a version of himself in the film, the leader of a small group of survivors.

# LIZ PHAIR

Anyone who reads this book will point out that I forgot to include many prominent artists from the decade. Truth is, there are a lot of artists from the '90s that I hated. Anytime I made it known there was an artist I didn't like (Dave Matthews, Sublime, Alanis), my friends would do everything in their power to convince me to like them. There were two artists from the '90s that no one could believe I didn't like: PJ Harvey and Liz Phair. I tried. Honestly, I tried. I've listened to PJ Harvey's album *Dry* more times than albums I actually love in hopes of liking it. No matter how many times I listened to these artists, I still came away with the same lukewarm opinion. Eventually, I stopped trying and moved on. In the writing of this book, I wanted it to be a personal account of my experiences during the '90s. Along with the bands that I liked were bands that I didn't like who made just as big of an impact on me. For this chapter, I conducted a music experiment. I decided to revisit Liz Phair and PJ Harvey one more time to see if my opinion of them has changed. For this challenge, whomever I liked more, I would give them a chapter in the book. I listened to both artists' complete nineties catalog and I'm sure it's rather obvious who won. I wouldn't say I became a Liz Phair fan, but I found myself more connected with her music than PJ Harvey. This list is based on her songs that connected with me the most during this listening exercise. These may not be her best songs, but they are the songs that made me get rid of PJ.

## Albums of the '90s:

*Exile In Guyville* (1993)
*Whip-Smart* (1994)
*Whitechocolatespaceegg* (1998)

## The 11 Best Songs By Liz Phair:

1. **6'1"** (*Exile In Guyville*)
2. **Rocket Boy** (*Stealing Beauty* OST)
3. **What Makes You Happy** (*Whitechocolatespaceegg*)
4. **Polyester Bride** (*Whitechocolatespaceegg*)
5. **Fuck And Run** (*Exile In Guyville*)
6. **Whitechocolatespaceegg** (*Whitechocolatespaceegg*)
7. **Divorce Song** (*Exile In Guyville*)
8. **Never Said** (*Exile In Guyville*)
9. **May Queen** (*Whip-Smart*)
10. **Perfect World** (*Whitechocolatespaceegg*)
11. **Supernova** (*Whip-Smart*)

**Fun Fact:** Liz Phair originally performed under the moniker Girly Sound in the Chicago rock scene. Popular among the local bands, Phair would commonly play on the same bill as bigger name Chicago artists like Material Issue and Urge Overkill.

**Fun Fact 2:** Liz Phair's debut album is a song by song reply to the rolling Stones album, *Exile On Main Street*.

# PRIMAL SCREAM

As I've mentioned, I am a big college basketball fan. In my defense, at UCLA, they teach you who John Wooden is before they give you a tour of the campus. In the spring of 1995, the UCLA basketball team made it to the national championship game against the Arkansas Razorbacks. I had tickets to the game in Seattle except for one huge problem. I had just been accepted to the UCLA graduate film program and my first screenwriting class was taking place at the same time as the national championship game. While every other teacher on campus gave their students the night off, my teacher refused. I had to attend the class for my film school future. I gave up my tickets to the game and went to class. Luckily, our professor let us out early. I bolted across campus, hopped in my car, and burned wheels across West L.A. to join my friends watching the game. My girlfriend had left her copy of Primal Scream's *Screamadelica*; in my car stereo. Stressed for time, I didn't change the music while I went full Mario Andretti in my Toyota Corolla. Primal Scream was exactly what I needed to keep movin'. Their euphoric music transformed my loaded stress into burning exuberance, leading me like a funky star to my destination. I arrived at my friend's house as the second half of the game began. UCLA was down ten and missing our point guard. The team mounted a comeback and won the game to become national champions. A few months later, my girlfriend and I broke up. I claimed I didn't know where her Primal Scream CD was, but I still have it and listen to it regularly.

# Albums of the '90s:

*Screamadelica* (1991)

*Dixie-Narco* (1992)

*Give Out But Don't Give Up* (1994)

*Vanishing Point* (1997)

*Star* (1997)

# The 11 Best Songs By Primal Scream:

1. **Loaded** (*Screamadelica*)
2. **Jailbird** (*Give Out But Don't Give Up*)
3. **Rocks** (*Give Out But Don't Give Up*)
4. **Slip Inside This House** (*Screamadelica*)
5. **Come Together** (*Screamadelica*)
6. **Movin' On Up** (*Screamadelica*)
7. **Burning Wheel** (*Vanishing Point*)
8. **Kowalski** (*Vanishing Point*)
9. **Screamdelica** (*Dixie-Narco*)
10. **Darklands** (*If They Move, Kill 'Em* single B-side)
11. **Swastika Eyes** (*XTRMNTR*)

**Fun Fact:**  Lead singer Bobby Gillespie played drums for the Jesus and Mary Chain on their first album, *Psychocandy*.

**Song Note (Loaded):**  Though it's their most famous hit, the song is a remix of another Primal Scream song, "I'm Losing More Than I'll Ever Have."  The remix includes song samples from "What I Am" by Edie Brickell, "I Don't Want to Lose Your Love" by the Emotions, and dialogue from the film *The Wild Angels*.

# PRIMUS

In the '90s, every band had a shot. With alternative rock taking over, the doors to the mainstream were kicked wide open for music that would have never had a chance in any other era. Could you imagine the radio in the '60s playing bands with names like the Butthole Surfers or the Ass Ponys? Could you imagine MTV in the '80s playing songs like "Detachable Penis" or "Rape Me?" In the '90s, film director Baz Luhrman had a hit with a spoken word song about not having enough sunscreen. The most successful of these odd shops of curiosities is Primus. Primus sang songs about spaghetti westerns, the DMV, pet beavers, and porno cats. They had a three-song trilogy about the perils of fishing. The band even encouraged their fanbase to chant "you suck" at concerts as an ode of solidarity and support. Primus doesn't have a lead guitarist; they have a lead bassist. Singer Les Claypool writes songs around his bass melodies. Claypool's rumbling, thump bass is as intense as any Mike Watt freak out, it's as cosmic as any Jaco jam, and it's as funky as anything Flea would bust a move to. What makes Claypool's bass playing so appealing is the progressive complexity that would make any crimson king turn pink. But despite all the strange things afoot, Primus found such success in the '90s that they rose to prominence and became the co-headliner for the 1993 Lollapalooza festival alongside Alice In Chains. Primus is a laundry list of everything that shouldn't work because, in the '90s, we embraced and celebrated everything that shouldn't be.

# Albums of the '90s:

*Frizzle Fry* (1990)
*Sailing The Seas Of Cheese* (1991)
*Miscellaneous Debris* (1992)
*Pork Soda* (1993)
*Tales From The Punchbowl* (1995)
*Brown Album* (1997)
*Rhinoplasty* (1998)
*The Antipop* (1999)

# The 11 Best Songs By Primus:

1. **Harold Of The Rocks** (*Frizzle Fry*)
2. **John The Fisherman** (*Frizzle Fry*)
3. **Wynonna's Big Brown Beaver** (*Tales From The Punchbowl*)
4. **Tommy The Cat** (*Sailing The Seas Of Cheese*)
5. **Fish On** (*Sailing The Seas Of Cheese*)
6. **Over The Electric Grapevine** (*Tales From The Punchbowl*)
7. **My Name Is Mud** (*Pork Soda*)
8. **Professor Nutter Butter's House Of Treats** (*Tales From The Punchbowl*)
9. **Spegetti Western** (*Frizzle Fry*)
10. **Jerry Was A Race Car Driver** (*Sailing The Seas of Cheese*)
11. **Making Plans For Nigel** (*Miscellaneous Debris*)

**Fun Fact:** Les Claypool went to high school with future Metallica guitarist Kirk Hammett in Richmond, CA.

# THE PROMISE RING

Many music subgenres would not exist without the independent record store. Emo was a genre that emerged in the late '90s. It was defined by emotive songs that embodied a punk ethos basically, punk love songs. The masses didn't really understand it, so the "emo" moniker became a generic sticker for any alternative-leaning music. I even heard the metal band Korn described as emo. When I first heard the Promise Ring, I didn't get emo either; I just knew that I liked the band. Singer Davey Von Bohlen crooned with sultry seduction, crisis, and pain. Rather than focus on a single sentiment, the Promise Ring's songs captured the multitude of emotions that encapsulated you at any moment. The Promise Ring was on a small label, the now-defunct Jade Tree. Big music store chains only carried major label releases. If you wanted to find an album on a small indie label, your only option was to go to an independent record store. In Hollywood, that was Aron's Records. I knew every time I walked into that store, I would find exactly what I wanted and a handful of albums I didn't know I needed. When I was looking for the Promise Ring's *Very Emergency*, it was Aron's where I found it. To sweeten the deal, it came with a free copy of the band's *Boys + Girls* EP just because Aron's was that freaking cool. Without independent record stores, I wouldn't be a fan of half the artists I love today. I would have never purchased a Promise Ring album. And, I still would have no idea what emo is.

# Albums of the '90s:

*30° Everywhere* (1996)
*The Horse Latitudes* (1997)
*Nothing Feels Good* (1997)
*Boys + Girls* (1998)
*Very Emergency* (1999)

# The 11 Best Songs By The Promise Ring:

1. **The Deep South** (*Very Emergency*)
2. **Why Did Ever We Meet** (*Nothing Feels Good*)
3. **Red Paint** (*30° Everywhere*)
4. **Skips A Beat (Over You)** (*Very Emergency*)
5. **B Is For Bethlehem** (*Nothing Feels Good*)
6. **Is This Thing On?** (*Nothing Feels Good*)
7. **Tell Everyone We're Dead** (*Boys + Girls*)
8. **A Picture Postcard** (*30° Everywhere*)
9. **Red & Blue Jeans** (*Nothing Feels Good*)
10. **Best Looking Boys** (*Boys + Girls*)
11. **Emergency! Emergency!** (*Very Emergency*)

**Fun Fact:** Frontman Davey Von Bohlen was a member of the seminal emo band Cap'n Jazz. He sang and played guitar in the band.

**Album Note (Very Emergency):** Davey Von Bohlen had a very difficult time recording the album due to constant debilitating headaches. It was later discovered that he had a benign brain tumor which was luckily removed.

# PUBLIC ENEMY

I first heard Public Enemy while at school, waiting for swim practice. My friend passed me their cassette *Fear Of A Black Planet* and whispered, "Good luck." Within seconds of listening, Chuck D's steel-enforced vocal confidence plowed through my brain like Samuel L. Jackson misfiring his gun in the back of a car. His militant wordplay felt like something a beat poet would have shouted at a coffee haus in the '50s rather than being MTV's video of the week. Chuck D's passionate outrage for the black community was every bit as jarring as it was eye-opening. He wasn't invoking a violent revolution; he was fighting for social change. The song "911 is a Joke," though played for comedy, exploits the fact that if you lived in a bad neighborhood and called 911, there is a good chance the police would not show up. The concept was so foreign to me that it caused me to realign my entire world view and gave me a profound appreciation for Public Enemy's message in their music. Years later, Public Enemy would create the soundtrack for the college basketball movie *He Got Game*. It was a blistering takedown of collegiate sports and how it enslaved a generation of black men to make millions of dollars for colleges while the players received little benefit. That soundtrack symbolized something big. This fearless band of dangerous militant rebels had become the first rap act asked by a major studio to make a soundtrack for a motion picture. Rap was no longer an underground entity; because of Public Enemy, it was now mainstream.

# Albums of the '90s:

*Fear Of A Black Planet* (1990)

*Apocalypse 91...The Empire Strikes Black* (1991)

*Muse Sick-N-Hour Mess Age* (1994)

*He Got Game* OST (1998)

*There's A Poison Goin' On* (1999)

# The 11 Best Songs By Public Enemy:

1. **By The Time I Get To Arizona** (*Apocalypse 91...The Empire Strikes Black*)
2. **Brothers Gonna Work It Out** (*Fear Of A Black Planet*)
3. **Welcome To The Terrordome** (*Fear Of A Black Planet*)
4. **Can't Truss It** (*Apocalypse 91...The Empire Strikes Black*)
5. **911 Is A Joke** (*Fear Of A Black Planet*)
6. **Who Stole The Soul?** (*Fear Of A Black Planet*)
7. **He Got Game** (*He Got Game* OST)
8. **What You Need Is Jesus** (*He Got Game* OST)
9. **Burn Hollywood Burn** (*Fear Of A Black Planet*)
10. **Shake Your Booty** (*He Got Game* OST)
11. **Give It Up** (*Muse Sick-N-Hour Mess Age*)

**Fun Fact:** Flavor Flav is a classically trained pianist. While on tour, Flav would commonly be found in his hotel lobby playing piano for the hotel guests and fans.

**Song Note (By The Time I Get To Arizona):** The song is an indictment of Arizona Governor Evan Mecham's refusal to honor the birthday of Martin Luther King Jr. as a national holiday.

# RADIOHEAD

It was my first time meeting someone from the internet, and I was nervous. I had heard horror stories that anyone you meet from the internet would likely be a creepy, 500-pound child molester who lives in his mother's basement. I was hoping that wasn't true because I was meeting this guy for a very important reason; he was selling me a bootleg of all of Radiohead's B-sides. I was meeting him at my campus radio station in case anything went wrong, so I could...well, I had no idea what I was going to do, but I just felt better about it. When the guy arrived, he was just a student, like me. The "evil internet man" rumors were merely propaganda. He was actually very nice; he even threw in a Radiohead concert bootleg for free. Radiohead had a huge collection of over 30 B-sides. Now, I had them all. The best track on the disc wasn't even a song; it was a live radio broadcast of a practical joke about Radiohead orchestrated by the Kevin & Bean morning show on KROQ in L.A. During the broadcast, after being teased for having a sleepy eye, Radiohead singer Thom Yorke instigated a fight with the DJs and severely injured himself, forcing them to cancel that night's concert. Surprise, surprise, this was just an April Fool's Day prank. Sadly, it was so believable that some ticket holders didn't go to the show because they thought it really was canceled. The station even received death threats from rabid fans who were pissed off for being duped. And I thought I was a hardcore fan because I paid a guy on the internet for some B-sides. Never thought I was the sane one.

# Albums of the '90s:

*Pablo Honey* (1993)
*The Bends* (1995)
*OK Computer* (1997)

# The 11 Best Songs By Radiohead:

1. **The Bends** (*The Bends*)
2. **Paranoid Android** (*OK Computer*)
3. **Karma Police** (*OK Computer*)
4. **Exit Music (From A Film)** (*OK Computer*)
5. **Street Spirit (Fade Out)** (*The Bends*)
6. **My Iron Lung** (*The Bends*)
7. **High And Dry** (*The Bends*)
8. **Polyethylene (Parts 1 & 2)** (*Paranoid Android* single B-side)
9. **Creep** (*Pablo Honey*)
10. **Electioneering** (*OK Computer*)
11. **Fake Plastic Trees** (*The Bends*)

**Fun Fact:**  Guitarist Jonny Greenwood and drummer Phil Selway were members of the band that plays at the Yule Ball in the film *Harry Potter And The Goblet Of Fire*.

**Song Note (Exit Music (From A Film)):**  This song was originally written to play over the closing credits for the Baz Luhrman film *Romeo + Juliet*.  The song was inspired by the Johnny Cash album, *At Folsom Prison*.

# RAGE AGAINST THE MACHINE

I saw over 1,000 bands perform live during the '90s. The best live band (and it's not even close) was Rage Against The Machine. Living in L.A., I had the privilege of seeing Rage play live before they were even signed to a label. And I went to see them every chance I had. Rage's live show wasn't just a concert; it was an experience. They brought the energy of a revolution, cranked to a million. With Tom Morello's feverish guitar scratching and Zac de la Rocha's lyrical assault, they could whip any audience into anarchy. When I heard they were coming to play a show at UCLA's on-campus pizzeria, The Cooperage, I lost my freaking mind. Most of the bands who had previously played the "Coop" performed acoustic sets. The Coop wasn't ready for Rage. On the night of the show, the place was packed; you couldn't move. The very moment Rage hit the stage, the audience exploded into rampant unrest. It was a sea of unbridled mayhem. I was punched, kicked, head-butted, thrown up in the air, and slammed down to the ground. I spent the show fighting for survival. By the end of the performance, The Coop was destroyed. Tables were smashed. Chairs busted. Light fixtures were hanging loose, while pieces of pizza were somehow stuck to the ceiling tiles. There were holes in the walls, broken glass, and some guy lost his pants. A twister would have done less damage. Because of Rage's destructive performance, the school banned all future live shows at The Coop. Rage was our proof that music had the power not just to inspire and motivate, but to ignite an uprising.

## Albums of the '90s:

*Rage Against The Machine* (1992)
*Evil Empire* (1996)
*The Battle For Los Angeles* (1999)

## The 11 Best Songs By Rage Against The Machine:

1. **Killing In the Name** (*Rage Against The Machine*)
2. **Bulls On Parade** (*Evil Empire*)
3. **Guerilla Radio** (*The Battle Of Los Angeles*)
4. **Know Your Enemy** (*Rage Against The Machine*)
5. **Bullet In The Head** (*Rage Against The Machine*)
6. **People Of The Sun** (*Evil Empire*)
7. **Sleep Now In The Fire** (*The Battle Of Los Angeles*)
8. **Down Rodeo** (*Evil Empire*)
9. **Bombtrack** (*Rage Against The Machine*)
10. **Year Of Tha Boomerang** (*Evil Empire*)
11. **Vietnow** (*Evil Empire*)

**Fun Fact:** In 1993, Rage Against The Machine was part of the Lollapalooza tour. At the Philadelphia stop, instead of performing, the band opted to protest censorship in music. For the entire 25-minute set, the band stood on stage naked, in silence, with the letters P. M. R. C. written on their chests. The P. M. R. C. is the Parents Music Resource Center that sought to put warning labels on explicit music and had been founded by then-Vice President Al Gore's wife, Tipper Gore.

# RED HOT CHILI PEPPERS

On the day Red Hot Chili Peppers' new album, *One Hot Minute* was released, I was sitting on my friend's studio apartment floor, skipping through the disc, looking for that one good song. After the massive success of *Blood Sugar Sex Magik*, I expected nothing short of Mozart. Listening to the new album, all I could think was, *What the hell is this?* People forget how big the Chili Peppers were in the early '90s. If the T-rex from *Jurassic Park* sang for Nirvana during a cameo on *Seinfeld*, the Chili Peppers would still have been bigger. They headlined Lollapalooza. They were played on MTV every 15 minutes. They were poised for '90s dominance until guitarist John Frusciante, the melodic backbone of the band, quit. How would the Chili Peppers survive? In a strange twist of fate, another L.A. band, Jane's Addiction broke up, leaving their classic guitarist Dave Navarro without a day job. When the Chili Peppers announced that Navarro had joined the band, it was more exciting than the time Billy Idol punched out that guy on the plane in *The Wedding Singer*. Like Joe Montana playing football for Kansas City Chiefs, this combination had amazing potential. Shockingly, all it had was potential. *One Hot Minute*, to put it likely, sucked. The Dave Navarro experiment failed out of the gates. The chemistry just wasn't there. Sure, there's a couple of songs that embodied the Chili's spirit but ultimately, it was destined for the $1 bin. This left Red Hot Chili Peppers with no choice but to reunite with Frusciante in 1999 and reclaim their stake to the alternative rock throne.

# Albums of the '90s:

*Blood Sugar Sex Magik* (1991)
*Out In L.A.* (1994)
*One Hot Minute* (1995)
*Californication* (1999)
.

# The 11 Best Songs By Red Hot Chili Peppers:

1. **Suck My Kiss** (*Blood Sugar Sex Magik*)
2. **Under The Bridge** (*Blood Sugar Sex Magik*)
3. **Love Rollercoaster** (*Beavis and Butthead Do America* OST)
4. **Parallel Universe** (*Californication*)
5. **I Could Have Lied** (*Blood Sugar Sex Magik*)
6. **Californication** (*Californication*)
7. **Give It Away** (*Blood Sugar Sex Magik*)
8. **Soul To Squeeze** (*Coneheads* OST)
9. **Around The World** (*Californication*)
10. **Coffee Shop** (*One Hot Minute*)
11. **Shallow Be Thy Game** (*One Hot Minute*)

**Fun Fact:** The band recorded the album, *Blood Sugar Sex Magic*, in a haunted house once owned by Harry Houdini called "The Mansion."

# R.E.M.

I had never seen R.E.M. play live. *Monster* was my least favorite R.E.M. album, but I was determined to see them play on this tour. It was winter 1995, and tickets were going on sale at 8 AM. I stumbled down to Tower Records Westwood with my friend Barry at 3 AM, where we were 8th in line. Only, instead of selling tickets on a first-come basis, Ticketmaster implemented a new lottery system, giving everyone a number, then at random, the store drew numbers to determine the official line positions. We went from 8th to 80th. The odds of us getting tickets went from "likely" to "no freaking way." We needed a plan B. We drove downtown to Ritmo Latino, a rumored secret place to get tickets without waiting in line. The secret was out. Their line was longer than Westwood. Our last option was the Ticketmaster Outlet in Hollywood. The line was long but manageable. When it was our turn to buy tickets, all the L.A. shows were sold out, but a few tickets were left for Anaheim. We bought them. I was finally going to see R.E.M. until...health issues began to plague the band, including Bill Berry's near-fatal brain aneurysm. The concert was postponed, from May to October 30th, the night before Halloween. Halloween or not, I was still going. We left Westwood at 5 PM for an 8 PM start time, only to hit horrible traffic delaying us three hours. After parking, getting into the venue, climbing to the very last row to find our seats (yes, last row!), we were just in time to see the first notes of R.E.M.'s set and I happily sang along to every song.

# Albums of the '90s:

*Out Of Time* (1991)
*Automatic For The People* (1992)
*Monster* (1994)
*New Adventures In Hi-Fi* (1996)
*Up* (1998)

# The 11 Best Songs By R.E.M.:

1. **Country Feedback** (*Out Of Time*)
2. **Losing My Religion** (*Out Of Time*)
3. **Leave** (*New Adventures In Hi-Fi*)
4. **Texarkana** (*Out Of Time*)
5. **The Wake-Up Bomb** (*New Adventures In Hi-Fi*)
6. **Walk Unafraid** (*Up*)
7. **Ignoreland** (*Automatic For The People*)
8. **Drive (**Automatic For The People*)
9. **Departure** (*New Adventures In Hi-Fi*)
10. **Circus Envy** (*Monster*)
11. **At My Most Beautiful** (*Up*)

**Fun Fact:** When not focusing on music, Michael Stipe is an active sculptor, crafting art pieces out of bronze and wood. One of his pieces, entitled "Foxes," is located outside a hotel in Atlanta, GA.

**Song Note (Losing My Religion):** Despite the title, the song has nothing to do with religion. The phrase "losing my religion" refers to obsession over unrequited love.

# THE ROOTS

It started as a rumor, whispers from student to student. "The Roots are coming to play on campus." It seemed too good to be true. When it was confirmed, the campus exploded with adrenaline and everybody wanted in. One of the main criticisms of rap music during this time was that it wasn't "real" music. It was just samples of other people's songs over computer beats with no real instruments. The Roots changed that. The Roots played actual instruments in the studio and live on stage. They upended the perception of what rap music could be. They interlaced rap and rock together in an audible lovemaking session, appealing to everyone. Because of that, everyone wanted to see them play. When they came to campus, the interest in the show was so popular, the line to get into the performance hall (Ackerman Grand Ballroom) looped around the building, twice. I refused to wait. The campus radio station was located in the back of the ballroom. Since the station was still operating, as a manager, security could not deny me access. So, when I walked up to the front of the line, I remained calm and showed them my station credentials. Without a word, they unlatched the velvet ropes and gave me unfettered access, despite hearing the roars of boos from the students in line. Snubbing my nose at authority to see a Roots concert felt like the appropriate thing to do. Though I had to watch the concert from the back of the room, the show was still dynamite, and I didn't want anything more.

## Albums of the '90s:

*Organix* (1993)
*Do You Want More?!!!??!* (1994)
*Illadelph Halflife* (1996)
*Things Fall Apart* (1999)

## The 11 Best Songs By The Roots:

1. **What You Want** (*The Roots Come Alive*)
2. **I Remain Calm** (*Do You Want More?!!!??!*)
3. **The Next Movement** (*Things Fall Apart*)
4. **You Got Me** (*Things Fall Apart*)
5. **Mellow My Man** (*Do You Want More?!!!??!*)
6. **Adrenaline!** (*Things Fall Apart*)
7. **The Session** (*Organix*)
8. **What They Do** (*Illadelph Halflife*)
9. **Respond/React** (*Illadelph Halflife*)
10. **Do You Want More?!!!??!** (*Do You Want More?!!!??!*)
11. **Dynamite!** (*Things Fall Apart*)

**Song Note (You Got Me):**   The song was written by a relatively unknown, Jill Scott.   MCA Records wanted a higher profile singer on the track, so Erykah Badu sang Scott's parts on the song instead.   Scott retained co-writing credit.

# SAINT ETIENNE

As 2 AM trickled by, driving under the Hollywood lights, I turned up into the hills, with the melodies of Saint Etienne's *Good Humor* to guide me home. It was the fall of 1999 when I moved into a house in the Hollywood Hills, in a place called Bronson Canyon. Secluded from the Hollywood scene, it felt exclusive. I lived down the street from Brad Pitt, Christina Ricci, and Fiona Apple. I felt like a movie star. I was in my early twenties, with no obligations, figuring out the rest of my life with unburdened freedom. I could walk out my front door and within a half-hour, I'd hike to the Hollywood sign or Griffith Observatory. If I wanted to hit Hollywood, I was moments from sipping a Blood & Sand at the Dresden or a Mai Tai at the Tiki-Ti. Bronson Canyon also had its own community. We'd grab a coffee at the Bourgeois Pig, we'd have drinks at Birds. We had our own bookstore, wine shop, and playhouse. It was a world unto itself. This era was so distinct I can still feel the optimism I had when I lived there. And the sound of that world, the album that captured this optimism was Saint Etienne's *Good Humor*. The '90s were ending. My youth was becoming my adulthood, and there was something charming about how Saint Etienne's music exhibited all that. It sounded like a new beginning. It was fresh. It was pure. It was like the sanguine personification of Audrey Hepburn put to song. This is why I played the album on the way home from my nights out. If it was a good night, the album's allure made me feel content; if it was a bad night, the songs gave me hope for a better tomorrow.

# Albums of the '90s:

*Foxbase Alpha* (1991)

*So Tough* (1993)

*Tiger Bay* (1994)

*Reserection* (1995)

*Continental* (1997)

*Good Humor* (1998)

*Fairfax High* (1998)

*The Misadventures Of Saint Etienne* (1999)

*Places To Visit* (1999)

# The 11 Best Songs By Saint Etienne:

1. **Lose That Girl** (*Good Humor*)
2. **Sylvie** (*Good Humor*)
3. **Burnt Out Car** (*Continental*)
4. **The Way I Fell For You** (*The Misadventures Of Saint Etienne*)
5. **Only Love Can Break Your Heart** (*Foxbase Alpha*)
6. **Erica America** (*Good Humor*)
7. **Split Screen** (*Good Humor*)
8. **Pale Movie** (*Tiger Bay*)
9. **Hobart Paving** (*So Tough*)
10. **Hit The Brakes** (*Fairfax High*)
11. **Nothing Can Stop Us** (*Foxbase Alpha*)

**Fun Fact:** Saint Etienne was originally an indie dance group with rotating singers. After songwriters Pete Wigs and Bob Stanley recorded with singer Sarah Cracknell, they chose to make her the band's permanent vocalist.

# SEBADOH

The movie *Kids* was hyped as the most controversial movie ever. Supposedly, it portrayed teens in the most accurate light to be put on film. I went to see *Kids* the day it was released. To say I was disappointed is an understatement. The movie felt forced. Also, boring as hell. It did have one redeeming quality: the soundtrack, which featured songs by The Folk Implosion, a side project by Sebadoh lead singer, Lou Barlow. As a fervent Sebadoh fan, I collected all their side projects, including Sentridoh, Animal Friends, and Dinosaur Jr. (though, technically, Sebadoh is a spin-off of them). One project escaped me: Deluxx Folk Implosion, which delivered my favorite track on the *Kids* soundtrack. There was no internet, so I had to delve into every article I could find to learn that Deluxx Folk Implosion was a combo of Folk Implosion and the band Deluxx, led by Sebadoh drummer, Bob Fay. I had to find their album. I purged L.A. stores without results. I tried Berkeley, Orange County, San Diego, but Deluxx was so obscure, most stores had never even heard of them. Finally, years later, on a trip to Seattle, I found the album randomly misplaced in the Depeche Mode section. I bought it immediately and returned to my friend's apartment to play it. Guess what? It sucked. It was a bunch of terrible bedroom demos, all completely unlistenable. It was a bigger disappointment than *Kids*. I never gave it a second listen. Like some CD shopping scavenger hunts, the chase is more exciting than the catch. In this case, I wish I was still looking.

# Albums of the '90s:

*Weed Forestin'* (1990)

*Sebadoh III* (1991)

*Smash Your Head On The Punk Rock* (1992)

*Bubble And Scrape* (1993)

*Bakesale* (1994)

*Harmacy* (1996)

*The Sebadoh* (1999)

# The 11 Best Songs By Sebadoh:

1. **Think (Let Tomorrow Bee)** (*Bubble And Scrape*)
2. **Rebound** (*Bakesale*)
3. **Willing To Wait** (*Harmacy*)
4. **Soul And Fire** (*Bubble And Scrape*)
5. **Magnet's Coil** (*Bakesale*)
6. **Vampire** (*Smash Your Head On The Punk Rock*)
7. **The Freed Pig** (*III*)
8. **Beauty Of The Ride** (*Harmacy*)
9. **Careful** (*Bakesale*)
10. **Love Is Stronger** (*The Sebadoh*)
11. **Spoiled** (*III*)

**Fun Fact:** In 1994, Deluxx Folk Implosion came together to record a full-length album. Lou Barlow kept the master tapes in his attic for 20 years before guitarist Mark Perretta convinced him to finally release the album in 2016. Only 1,000 copies were made, and I own one of them.

# TUPAC SHAKUR

I watched a lot of MTV in the '90s. We all did. It was like an involuntary muscle reaction. Like Pavlov's dog playing fetch with the postman, if you walked into a room with a television, you mindlessly turned it on and flipped it to MTV. You thought people in the 2000s were obsessed with looking at their phones? For anyone under the age of 25 in the '90s, MTV was on all the time. People left it playing when they went to bed at night. MTV was our 24-hour news cycle. We all knew the top twenty videos, we all had our favorite VJs (mine was Kurt Loder), and we all knew the shows. Though *120 Minutes* and *Headbangers Ball* were popular, *Yo! MTV Raps* were masters of their domain. At this time, very few radio stations played rap music. If you wanted to discover the freshest rapper, you watched *Yo! MTV Raps*. *Yo! MTV Raps* didn't just play rap videos; it dictated rap culture. Hosts Ed Lover and Doctor Dre (not Dr. Dre from N.W.A.) would break down everything happening on the scene, what was true and what was real. All the attention on the show wasn't always a dope thang. I remember watching *Yo! MTV Raps*, when Tupac Shakur was a guest. During his appearance, Tupac bragged about beating down film director Allen Hughes. Unfortunately, the police took Tupac's boasting as a confession and used it to send him to jail for two weeks. And if the police watched *Yo! MTV Raps*, then you know it had infiltrated society on every level. Even Tupac could not get around its power. We wanted our MTV...well, we got it.

## Albums of the '90s:

*2Pacalypse Now* (1991)

*Strictly 4 My N.I.G.G.A.Z.* (1993)

*Me Against The World* (1995)

*All Eyez On Me* (1996)

*The Don Killuminati: The 7 Day Theory* (1996)

*R U Still Down (Remember Me?)* (1997)

## The 11 Best Songs By Tupac Shakur:

1. **To Live And Die In L.A.** (*The Don Killuminati: The 7 Day Theory*)
2. **I Get Around** (*Strictly 4 My N.I.G.G.A.Z...*)
3. **California Love** (*All Eyez On Me*)
4. **Me Against The World** (*Me Against The World*)
5. **Dear Mama** (*Me Against The World*)
6. **Keep Ya Head Up** (*Strictly 4 My N.I.G.G.A.Z...*)
7. **Brenda's Got A Baby** (*2Pacalypse Now*)
8. **I Ain't Mad At Cha** (*All Eyez on Me*)
9. **2 Of Amerikaz Most Wanted** (*All Eyez On Me*)
10. **Hail Mary** (*The Don Killuminati: The 7 Day Theory*)
11. **Words Of Wisdom** (*2Pacalypse Now*)

**Fun Fact:** Tupac wanted his career to expand into acting. He auditioned for the role of Bubba in *Forrest Gump,* and it was rumored that George Lucas wanted him to read for the role of Mace Windu in *Star Wars Episode I: The Phantom Menace.*

215

# SLEATER-KINNEY

I had a crush on a girl. She had spunk, charm, and no accounting for grace. She had no respect for authority and never obeyed the rules. As the host of the punk show for the UCLA radio station, she dubbed herself the queen of the "Riot Grrls" (a '90s term to describe female punks). Her favorite band was Sleater-Kinney, and I wanted to be her Joey Ramone. When Sleater-Kinney's new album, *Dig Me Out* was released, I had the perfect opportunity. I called the label for tickets to their show at the Troubadour. When I told the Riot Grrl I had tickets, she flipped. It was a date. The night of the show, Sleater-Kinney killed it. They were loud, dynamic, and played with end of the world urgency as if Bruce Willis was riding an asteroid set to crash on Earth. Janet Weiss's precision drumming was the foundation for Corin Tucker's rocket-fueled riffs and Carrie Brownstein's ear-melting melodies. During the heat of the show, the Riot Grrl grabbed my hand and pulled me into the mosh pit. Even though she was doing it so we could stay together, I only cared that she had just held my hand. We pushed through the crowd to the front of the stage, where we watched the band, craving every last scream, shriek, and howl. After the show, I asked the Riot Grrl to grab a bite at an all-night diner for some unhealthy carb-heavy food. She said no. She had to get home because she and her boyfriend had to be up early for brunch. I don't know what broke my heart more, that she had a boyfriend or that she ate brunch. At least, I saw Corin, Carrie, and Janet turn it on live.

# Albums of the '90s:

*Sleater-Kinney* (1995)
*Call The Doctor* (1996)
*Dig Me Out* (1997)
*The Hot Rock* (1999)

# The 11 Best Songs By Sleater-Kinney:

1. **Turn It On** (*Dig Me Out*)
2. **I Wanna Be Your Joey Ramone** (*Call The Doctor*)
3. **Dance Song '97** (*Dig Me Out*)
4. **Good Things** (*Call The Doctor*)
5. **Stay Where You Are** (*Call The Doctor*)
6. **It's Enough** (*Dig Me Out*)
7. **The Drama You've Been Craving** (*Dig Me Out*)
8. **Call The Doctor** (*Call The Doctor*)
9. **Dig Me Out** (*Dig Me Out*)
10. **Start Together** (*The Hot Rock*)
11. **Banned From The End of the World** (*The Hot Rock*)

**Fun Fact:** Singer/guitarist Carrie Brownstein produced and starred in the comedy sketch series, *Portlandia* with Fred Armisen. The show focused on the weird world of Portland and its "'90s" mentality. Many rockers made cameos in the show, including Isaac Brock of Modest Mouse, J Mascis of Dinosaur Jr., Eddie Vedder of Pearl Jam, Jello Biafra of the Dead Kennedys, James Mercer of the Shins, and Sleater-Kinney bandmates, Corin Tucker and Janet Weiss. The show was a hit and ran for eight seasons.

# THE SMASHING PUMPKINS

The Smashing Pumpkins are often considered the after-thought of the grunge era; the tag-along, the step-brother, the "oh yeah, those guys." That's because time has been unfair to them. During the mid-'90s, the Smashing Pumpkins were the biggest band in the world. In the fall of 1995, the Pumpkins released their double album, *Mellon Collie And The Infinite Sadness*. The sheer audacity of a rock band to throw down a double album hadn't been done since Guns N' Roses dropped *Use Your Illusion* in 1991. The release of *Mellon Collie* was an equally monumental moment. It became a religious ritual to listen to it on endless repeat, exploring every track on the sprawling 28-song, two-hour journey. We had nightly listening parties, where we would gather, drink, and listen to the album, arguing over our favorite songs. Radio stations played every song. MTV played all the videos. They sold out concerts, album sales flew high, and Billy Corgan was knighted the new grunge king. They could do no wrong, until they did. It was called *Adore*. *Adore* was their follow-up album, which saw The Pumpkins ditching their guitars for electronics and a drum machine. It was a cold, emotionless whirlpool of somber despair. Even though loyal fans studied the effort, it failed to connect with a wider audience. The band's global popularity drowned in the vast ocean of changing musical trends. As time has passed, it's *Adore* that has the greatest musical influence on modern music. Though the Pumpkins don't get the respect they deserve, today's landscape is built on their efforts.

# Albums of the '90s:

*Gish* (1991)

*Siamese Dream* (1992)

*Earphoria* (1994)

*Pisces Iscariot* (1994)

*Mellon Collie And The Infinite Sadness* (1995)

*The Aeroplane Flies High* (1996)

*Adore* (1998)

## The 11 Best Songs By The Smashing Pumpkins:

1. **Starla** (*Pisces Iscariot*)
2. **Disarm** (*Siamese Dream*)
3. **I Am One** (*Gish*)
4. **Drown** (*Singles* OST)
5. **Quiet** (*Siamese Dream*)
6. **Galapogos** (*Mellon Collie And The Infinite Sadness*)
7. **Bullet With Butterfly Wings** (*Mellon Collie And The Infinite Sadness*)
8. **Siva** (*Gish*)
9. **Rocket** (*Siamese Dream*)
10. **Mayonaise** (*Siamese Dream*)
11. **Porcelina of the Vast Oceans** (*Mellon Collie And The Infinite Sadness*)

**Fun Fact:** Billy Corgan is obsessed with the music on their albums sounding perfect. During the recording of *Siamese Dream*, Corgan played all the instruments on the album but still gave credit to the other band members.

# ELLIOTT SMITH

In the winter of 1997, I received a copy of Elliott Smith's new album, *Either/Or*. Elliott's ability to articulate his emotional vulnerability with such open honesty was unmatched. I rallied a friend to see him play at the now-defunct Spaceland in Silverlake. We arrived when the doors opened. It was early. Too early. We were the only ones in the joint. With an empty pool table at our disposal, we found a way to pass the time. A borderline homeless man was watching us play, so we invited him to join. Surprisingly, this homeless man could play. After our game, he thanked us and shuffled off. When the show started, to our surprise, the homeless man was actually Elliott Smith. I had just played pool with Elliott Smith, which made the show even more memorable. That night, Elliott was stronger, more confident, and more personal than I would ever see him again. After his national exposure from his Oscar® nomination for *Good Will Hunting*, Elliott became a different performer. The next time I saw him at Spaceland, the place was packed with Hollywoodites pretending they had been fans all along. Minnie Driver even crashed our table, stealing my friend's seat as if she had earned her right to be there. Elliott wasn't the same. There was an emotional distance in his performance, like he was trying to live up to his rock star status rather than be the artist he had always been. The authenticity in his music made him a star, but it was also this expectation that would contribute to his early death in 2003. Sadly, sometimes honesty comes with a price.

## Albums of the '90s:

*Roman Candle* (1994)
*Elliott Smith* (1995)
*Either/Or* (1997)
*XO* (1998)

## The 11 Best Songs By Elliott Smith:

1. **Waltz #2 (XO)** (*XO*)
2. **Angeles** (*Either/Or*)
3. **Pictures Of Me** (*Either/Or*)
4. **Miss Misery** (*Good Will Hunting* OST)
5. **Ballad Of Big Nothing** (*Either/Or*)
6. **Between The Bars** (*Either/Or*)
7. **Single File** (*Elliott Smith*)
8. **Independence Day** (*XO*)
9. **Say Yes** (*Either/Or*)
10. **Coming Up Roses** (*Elliott Smith*)
11. **Division Day** (Non-album single)

**Fun Fact:** Smith attended and graduated from Hampshire College in Massachusetts with a degree in political science and philosophy.

**Song Note (Miss Misery):** In 1998, this song was nominated for an Oscar® for Best Song From a Movie for its inclusion in the film *Good Will Hunting*. Elliott lost to Celine Dion for her song "My Heart Will Go On" from the movie *Titanic*.

# SHAWN SMITH

When I heard Stone Gossard had a side project, I flipped. Stone Gossard's day job was playing guitar for Pearl Jam. It was spring of 1993; Pearl Jam hadn't even put out their second album and we were already getting a side project. I didn't care what it sounded like; it had something to do with Pearl Jam, and that's all I needed to know to buy it. Expecting the music to be Pearl Jam-like, Brad delivered something from the other end of the musical spectrum. It wasn't grunge rock; it was grunge gospel. Singer Shawn Smith had a voice that angels would listen to when they needed inspiration. It had an otherworldly yet foreboding mood about it. There was darkness in the light and light in the morose. Shawn Smith was a banshee of the blues, a siren of the suffering soul, a vagabond of the tortured psyche. Smith had four musical entities in the '90s: his solo work, Brad, Pigeonhed, and Satchel (which was Brad without Stone Gossard). I went to see Brad in concert to see Stone Gossard, but I left enamored with Smith. He was like a sumo wrestler who had just barreled out of a sushi joint, drunk off his ass, and stumbled into a karaoke bar, where he tore the mic away from a pack of sorority girls and demanded to sing Harry Nilsson. Smith was unique. He danced across the stage, channeling his inner Prince. He preached, he charmed, he pounded the piano like it was his last will and testament. There was no other voice in the '90s that could match Smith's unearthly poetry of his wounded heart. Smith's music was a brilliant lighthouse in the alt rock ocean.

# Albums of the '90s:

Pigeonhed - *Pigeonhed* (1993)

Brad - *Shame* (1993)

Satchel - *EDC* (1994)

Satchel - *The Family* (1996)

Brad - *Interiors* (1997)

Pigeonhed - *The Full Sentence* (1997)

Shawn Smith - *Let It All Begin* (1999)

# The 11 Best Songs By Shawn Smith:

1. **Suffering** (*EDC*)
2. **The Day Brings** (*Interiors*)
3. **Screen** (*Shame*)
4. **Secret Girl** (*Interiors*)
5. **Good News** (*Shame*)
6. **Buttercup** (*Shame*)
7. **On The Banks** (*Let It All Begin*)
8. **Circle & Line** (*Interiors*)
9. **Land Of Gold** (*Let It All Begin*)
10. **Her** (*Pigeonhed*)
11. **The Full Sentence** (*The Full Sentence*)

**Fun Fact:** Shawn Smith died on April 5th, 2019. He is the third Seattle rocker to die on that date. Kurt Cobain of Nirvana died on that date in 1994, and Layne Staley of Alice in Chains passed away on that date in 2002.

# SNOOP DOGGY DOGG

In 1993, I looked like every typical white American college student. My hair was long, my goatee was scruffy, and I was drenched in plaid after raiding my dad's closet of all his flannel shirts. I had a car. It was my parent's old Toyota sedan, but it was so old that when my parents bought it, it didn't come with a CD player. It was the '90s, I needed a CD player, so I had one installed after-market. Since stereos were hot-ticket items for car thieves, I had a removable stereo installed. Every time I exited the car, I had to remove the stereo and drag it around with me. Despite the nuisance, I was very proud of that stereo. I always rolled down my windows so other cars could hear the cool tunes I was playing. Getting a head nod from a passenger in the car next to me was akin to getting a *like* for a social media post. I got thumbs down, too, like when I was pumping Snoop Dogg's debut album, *Doggy Style*. Snoop wasn't like other rappers; Snoop's persona wasn't about being tough, it was about being cool. He had style, swing, and sway. He invited us into his world, to be a part of it. He made it okay for a kid that looked like me to blast his album in upscale Beverly Hills. I did that, sitting at a red light, blaring "Gin and Juice" like I had a refrigerator full of 40-ounce beers at home. I thought I was cool until a police car pulled up next to me. The officer took one look at me and shook his head in pity. It wasn't because I was listening to rap music; he pitied me because I looked like an absolute moron playing rap music. I cut my hair the next day.

# Albums of the '90s:

*Doggystyle* (1993)

*Tha Doggfather* (1996)

*Da Game Is To Be Sold, Not To Be Told* (1998)

*Smoke Fest World Tour* (1998)

*No Limit Top Dogg* (1999)

# The 11 Best Songs By Snoop Doggy Dogg:

1. **Who Am I (What's My Name)?** (*Doggystyle*)
2. **Snoopafella** (*No Limit Top Dogg*)
3. **Gin And Juice** (*Doggystyle*)
4. **Gz And Hustlas** (*Doggystyle*)
5. **2001** (*Tha Doggfather*)
6. **Tha Shiznit** (*Doggystyle*)
7. **Snoop's Upside Ya Head** (*Tha Doggfather*)
8. **Snoop Bounce** (Rock & Roll Remix) (*Doggfather* single B-side)
9. **Cee Walkin** (*Smoke Fest World Tour*)
10. **Just Dippin'** (*No Limit Top Dogg*)
11. **Snoop World** (*Da Game Is To Be Sold, Not To Be Told*)

**Fun Fact:** *Doggystyle* debuted at No. 1 on the Billboard 200, selling 806,858 copies in its first week in the United States, which, at the time, was the record for a debut artist and the fastest-selling hip-hop album ever.

# SONIC YOUTH

When Sonic Youth guest-starred on *The Simpsons*, it was one of the most subversive TV moments of the decade. Though animated, *The Simpsons* was the most accurate portrayal of the American family ever to be put on television. They may have been yellow, but they had more in common with average Americans than the Conners, the Taylors, or the Bundys. Every Sunday night, 25 million American households collectively sat down in front of our TVs and watched Homer strangle Bart because of some new shenanigans. *The Simpsons* were a cultural touchstone, which was apparent by their guest stars, including Paul McCartney, Buzz Aldrin, and even Bob Hope. In season seven, *The Simpsons* cast Sonic Youth for the lollapalooza-parody, *Homerpalooza*. While alternative rock dominated, indie rock lived in the underground for those too cool to listen to Weezer. Sonic Youth was the el Presidente of the indie rock scene, whose noise rock melodies were like listening to feedback, wrapped up in distortion, inside an avant-rock enigma. This is why their inclusion in the show was such a kool thing. It illustrated the show's adept ability to tap into the greater social zeitgeist. Though Smashing Pumpkins and Cypress Hill also appeared in the episode, by including Sonic Youth, it was the show acknowledging my generation by saying, *we get you*. That's why *The Simpsons* and Sonic Youth lasted for over 30 years. It was because they listened to what their audiences wanted rather than forcing their audiences to listen to them.

# Albums of the '90s:

*Goo* (1990)

*Dirty* (1992)

*Whore's Moaning* (1993)

*Experimental Jet Set, Trash And No Star* (1994)

*TV Shit* (1994)

*Washing Machine* (1995)

*A Thousand Leaves* (1998)

*Silver Session For Jason Knuth* (1998)

# The 11 Best Songs By Sonic Youth:

1. **The Diamond Sea** (*Washing Machine*)
2. **Kool Thing** (*Goo*)
3. **100%** (*Dirty*)
4. **Sunday** (*A Thousand Leaves*)
5. **Dirty Boots** (*Goo*)
6. **Sugar Kane** (*Dirty*)
7. **My Friend Goo** (*Goo*)
8. **Bull In The Heather** (*Experimental Jet Set, Trash And No Star*)
9. **Disappearer** (*Goo*)
10. **Mote** (*Goo*)
11. **Screaming Skull** (*Experimental Jet Set, Trash And No Star*)

**Fun Fact:** Thurston Moore played guitar in the Backbeat band for the film *Backbeat*, about the Beatles pre-fame days. The band also included Mike Mills (R.E.M.), Dave Pirner (Soul Asylum), and Dave Grohl (Nirvana).

# SET-BREAK / THE BATTLE OF JASON EVERMAN

Who is Jason Everman? Some call him the unluckiest man in rock and roll. Others call him a hero.

Even though it came out first, Nirvana's *Bleach* wasn't the first Nirvana album I purchased. It wasn't even the second. And if the *Hormoaning* EP counts, then it wasn't even the third. I picked up *Bleach* during the summer of 1993 in anticipation of the release of *In Utero* that was still a few weeks away. I had listened to *Bleach* before, but I had never fully taken a dive into it. In prep for the new Nirvana album, it was as good of a time as any. After purchasing *Bleach* at one of my usual music store haunts, I noticed something immediately. I had seen the front cover of the album plenty of times. It was a photo negative of Nirvana in mid-jam, threshing their hair like an electrical charge had backfired through their equipment in a frenetic surge. For the first time today, I looked closer at the back cover. It listed the songs on the albums and the band members. Kurdt Kobain with vocals and guitar (deliberate misspelling), Chris Novoselic on bass, Chad Channing on drums, and...Wait... *And*? Who? Jason Everman? Nirvana had a fourth member? Who the hell was Jason Everman?

Now, I knew that Nirvana's original drummer was Chad Channing and was replaced with Dave Grohl before the recording of *Nevermind*, but I never knew that Nirvana had a second guitarist named Jason Everman.

This was 1993. It was pre-internet, so there was no way to look this guy up. You had to rely on word of mouth. As we all know, most people are idiots. I had one friend who was a pseudo-reliable source when it came to music and he lived in Seattle, so I gave him a call. He was fuzzy on the guy but thought that Everman owed money to Cobain, so Cobain put him on the cover as a trade-off. He was pseudo-right. Turns out Jason Everman was a local Seattle musician. Before the release of *Bleach*, Cobain wanted to add a second guitarist to the band so he could concentrate more on singing when he was on stage. The band had already wrapped the recording of *Bleach* but had run out of money, so they couldn't pay the studio for the recording fees, which was holding up the album from being released. Cobain struck a deal with Everman. Everman would pay the remaining fees on the recording bill and in return would become a member of the band. Everman was included on all the album packaging and joined the band on tour. So yes, Jason Everman was an official member of Nirvana but...for only one summer. Midway through the promotional tour for *Bleach*, Everman and Cobain began butting heads, which led to Everman being kicked out of the band before the tour ended. Nirvana would go on to superstardom and Everman would be a mere footnote, having only recorded one song with the band for a Kiss tribute album.

This is not the end of Everman's tale. It's barely the beginning.

Before joining Nirvana, Everman was a well-respected musician and was friends with many other Seattle bands. After leaving Nirvana, a friend called him about a band looking for someone to replace their bassist. Everman agreed and joined this new band. The new band was

Soundgarden.    Unfortunately,   Everman's   tenure   in Soundgarden didn't last much longer.  And he once again found himself kicked out.

In just a year, Jason Everman had been kicked out of two of the decade's biggest bands.  And all he had to show for it was a liner note on the back of a CD.  So, why am I writing about Jason Everman?  Is it because while most people get one crack at stardom, he actually had two and screwed them both up?   No, Everman isn't a failure; he is the living example of who we were in the '90s.  He is the poster boy for our generation.  He is everything right with Gen-X. Jason Everman is a hero.

What's interesting about the Seattle scene isn't that Everman's path was unusual, but his journey was quite normal in that musical community. Stone Gossard and Jeff Ament of Pearl Jam were in Green River with Mark Arm and Steve Turner of Mudhoney.  But so was Bruce Fairweather, who joined Gossard and Ament in Lords of the Wasteland and Mother Love Bone before splitting off with Greg Gilmore to form Blind Horse and ultimately heading off on his own and joining Love Battery.   Greg Gilmore was another journeyman who played in 10 Minute Warning with of all people, Duff McKagan of Guns N' Roses before joining Mother Love Bone, Blind Horse, and finally landing in Son of Man with Dave Krusen, who might have the most hard-luck story of everyone.  Krusen played drums in half a dozen Seattle bands before finding a home in Pearl Jam.  He's actually their original drummer and played on their debut album, *Ten*.  But he was kicked out before the recording of their second album.  Krusen joined Son of Man with Gilmore before ending his musical journey as the drummer in Candlebox.  This isn't an indictment of Fairweather, Gilmore, or Krusen. All of them were well-liked and well-respected musicians. Stone Gossard and Jeff Ament were in plenty of bands before Pearl Jam. All of them disbanded. Drummer Matt Cameron bounced from band to band before finding Soundgarden. Were Gossard, Ament, and Cameron better than Fairweather, Gilmore, and Krusen, or just lucky? That doesn't matter because what matters is persistence. This is where Everman succeeded.

While band-hopping isn't an unusual thing in an enclosed music community, for Seattle, it was much more. Seattle was a community that never thought they were going to be global rock stars. No one thought they were going to be big MTV stars. The most any band could hope for was being signed to the local music label, Sub Pop. Within that community, jealousy didn't exist. They supported each other, rooted for each other. It was encouragement over competition. The worldwide success that would eventually come from it was rooted in the purity of the music. They weren't trying to write radio hits, they weren't having naked girls dance in their videos, they weren't riding dolphins down Sunset Blvd. They weren't trying to be anything other than themselves.

This is where Jason Everman comes back into our story.

After bouncing around Seattle trying to make his way in other bands, Everman made a forked life choice and joined the United States Army working his way up to the Special Forces, where he fought in Iraq and Afghanistan. Due to the highly classified nature of his role in the military, very little is known about his service except that his fellow soldiers have nothing but high praise and respect for him. General Stanley McChrystal wrote a letter of recommendation for

Everman when he applied to Columbia University, where he would eventually earn a degree in philosophy. His love for philosophy was inspired by the time he spent in Tibet, studying at a Buddhist Monastery in between his Special Forces enlistments. Seriously!

In the '90s, we didn't care what other people thought of us. We didn't care about getting likes on social media. The closest we came to getting a "like" was getting a literal "thumbs up" from a friend. We didn't have the barriers of social acceptance to alter our personas. All we had was ourselves. That had to be good enough because there were no other options. And it wasn't just a prelude to how the future would change things; it was also a rejection of the past. The '80s were all about looks, fame, and fortune. The '90s said screw that, none of that shit matters. It's all fake. We just want to be human. And for this one decade, that's what we were.

This is why the music of the '90s is so eclectic, strange, but daring. It's unrefined, unpolished, and unclassifiable. Our generation had rejected the traditional molds of what was socially acceptable. How else do you explain weirdo bands like Mr. Bungle, Ween, Gwar, or Green Jellÿ? We didn't care about the image; we cared about the music, and the less polished, the better. Because of this, we would look for music everywhere. An acoustic performance in a coffee cafe was more riveting than seeing a major artist in a massive stadium. We had more affinity for the intimacy. The ability to speak to the performer after the show, to connect with them, that bond was everything. The '90s rejected the distance that had previously divided us by societal ranking. In the '90s, we realized we needed humanity to be fulfilled. We craved it. We ignored the divide because everyone was welcome. We didn't label ourselves because we realized it was the labels that limited us. It was the labels that held us back. Without labels, we were without limits. We could do anything we wanted.

This is why Jason Everman is our hero. He didn't let the music setbacks hold him back. Honestly, I don't believe he ever saw them as setbacks. Because if you don't believe in labels and being judged, then being kicked out of Nirvana and Soundgarden weren't failures but just wrong turns. He backed up, turned around, and transformed himself. Success wasn't measured in how many albums you sold; it was measured in your personal achievements. I'm sure there's a part of Everman that fantasizes about the spoils of being a rock star; I mean, who doesn't? My point is, he didn't let this hold him back, he found a new path, the path he was meant to be on. That was the motive that inspired our generation to forge our own path that came from within and not from the pressure of the peanut gallery.

There is a sliver of light for Everman. In 2004, when Nirvana released their box set of unreleased material, *With The Lights Out*, two of the songs feature Everman on guitar. It may be a couple of songs out of an entire catalog, but in the annals of history, Jason Everman's guitar playing is featured on an official Nirvana album. Everman is officially a part of the Nirvana legacy, but it might be more fitting to say that Nirvana is a piece of Everman's legacy.

The '90s were a time when the road didn't have an end, when the mountain didn't have a peak, we adored the bold over the beautiful, the many versus the one, it was a time where we all fit in somewhere. There was no pressure to find where you fit in because it was about enjoying the journey to find it. The music gave us the courage to defy tradition, to forge our own paths, and that a great idea came come from anywhere. It may be a cliché to say it, but the '90s had spirit, an independent spirit that inspired every person to never give up because giving up just didn't exist.

# SOUNDGARDEN

During the summer of 1994, it was Soundgarden's world, and the universe spun around the gravitational pull of their Cream makes love to the Beatles inspired psychedelic trip, "Black Hole Sun." In the muck and mire of the disgruntled grunge tornado, "Black Hole Sun" emerged as the perfect storm, amassing alt rock's soul into a nitrogen-fueled cigarette lighter, fist-pumping finale to the impending end of the genre. A genre that arrived with a spirited roar of teenage rebellion was on the verge of its inevitable demise, and "Black Hole Sun" was the serenade prophesying the tsunami of fake emotions and plastic empathy that would one day drown the musical world. For Soundgarden, "Black Hole Sun" was its calling card and its albatross. Fans who had followed the band through their early screaming life declared "Black Hole Sun" to be Soundgarden's sell-out moment. When Nirvana, Pearl Jam, and Alice In Chains dominated alternative music, Soundgarden was the cool kid, hanging out in the background, drinking whiskey behind the gym. They played harder, screamed louder, and didn't care about any music video countdown. When they finally obtained chart success, their fans felt betrayed. But "Black Hole Sun" wasn't designed for pop radio stardom and it still might be one of the most peculiar songs to achieve that. If anything, it was Soundgarden diving deeper down the rabbit hole only to go all the way around the Möbius strip and come out on the other side. Soundgarden didn't achieve success with a pop song; they did with a Soundgarden song.

# Albums of the '90s:

*Badmotorfinger* (1992)

*Somms* (1993)

*Superunknown* (1994)

*Down The Upside* (1996)

# The 11 Best Songs By Soundgarden:

1. **Searching With My Good Eye Closed** (*Badmotorfinger*)
2. **Burden In My Hand** (*Down On The Upside*)
3. **Outshined** (*Badmotorfinger*)
4. **Slaves & Bulldozers** (*Badmotorfinger*)
5. **The Day I Tried To Live** (*Superunknown*)
6. **Like Suicide** (*Superunknown*)
7. **Rusty Cage** (*Badmotorfinger*)
8. **Birth Ritual** (*Singles* OST)
9. **Fell On Black Days** (*Superunknown*)
10. **No Attention** (*Down On The Upside*)
11. **Black Hole Sun** (*Superunknown*)

**Fun Fact:** Singer Chris Cornell had an incredibly unique singing voice with such a wide octave range that it required multiple microphones to capture it properly. On top of that, Cornell was known to sing louder than most vocalists and would commonly blow through microphones while recording, requiring them to be constantly replaced.

# SPIRITUALIZED

During the '90s, when a web company would go public, its stock would explode and make every investor an overnight millionaire. Everyone wanted in on the action, and investors would airdrop piles of money to any kid who knew HTML. After college, I was a DJ for an internet radio station called Spike Radio, the first global radio station. Spike had been given two years of funding in advance, which the execs at the station spent in lavish ways. They rented out mansions to throw massive parties. They treated the crew to dinners at the best restaurants. They bought random useless things like an industrial CD burner and a color copier. Armed with a CD burner and an unlimited supply of free blank CDs, I could burn any CD from our station's library, and using the color copier, I could make an exact replica of the CD jacket. I used it to fill my personal library with replica CDs. One late night, I made a copy of Spiritualized's *Ladies And Gentlemen We Are Floating Through Space*. One of the station's programmers saw my "copied" CD case, picked it up, and thought it was the real thing. She went on to tell me about a Spiritualized concert she saw in London. She said it was like having a religious experience. Thinking I was a Spiritualized fan, she *asked me* to go to sushi. I agreed but neglected to tell her I had never listened to Spiritualized. Turns out, we had nothing in common and our first date was also our last. Six months after launch, Spike Radio folded. The multi-million dollar station couldn't make it one year, but twenty years later I still have my fake Spiritualized CD and it works fine.

# Albums of the '90s:

*Lazer Guided Melodies* (1992)
*Pure Phase* (1995)
*Ladies And Gentlemen We Are Floating In Space* (1997)

# The 11 Best Songs By Spiritualized:

1. **Medication** (*Pure Phase*)
2. **Ladies And Gentlemen We Are Floating In Space** (*Ladies and Gentlemen We Are Floating In Space*)
3. **Electricity** (*Ladies and Gentlemen We Are Floating In Space*)
4. **Broken Heart** (*Ladies and Gentlemen We Are Floating In Space*)
5. **Run** (*Lazer Guided Melodies*)
6. **Lay Back In The Sun** (*Pure Phase*)
7. **I Think I'm In Love** (*Ladies and Gentlemen We Are Floating In Space*)
8. **Shine A Light** (*Lazer Guided Melodies*)
9. **Cop Shoot Cop** (*Ladies and Gentlemen We Are Floating In Space*)
10. **Stay With Me** (*Ladies and Gentlemen We Are Floating In Space*)
11. **Sway** (*Lazer Guided Melodies*)

**Fun Fact:** Frontman Jason Pierce was dating keyboardist Kate Radley until she left him for Richard Ashcroft of the Verve. Pierce wrote *Ladies And Gentlemen We Are Floating In Space* as an emotional reaction to the break up. Radley left the band shortly after its release.

# STONE TEMPLE PILOTS

My first DJ gig at the UCLA radio station was co-hosting a "Rare Songs" show. A fellow DJ and I were big collectors of rare tracks, which was not a simple task in the '90s. In a time before the internet, I had to scour every music store, import rack, and mail order catalog to find a compilation album, CD single, 12-inch vinyl, or bootleg that featured a coveted rare track. Between my co-host and I, we had amassed a library of rare songs from Pearl Jam's "I've Got A Feeling" to Nirvana's "Opinion" to the Beastie Boys "Rock Hard." We had almost every one of our favorite bands covered, except Stone Temple Pilots. Our program director was a rabid STP fan and had challenged us to find a rare track, which he claimed didn't exist. And, their cover of "Dancing Days" from the Led Zeppelin tribute album didn't count. Around that time, MTV aired Stone Temple Pilots' unplugged session. During the performance, the band played a cover of David Bowie's "Andy Warhol," which wasn't on any of their albums. But how could I play this TV performance on the radio? I had a plan. I hooked up my cassette recorder to my TV, waited for MTV to re-air the episode, and recorded it. I brought the cassette into our next show and played it. It was a huge hit. The program director loved it so much that the following year when I was being considered to be the general manager of the station, it was the program director's deciding vote that put me in. "Andy Warhol" would eventually be released as an official B-side, but because I played it first, it had put me plush in his good graces.

## Albums of the '90s:

*Core* (1992)
*Purple* (1994)
*Tiny Music From The Vatican Gift Shop* (1996)
*No. 4* (1999)

## The 11 Best Songs By Stone Temple Pilots:

1. **Vasoline** (*Purple*)
2. **Trippin' On A Hole In A Paper Heart** (*Tiny Music From The Vatican Gift Shop*)
3. **Big Empty** (*Purple*)
4. **Sex Type Thing** (*Core*)
5. **Army Ants** (*Purple*)
6. **Interstate Love Song** (*Purple*)
7. **Big Bang Baby** (*Tiny Music From The Vatican Gift Shop*)
8. **Unglued** (*Purple*)
9. **I Got You** (*No. 4*)
10. **Andy Warhol** (*Vasoline* single B-side)
11. **Creep** (*Core*)

**Fun Fact:** Singer Scott Weiland was a big fan of the musical *Hedwig And The Angry Inch*. During multiple STP shows, he dressed up and performed as Hedwig.

**Personal Note:** In 2015, I sat next to Scott Weiland on a plane on the way to the Sundance Film Festival, where he was performing. The entire time on the flight, he was diligently working on music.

# SUNNY DAY REAL ESTATE

How intense were Sunny Day Real Estate fans? They make Annie Wilkes in *Misery* look like an eccentric bed and breakfast owner. They make Max Cady in *Cape Fear* look like a lovesick ex-boyfriend. They make Hannibal Lector look like a foodie with unusual tastes. One of my post-college gigs was writing music reviews. In an interview to join Blender magazine, I was asked what I thought about Sunny Day Real Estate. I was honest; I said I thought they were overrated. The interviewer blurted out, "You're just not emo enough to understand them." He said it in a tone so smug, Shannon Doherty would have returned to *90210* just to avoid it. I don't know what's more emo, the band or that response. Of course, I didn't get the job. It did motivate me to crack the SDRE code. What was it that drove their fans to such aggressive stances? I downloaded all of their albums and I listened, absorbed, and deciphered. There was a vulnerable sweetness in the depths of singer Jeremy Enigk's vocal strain that shouted through the post-hardcore grind of grizzled guitars like a lost child screaming for help in a factory filled with the din of clanging metal. In the late '90s, we witnessed the rise of the machines from the internet to cell phones, in an era where we could communicate better, we struggled with our inability to connect. SDRE's music was a plea to the world to try to hold together; this is what inspired their fans' undying devotion. Sadly, SDRE fell victim to the changing world and broke up. Their genuine emo heart just couldn't beat in the apathetic digital frontier of tomorrow.

# Albums of the '90s:

*In Circles* (1994)
*Diary* (1994)
*Sunny Day Real Estate (LP2)* (1995)
*How It Feels To Be Something On* (1998)

# The 11 Best Songs By Sunny Day Real Estate:

1. **Pillars** (*How It Feels To Be Something On*)
2. **Seven** (*Diary*)
3. **Rodeo Jones** (*LP2*)
4. **9** (*In Circles*)
5. **8** (*Diary*)
6. **Shadows** (*Diary*)
7. **How It Feels To Be Something On** (*How It Feels To Be Something On*)
8. **Spade and Parade** (*LP2*)
9. **In Circles** (*Diary*)
10. **Guitar and Video Games** (*How It Feels To Be Something On*)
11. **Song About An Angel** (*Diary*)

**Fun Fact:** Drummer William Goldsmith and bassist Nate Mendel joined the Foo Fighters for their first tour. During the recording of the Foo Fighters' second album, *The Colour And The Shape*, Dave Grohl re-recorded all of William Goldsmith's drum parts. This prompted Goldsmith to leave the band and reunite with Sunny Day Real Estate. Nate Mendel remained with the Foo Fighters.

# SUPERCHUNK

Tower Records was my great escape, my oasis, my nirvana. I visited Tower three times a week, whether I bought a CD or not. Just to be in that environment was more soothing to me than a yoga retreat on the beaches of Bali. The click-clack of the CDs smacking against each other as my fingers flipped through the titles might be my favorite beat of the decade. It was cathartic. In between my TV gigs, I even tried to get a job at Tower Sunset, the coolest Tower Records in L.A., and second only to the Tower in San Francisco, where my mom worked while she was in college. I was offered the job, but only if I opted not to go back to work in TV. I had to turn it down. The manager was cool. He felt bad, so he offered me two tickets to Superchunk. I had never seen Superchunk and after hearing all the high praise from my friends about their live shows, this was an unbelievable consolation prize. The show exceeded every expectation. Superchunk took the stage with such ferocious passion, it literally knocked us on our collective asses. The entire floor of the venue shook. The wood beneath our feet was vibrating so wildly that it was setting off Geiger counters all over the city, causing people to duck under doorways afraid that the big one had arrived. The concert was a non-stop avalanche of heart-pounding, sweat-inducing, unwavering power rock. As an indie rock titan of the decade, Superchunk did not disappoint. This is how cool Tower Records was; they gave me Superchunk tickets when I didn't take the job. I can only imagine what would have happened if I had worked there.

# Albums of the '90s:

*Superchunk* (1990)
*No Pocky For Kitty* (1991)
*On The Mouth* (1993)
*Foolish* (1994)
*Here's Where The Strings Come In* (1995)
*Indoor Living* (1997)
*Come Pick Me Up* (1999)

# The 11 Best Songs By Superchunk:

1. **Precision Auto** (*On The Mouth*)
2. **Slack Motherfucker** (*Superchunk*)
3. **Cursed Mirror** (*Come Pick Me Up*)
4. **Detroit Has A Skyline** (*Here's Where The Strings Come In*)
5. **Driveway To Driveway** (*Foolish*)
6. **Animated Airplanes Over Germany** (*Here's Where The Strings Come In*)
7. **Skip Steps 1 & 3** (*No Pocky For Kitty*)
8. **Basement Life** (*Dope Guns 'N Fucking In The Streets Vol. 8*)
9. **Seed Toss** (*No Pocky For Kitty*)
10. **Why Do You Have To Put A Date On Everything** (*Foolish*)
11. **Unbelievable Things** (*Indoor Living*)

**Fun Fact:** Singer Mac McCaughan met bassist Laura Ballance while the two of them worked together at a pizza place in Chapel Hill, North Carolina, called Pepper's Pizza.

# SWELL

As the General Manager of the UCLA radio station, I oversaw everything. I oversaw the DJs, program schedule, sports department, talks shows, and the music department. Though I let my music director and program director pick the songs for rotation, I did have executive power and could intervene at any time. As a good leader, I rarely exercised that nuclear option, but I did occasionally hunt for any overlooked artist or song. Weekly, I would flip through our crates of discarded CDs, searching for a hidden gem that had fallen into our crap bin. This is how I discovered the band Swell. It was 1997, and Swell was part of a small sub-genre called post-grunge. Like grunge, post-grunge embodied the fuzzed-out, feedback hungry guitars, just without the anger. The moment that Swell's album, *Too Many Days Without Thinking*, seeped through my stereo speakers, they became my favorite new band, yet when I played the album for my fellow staff members, I was met with shrugs and a lack of enthusiasm. One girl said the music sounded like Seattle classic rock. And yes, she was referring to Nirvana from three years earlier. Despite the malaise, I trusted my instincts and I added Swell's song "Going Up (To Portland)" to our rotation. It caught on. Within weeks, it was one of the most played tracks at the station. I felt vindicated. Swell went on to be one of my favorite bands of the late '90s before they disappeared into obscurity. This is what made the music of the '90s so unique; no matter where you looked, there was great music everywhere, even in the discard pile.

# Albums of the '90s:

*Swell* (1990)

*...Well?* (1991)

*Room To Think* (1993)

*41* (1994)

*Too Many Days Without Thinking* (1997)

*For All The Beautiful People* (1998)

# The 11 Best Songs By Swell:

1. **Going Up (To Portland)** (*Too Many Days Without Thinking*)
2. **F\*ck Even Flow** (*Too Many Days Without Thinking*)
3. **Come Tomorrow** (*Swell*)
4. **Make Up Your Mind** (*For All The Beautiful People*)
5. **Down** (*...Well?*)
6. **Kinda Stoned** (*41*)
7. **At Lennies** (*Too Many Days Without Thinking*)
8. **Throw The Wine** (*Too Many Days Without Thinking*)
9. **(I Know) The Trip** (*Too Many Days Without Thinking*)
10. **Love You All** (*Swell*)
11. **Everything Is Good** (*For All The Beautiful People*)

**Fun Fact:** In support of their first album, the band took an unusual approach to promote it. Instead of touring in the traditional sense, the band spent the summer busking around Spain playing their music to street crowds.

# SWING MUSIC

The line of snazzy hipsters stretched down Hillhurst Ave. and around the corner onto Los Feliz Blvd. It was a sea of bowling shirts, zoot suits, black fedoras, vintage cowl neck dresses, and the brightest red lipstick you've ever seen. It was an hour before the joint opened and I was already trying not to blow my wig whether I was going to make it in. This wasn't my first romp to the Derby, but I had never seen it so wall-to-wall nuts. My babe was meeting me here, and she was a real looker. I had been dizzy with this dame for months and she finally agreed to a date because I promised her swing dancing. If I couldn't deliver, it would be curtains. Since the release of Jon Favreau's film, *Swingers*, the Derby was host to the hottest wingdings in L.A. While rock clubs were struggling to get a half-full crowd to check out another Green Day-knock-off, the Derby was packing in the hip cats, night after night. This was the swing revival. It was filling a void that had been drained by the hard rock animalism. You didn't dance to alternative rock; you slammed into each other at high speeds. If you wanted to boogie-woogie, your only options were rap clubs and drug-heavy electronica raves. The swing revival changed that. Going to the Derby wasn't just about the dancing; it was about being transported back to the days of our grandparents. If you were going out for a night on the town, you dressed up smooth for it, togged to the bricks. The line outside the Derby looked identical to the crowd from my grandfather's era when he would visit L.A. during his military days. Everyone in town who owned a pair of white and black patent-leather shoes was in line in front of me. Turns out, that night, the Derby booked a special guest, Big Bad Voodoo Daddy, only the most swell artist of the Swing Revival. It was my first date with this doll and swing's big daddy was gumming up the works. When my broad showed up, she was in a fit over how far back we were in line. After waiting an hour, we made it to the front doors when the joint hit capacity and we got the kiss-off. The bouncer closed the line and told us to make tracks back to my cave. I tried to salvage the date with some booze at the Dresden, listening to the cool tunes by Marty and Elayne, but my date had already soured. I don't blame Big Bad Voodoo Daddy for putting the kibosh on my rendezvous; if anything, it was one of the best bad first dates I've ever had.

## The 11 Best Swing Revival Albums:

1. Big Bad Voodoo Daddy - *Americana Deluxe* (1998)
2. Atomic Fireballs - *Torch This Place* (1999)
3. The Lucky Strikes - *Song & Dance* (1998)
4. Big Rude Jake - *Butane Fumes & Bad Cologne* (1993)
5. Cherry Poppin' Daddies - *Zoot Suit Riot* (1997)
6. Squirrel Nut Zippers - *Hot* (1996)
7. Royal Crown Revue - *The Contender* (1998)
8. Brian Setzer Orchestra - *The Dirty Boogie* (1998)
9. Big Bad Voodoo Daddy - *This Beautiful Life* (1999)
10. Deluxtone Rockets - *Deluxtone Rockets* (1999)
11. Steve Lucky & The Rhumba Bums - *Come Out Swingin'!* (1998)

# TLC

It was the summer of 1992 and I was on a road trip up to Northern California to see Lollapalooza at the Shoreline Amphitheatre in Mountain View. During our car ride from L.A., my friends and I took turns playing CDs. We were focusing on the bands who were playing at the festival, like the Red Hot Chili Peppers, The Jesus and Mary Chain, and Pearl Jam. When my friend put in TLC's *Oooooh On The TLC Tip*, it was met with a flurry of groans and ridicule. But in guy code, a deal's a deal. It was his turn, so we had to suck it up. As much as I wasn't a fan of R&B, there were a few songs I did enjoy. If "Motownphilly" by Boyz II Men or "Do Me" by Bel Biv Devoe came on the radio, I wouldn't switch stations. For TLC, I was probably the biggest critic in the car, comparing the listening session to a military interrogation. Surprisingly, the album wasn't bad, and I even found myself head-bobbing along. It wasn't enough to motivate me to buy the album, but it did intrigue me when their second album dropped. *CrazySexyCool* was an ambitious leap forward in sound and maturity, but one song that stood out. The final song on the album, "Sumthin' This Way Comes," featured a chilling rap by Outkast's Andre 3000 that sealed me as a fan. The song was dark. Tim Burton dark. It dove into uncharted waters for the group, digging into the layers of personal trauma like a mafia therapist. I connected with the music in a way that had only happened with rock music. These funky divas had freed my mind with their unbreakable music, making them one of my real loves.

## Albums of the '90s:

*Ooooooh... On The TLC Tip* (1992)
*CrazySexyCool* (1994)
*FanMail* (1999)

## The 11 Best Songs By TLC:

1. **Sumthin' Wicked This Way Comes** (*CrazySexyCool*)
2. **What About Your Friends** (*Ooooooh... On The TLC Tip*)
3. **Creep** (*CrazySexyCool*)
4. **No Scrubs** (*FanMail*)
5. **Kick Your Game** (*CrazySexyCool*)
6. **Hat 2 Da Back** (*Ooooooh... On The TLC Tip*)
7. **Waterfalls** (*CrazySexyCool*)
8. **His Story** (*Ooooooh... On The TLC Tip*)
9. **Ain't 2 Proud 2 Beg** (*Ooooooh... On The TLC Tip*)
10. **My Life** (*FanMail*)
11. **Depend On Myself** (*Ooooooh... On The TLC Tip*)

**Fun Fact:** Even though *CrazySexyCool* was Diamond-certified, the way their record deal was structured, the band received almost no royalties from the sales. TLC tried holding Clive Davis up at gunpoint to get a royalty boost, but it wasn't enough to save the band from having to declare bankruptcy the following year.

**Song Note (Waterfalls):** Cee-Lo Green provides background vocals on this track.

# TRICKY

When first listening to Tricky's debut album, *Maxinquaye*, what impressed me the most wasn't the cultural importance it had for trip hop, it was the use of the sample of the Smashing Pumpkins song, "Suffer," for the song "Pumpkin." The art of sampling, if you can even call it an art, was still in the toddler phase. An overwhelming majority of samples came from '70s songs with monstrous grooves. As grunge enveloped society in a blanket of flannel, it was largely considered a passing fad rather than a substantial contributor. For Tricky to sample Smashing Pumpkins, it had a greater meaning. By using this song, Tricky was acknowledging the legitimacy of the musical legacy of not just the Smashing Pumpkins but the entire grunge genre. With its dizzy guitar swirl and shoegaze-adjacent melody, "Pumpkin" is the song that lured me into the entire album. Listening to *Maxinquaye* was like descending an old wooden staircase in the back of an aging Chinese restaurant and stumbling upon a drug den of blurred beats, mesmerizing chants, and hypnotic vocals. It was like the theme music to a sensual underbelly of grimy street life, like a secret door into a confused psyche. Even though he had broken his training wheels in Massive Attack, Tricky's solo album felt fresh and original. In 1995, there was no band bigger than the Smashing Pumpkins. This is why the Pumpkins sample fit. *Maxinquaye* was a snapshot of that era, encompassing all the sights, sounds, and emotions that existed in society, even Billy Corgan.

# Albums of the '90s:

*Maxinquaye* (1995)

*Nearly God* (1996)

*Grassroots* (1996)

*Pre-Millennium Tension* (1996)

*Angels With Dirty Faces* (1998)

*Juxtapose* (1999)

# The 11 Best Songs By Tricky:

1. **Black Steel** (*Maxinquaye*)
2. **Makes Me Wanna Die** (*Pre-Millennium Tension*)
3. **Overcome** (*Maxinquaye*)
4. **I Sing For You** (*Nearly God*)
5. **Hell Is Around The Corner** (*Maxinquaye*)
6. **Pumpkin** (*Maxinquaye*)
7. **Broken Homes** (*Angels With Dirty Faces*)
8. **Call Me** (*Juxtapose*)
9. **Aftermath** (*Maxinquaye*)
10. **Christiansands** (*Pre-Millennium Tension*)
11. **Brand New You're Retro** (*Maxinquaye*)

**Fun Fact:**  Tricky named his album, *Maxinquaye* after his mother Maxine Quaye, who passed away when he was four years old.

**Fun Fact 2:**  Tricky used the same lyrics in his solo material as he did in Massive Attack to create a symbiotic connection between his two musical pathways.

#  U2

Though multiple actors have played Batman, to a '90s kid, Michael Keaton is the only true Batman. After two incredible Batman films, Keaton stepped away from the role. This was devastating to fans who saw Keaton elevate the Batman brand as Christopher Reeves did for Superman. No one could replace Keaton in our minds. I was working at my movie theater job when we were playing the trailer to *Batman Forever* with Val Kilmer as the caped crusader. In a random occurrence, Michael Keaton walked out of the theater, up to the concessions counter, and said, "Alright guys, what do you think of the new *Batman* trailer?" I was floored. I wanted to scream, you're Batman! But I held my tongue and gave a more measured response, "It looks okay but not as good as the first two films." Keaton being a professional, half-smiled and said, "I think Val's going to do a good job." Despite Val Kilmer's decent take on Batman, the movie is largely considered a bust except for its critically acclaimed soundtrack. With unreleased tracks by The Offspring, Massive Attack, and Seal, the biggest praise went to U2. After the head-scratching release of their album *Zooropa*, U2 needed something to remind us what made them great. Their contribution to the soundtrack "Hold Me, Thrill Me, Kiss Me, Kill Me" was the sultry swagger that we yearned for. It was only one song, but it was strong enough to keep us excited for the next album. In a decade that saw U2 transform, rattle, and pop, they always found a way to get us to stand at attention.

# Albums of the '90s:

*Achtung Baby* (1991)

*Pop* (1993)

*Zooropa* (1997)

# The 11 Best Songs By U2:

1. **Until The End Of The World** (*Achtung Baby*)
2. **One** (*Achtung Baby*)
3. **Stateless** (*Million Dollar Hotel* OST)
4. **Ultraviolet (Light My Way)** (*Achtung Baby*)
5. **Gone** (*Pop*)
6. **The Fly** (*Achtung Baby*)
7. **Last Night On Earth** (*Pop*)
8. **Hold Me, Thrill Me, Kiss Me, Kill Me** (*Batman Forever* OST)
9. **Do You Feel Loved** (*Pop*)
10. **The First Time** (*Zooropa*)
11. **Love Is Blindness** (*Achtung Baby*)

**Fun Fact:** At a 1993 show in Australia, bassist Adam Clayton was so severely hung-over, he couldn't perform and was replaced by his bass tech, Stuart Morgan. This is the only show ever where U2 played without their original line-up.

**Song Note (One):** The song is about a son coming out to his religious father about his sexual orientation.

# UNCLE TUPELO

My grandfather was dying of cancer. He had been fighting liver cancer and it was finally taking over. I visited him in San Francisco where he was on home hospice care. While he slept, I would care for my grandmother's needs, like taking her to get groceries and other life stuff that they used to do together. I did spend a lot of time in his room, watching him sleep, reading books, or listening to music, whatever it took to be present. I loved my grandfather, but there came a point where even I needed an emotional break. San Francisco had one of the most iconic Tower Records in the country. Just walking through the aisles was a cathartic activity that helped me cope. The rhythmic sound of the plastic CD cases clicking together as I flipped through them was soothing to my anxiety. On that day, I stopped on the cover of Uncle Tupelo's *Anodyne*, fixated on the black and white photo of the wall of guitars. I don't know what prompted me to buy the album, but it called to me at that moment. Later that night, I sat at my grandfather's bedside and listened to the album. The sedative monotone of Jay Farrar's voice coupled with the cracked tenderness in Jeff Tweedy's yowl was comforting. The profound emotions, layered like a brick wall, permeated through the pores of every song, setting a peaceful tone to the room. I stayed by my grandfather's side through the night with Uncle Tupelo's music holding my hand through the severe gravity of the situation. If there's ever an example of how music has the power to be an emotional support, I can't think of a better one than this.

# Albums of the '90s:

*No Depression* (1990)
*Still Feel Gone* (1991)
*March 16-20, 1992* (1992)
*Anodyne* (1993)

# The 11 Best Songs By Uncle Tupelo:

1. **Anodyne** (*Anodyne*)
2. **Gun** (*Still Feel Gone*)
3. **The Long Cut** (*Anodyne*)
4. **Moonshiner** (*March 16-20, 1992*)
5. **Whiskey Bottle** (*No Depression*)
6. **Black Eye** (*March 16-20, 1992*)
7. **New Madrid** (*Anodyne*)
8. **I Got Drunk** (*No Depression*)
9. **We've Been Had** (*Anodyne*)
10. **Graveyard Shift** (*No Depression*)
11. **Chickamauga** (*Anodyne*)

**Fun Fact:** Uncle Tupelo's album, *No Depression*, is considered the first seminal alternative country album and the true originator of the genre. It is so highly acclaimed within the genre that the alt-country magazine, *No Depression*, derived their name from it.

**Album Note (*March 16-20, 1992*):** Peter Buck of R.E.M. produced the album and provided guitar feedback where necessary.

# WILCO

It was a road trip to Vegas when I learned the embarrassing truth. "Where's disc two?" my friend on the passenger side said, holding up my CD case for Wilco's album, *Being There*. "What disc two?" I replied, confused. Then, he laid it on me. For years I thought Wilco's *Being There* was a single disc album. Initially, Wilco's drunken cowpoke twang veered too country for me. It wasn't until their rock-oriented album, *Summerteeth*, where they found a balance between the Dylanesque-drawl and the Cheap Trick-makes-love-to-the-Beatles harmonies that I became a fan. Because of my new-found love for Wilco, I dove into their back catalogue. In the '90s, unless an album was a new release, you never bought it new. Anything older than three months was surely in a used CD bin somewhere. When purchasing *Being There*, I experienced one of the dangers of such an activity. It turns out that my copy of *Being There* was missing its second disc. Since I didn't know that *Being There* was a two-disc set, I didn't know that disc two was missing until I was on that Vegas trip. Seeing the disappointment on my friend's face when he learned that we weren't going to be able to listen to the second half of the album was like watching someone's reaction to the end of the movie *Seven*. I did what I had to do. When we reached Vegas, I sought out a CD store and I purchased a brand new copy of *Being There*. We listened to disc two very appropriately on the way home. I didn't win any money on that Vegas trip but discovering an entire disc of Wilco music was an even better jackpot.

# Albums of the '90s:

*A.M* (1995)
*Being There* (1996)
*Summerteeth* (1999)

# The 11 Best Songs By Wilco:

1. **How To Fight Loneliness** (*Summerteeth*)
2. **Monday** (*Being There*)
3. **Box Full Of Letters** (*A.M.*)
4. **Nothing'severgonnastandinmyway (Again)** (*Summerteeth*)
5. **Outtasite (Outta Mind)** (*Being There*)
6. **I Got You (At The End Of The Century)** (*Being There*)
7. **Via Chicago** (*Summerteeth*)
8. **I Thought I Held You** (*A.M.*)
9. **Blue Eyed Soul** (*A.M.*)
10. **I Must Be High** (*A.M.*)
11. **The Lonely 1** (*Being There*)

**Fun Fact:** Wilco combined forces with folk artist Billy Bragg to write and record two albums based on unused Woody Guthrie lyrics. Bragg and Wilco composed new music for the lyrics with Bragg and Wilco singer, Jeff Tweedy, trading off singing duties. These albums were called *Mermaid Avenue 1 & 2*. A third disc of material emerged on the *Mermaid Avenue* box set in 2012.

# WU-TANG CLAN FAMILY

Wu-Tang Clan's music was so unique it defied tradition. Chorus? What chorus? Melody? What melody? Wu-Tang songs were re-invented rap battle cypher slug-outs. With nine lead rappers and each insisting on spitting rhymes on every song, the structure was almost never verse, chorus, verse. It wasn't uncommon for a song to be verse, verse, verse, verse, verse, verse, verse, verse, verse, next song. One of the few times Wu-Tang released a traditional song ("C.R.E.A.M."), it slayed the charts and became one of the biggest hip-hop hits of the decade. Each MC in the group exhibited their own unique personality that rarely flowed gracefully from one rapper to the next. It was like being caught in a cyclone of lyrics that came at your ears from every direction. The lyrics fit together like an upside-down puzzle. You couldn't see how the picture would come together, but you just knew that it would. Wu-Tang's style is so distinct and such a completely radical departure from the norm, their success is nothing short of an anomaly. Since their debut, there has never been another group to attempt what the Wu has accomplished. Imagine walking into a record label and pitching a rap group with ten members obsessed with Shaolin kung fu fighting, martial arts films, comic books, and rap as a collective with no apparent song structure. I remember getting a call from the label rep asking if I had listened to the Wu's debut album, *Enter The 36 Chambers*, and if my station was planning to add any of the tracks. I said I didn't find anything radio-friendly. I will never forget the label rep's response. "They are the least radio-friendly group of all time." But, they're one of the best. Wu-Tang only released two albums during the '90s, but their creative energy was uncontainable and ignited the members to seek out a spotlight of their own. With a group this ground-breaking, it wasn't fair to hold them to just 11 songs, so instead, I've compiled 111 songs from their studio albums, their B-side albums, and their multitude of solo albums for the most epic Wu-Tang list ever created.

## Wu-Tang Clan & Members Albums of the '90s:

*Words From The Genius* - GZA (1991)
*Enter The Wu-Tang (36 Chambers)* - The Wu-Tang Clan (1993)
*Tical* - Method Man (1994)
*Liquid Swords* - GZA (1995)
*Only Built 4 Cuban Linx* - Raekwon (1995)
*Return To The 36 Chambers* - Ol' Dirty Bastard (1995)
*Ironman* - Ghostface Killah (1996)
*Wu-Tang Forever* - The Wu-Tang Clan (1997)
*Bobby Digital In Stereo* - RZA (1998)
*The Pillage* - Cappadonna (1998)
*The Swarm* - Wu-Tang Killa Bees (1998)
*Tical 2000: Judgement Day* - Method Man (1998)
*Beneath The Surface* - GZA (1999)
*Golden Arms Redemption* - U-God (1999)
*Immobilarity* - Raekwon (1999)
*Nigga Please* - Ol' Dirty Bastard (1999)
*Uncontrolled Substance* - Inspectah Deck (1999)
*Wu-Chronicles* - The Wu-Tang Clan (1999)

# The 111 Best Songs By The Wu-Tang Clan:

1. **Protect Ya Neck** (*Enter The Wu-Tang (36 Chambers)*)
2. **A Better Tomorrow** (*Wu-Tang Forever*)
3. **Shame On A Nigga** (*Enter The Wu-Tang (36 Chambers)*)
4. **For Heavens Sake** (*Wu-Tang Forever*)
5. **C.R.E.A.M.** (*Enter The Wu-Tang (36 Chambers)*)
6. **Reunited** (*Wu-Tang Forever*)
7. **Got Your Money** (*Nigga Please*)
8. **Bells Of War** (*Wu-Tang Forever*)
9. **Triumph** (*Wu-Tang Forever*)
10. **Method Man** (*Enter The Wu-Tang (36 Chambers)*)
11. **After The Laughter Comes Tears** (*Protect Ya Neck* single B-side)
12. **Shimmy Shimmy Ya** (*Return To The 36 Chambers*)
13. **Retro Godfather** (*Tical 200: Judgement Day*)
14. **Da Mystery Of Chessboxin'** (*Enter The Wu-Tang (36 Chambers)*)
15. **Shadowboxin'** (*Liquid Swords*)
16. **Release Yo' Delf** (*Tical*)
17. **Criminology** (*Only Built 4 Cuban Linx…*)
18. **Wu-Tang Ain't Nuthing ta F' Wit** (*Enter The Wu-Tang (36 Chambers)*)
19. **B.I.B.L.E. (Basic Instructions Before Leaving Earth)** (*Liquid Swords*)
20. **260** (*Ironman*)
21. **Milk the Cow** (*The Pillage*)
22. **Jury** (*Immobilarity*)
23. **Liquid Swords** (*Liquid Swords*)
24. **Bring Da Ruckus** (*Enter The Wu-Tang (36 Chambers)*)
25. **Bring The Pain** (*Tical*)

26. **Cash Still Rules/Scary Hours (Still Don't Nothing Move But the Money)** (*Wu-Tang Forever*)
27. **Brooklyn Zoo** (*Return To The 36 Chambers*)
28. **My Lovin' Is Digi** (*Bobby Digital In Stereo*)
29. **It's Yourz** (*Wu-Tang Forever*)
30. **I'll Be There For You/You're All I Need** (*Tical*)
31. **Bizarre** (*Golden Arms Redemption*)
32. **Black Jesus** (*Ironman*)
33. **Heart To Heart** (*Immobilarity*)
34. **Pleasure Or Pain** (*Golden Arms Redemption*)
35. **Daytona 500** (*Ironman*)
36. **Hippa To Da Hoppa** (*Return To The 36 Chambers*)
37. **Break Ups 2 Make Ups** (*Tical 200: Judgement Day*)
38. **Publicity** (*Beneath The Surface*)
39. **Guillotine (Swordz)** (*Only Built 4 Cuban Linx…*)
40. **Iron Maiden** (*Ironman*)
41. **Friday** (*Immobilarity*)
42. **Incarcerated Scarfaces** (*Only Built 4 Cuban Linx…*)
43. **Cold Blooded** (*Nigga Please*)
44. **Verbal Intercourse** (*Only Built 4 Cuban Linx…*)
45. **I Get My Thang In Action** (*Tical*)
46. **Motherless Child** (*Ironman*)
47. **Breaker, Breaker** (*Beneath The Surface*)
48. **All That I Got Is You** (*Ironman*)
49. **Living In The World Today** (*Liquid Swords*)
50. **Movas & Shakers** (*Uncontrolled Substance*)
51. **Heaven & Hell** (*Only Built 4 Cuban Linx…*)
52. **97 Mentality** (*The Pillage*)
53. **Severe Punishment** (*Wu-Tang Forever*)
54. **N.Y.C. Everything** (*Bobby Digital In Stereo*)
55. **Beneath The Surface** (*Beneath The Surface*)
56. **Glaciers Of Ice** (*Only Built 4 Cuban Linx…*)
57. **Slang Editorial** (*The Pillage*)
58. **Impossible** (*Wu-Tang Forever*)

59. **Soul Dazzle** (*Golden Arms Redemption*)
60. **Black Boy** (*The Pillage*)
61. **Love Jones** (*Bobby Digital In Stereo*)
62. **Ice Cream** (*Only Built 4 Cuban Linx…*)
63. **Duel Of The Iron Mic** (*Liquid Swords*)
64. **Baby C'Mon** (*Return To The 36 Chambers*)
65. **Raw** (*Immobilarity*)
66. **Tearz** (*Enter The Wu-Tang (36 Chambers)*)
67. **Rainy Dayz** (*Only Built 4 Cuban Linx…*)
68. **Investigative Reports** (*Liquid Swords*)
69. **Protect Ya Neck II The Zoo** (*Return To The 36 Chambers*)
70. **Wu-Tang: 7th Chamber Part II** (*Enter The Wu-Tang (36 Chambers)*)
71. **Glide** (*Golden Arms Redemption*)
72. **R.E.C. Room** (*Uncontrolled Substance*)
73. **Meth Vs. Chef** (*Tical*)
74. **Clan In Da Front** (*Enter The Wu-Tang (36 Chambers)*)
75. **As High As Wu-Tang Get** (*Wu-Tang Forever*)
76. **I Gotcha Back** (*Liquid Swords*)
77. **Little Ghetto Boys** (*Wu-Tang Forever*)
78. **Torture** (*Tical 200: Judgement Day*)
79. **Wu-Gambinos** (*Only Built 4 Cuban Linx…*)
80. **Gold** (*Liquid Swords*)
81. **Kiss Of A Black Widow** (*Bobby Digital In Stereo*)
82. **I Can't Wait** (*Nigga Please*)
83. **The Riddler** (*Batman Forever* OST)
84. **Everything Is Everything** (*The Pillage*)
85. **Show N Prove** (*Uncontrolled Substance*)
86. **Killin' Fields** (*Tical 200: Judgement Day*)
87. **The City** (*Wu-Tang Forever*)
88. **Fish** (*Ironman*)

89. **Can It All Be So Simple** (*Enter The Wu-Tang (36 Chambers)*)
90. **Turbo Charge** (*Golden Arms Redemption*)
91. **Run** (*The Pillage*)
92. **What The Blood Clot** (*Tical*)
93. **Yae Yo** (*Immobilarity*)
94. **Lovin' You** (*Uncontrolled Substance*)
95. **The Table** (*Immobilarity*)
96. **Nigga Please** (*Nigga Please*)
97. **After The Smoke Is Clear** (*Ironman*)
98. **Tragedy** (*Wu-Chronicles*)
99. **Wu-Tang: 7th Chamber Part I** (*Enter The Wu-Tang (36 Chambers)*)
100. **Judgement Day** (*Tical 200: Judgement Day*)
101. **Word On The Street** (*Uncontrolled Substance*)
102. **Sneakers** (*Immobilarity*)
103. **Rollin' Wit You** (*Nigga Please*)
104. **Snakes** (*Return To The 36 Chambers*)
105. **Victim** (*Beneath The Surface*)
106. **Suspect Chin Music** (*Tical 200: Judgement Day*)
107. **Dog Sh*t** (*Wu-Tang Forever*)
108. **Live From New York** (*Immobilarity*)
109. **Damage** (*Return To The 36 Chambers*)
110. **Dart Throwing** (*The Pillage*)
111. **4 Sho Sho** (*Ghost Dog* OST)

# YO LA TENGO

*I Can Hear The Heart Beating As One* was the first full album I downloaded from Napster. At the time, I was working on a TV show for Sony. Our college intern introduced the office to this new file-sharing software called Napster. With Napster, I could download any song I wanted within seconds, for free. With CD prices approaching $20 a disc, the concept that every song I've ever wanted could be mine for free was too good to be true. Everyone in the office was obsessed; the writers, directors, and producers, all had their own scavenger hunt. My executive producer even had the IT department install a CD burner on his computer so we could burn the music that we downloaded onto CDs. Napster lasted for three years and at that time, the record industry had its biggest sales numbers of all time. This is 100% true. Though the music industry accused Napster of "stealing," it was also a way for people to discover new music before purchasing a physical copy. I had bonded with one of the show's actresses over our shared musical tastes. One night she pulled me into her car and played me "Stockholm Syndrome" by Yo La Tengo. Hanging out in her car, letting the music absorb me, I was intrigued but still wasn't convinced to buy the album. Introducing...Napster. I hopped on my computer and went to work grabbing all the songs. Within minutes, I had acquired the complete album. After downloading the album and listening to it, I liked it so much, I went out and bought it. Yo La Tengo had a new fan and it was all because of illegal file-sharing.

# Albums of the '90s:

*Fakebook* (1990)
*May I Sing With Me* (1992)
*Painful* (1993)
*Electr-O-Pura* (1995)
*I Can Hear The Heart Beating As One* (1997)

# The 11 Best Songs By Yo La Tengo:

1. **Stockholm Syndrome** (*I Can Hear The Heart Beating As One*)
2. **Autumn Sweater** (*I Can Hear The Heart Beating As One*)
3. **Tom Courtenay** (*Electr-O-Pura*)
4. **Big Day Coming** (*Painful*)
5. **The Summer** (*Fakebook*)
6. **Blue Line Swinger** (*Electr-O-Pura*)
7. **Moby Octopod** (*I Can Hear The Heart Beating As One*)
8. **Sugarcube** (*I Can Hear The Heart Beating As One*)
9. **Detouring America With Horns** (*May I Sing With Me*)
10. **From A Motel 6** (*Painful*)
11. **Barnaby, Hardly Working** (*Fakebook*)

**Fun Fact:** Yo La Tengo is Spanish for "I Got It." This phrase was shouted by New York Mets' shortstop Elio Chacón when he would attempt to catch a foul ball. The band liked it so much, they adopted it as their name.

# NEIL YOUNG

My first introduction to Neil Young was in 1989 when the classic rocker won MTV's Video of the Year award for his song, "This Note's For You" (a video that had been banned by MTV, and a video that I had never seen). I was pissed when he won. Who the hell was this old guy? What was MTV thinking? This left such a sour taste in my mouth, it wouldn't be until another MTV moment that I gave Young a second chance. It was at the end of the 1993 MTV Video Music Awards. Pearl Jam was the final performance of the show and they invited Young to join them on stage for a feedback-heavy version of Young's song, "Rockin' In The Free World." Pearl Jam seamlessly vibed with Young's rustic style. It was at that moment that Young was christened the Godfather of grunge. And overnight, everyone I knew had suddenly become a Neil Young fan. "I have all his albums," said one friend (he didn't). "I saw him play with Buffalo Springfield," said another friend (he didn't). "I loved him in *The Jazz Singer*," said yet another friend (wrong Neil). Young connected with our generation because he was a rebel, a fighter, a non-conformist. He was a leader for youths who didn't comb their hair or purchase clothes that fit. When Pearl Jam legitimized Young on the stage that night, it elevated his past antics into that of a folk hero. A few years later when Pearl Jam would double as Young's backing band on his album, *Mirror Ball*, the symmetry had been completed. Young was our Yoda, our Morpheus, our Dumbledore, but most importantly, he was no longer a '70s rocker; he was now one of ours.

# Albums of the '90s:

*Ragged Glory* (1990)
*Harvest Moon* (1992)
*Sleeps With Angels* (1994)
*Mirror Ball* (1995)
*Broken Arrow* (1997)

# The 11 Best Songs By Neil Young:

1. **Harvest Moon** (*Harvest Moon*)
2. **Unknown Legend** (*Harvest Moon*)
3. **Train Of Love** (*Sleeps With Angels*)
4. **One Of These Days** (*Harvest Moon*)
5. **I'm The Ocean** (*Mirror Ball*)
6. **War Of Man** (*Harvest Moon*)
7. **Mansion On The Hill** (*Ragged Glory*)
8. **Throw Your Hatred Down** (*Mirror Ball*)
9. **From Hank To Hendrix** (*Harvest Moon*)
10. **Prime Of Life** (*Sleeps With Angels*)
11. **Days That Used To Be** (*Ragged Glory*)

**Fun Fact:**  It took Young 54 years to finally achieve U.S. citizenship. The Canadian-born singer became an American citizen on January 22, 2020.

**Album Note (Harvest Moon):** The album is the spiritual sequel of Young's 1972 album, *Harvest*. The new album features Linda Ronstadt and James Taylor, who were also guests on *Harvest*.

# 1990

## Big Music Events of 1990:

MTV's Unplugged debuts. Jamaica declares Bob Marley's birthday a national holiday. Gloria Estefan's tour bus crashes, breaking her back. Elton John dedicates "Candle in the Wind" to child Aids victim Ryan White, Ryan dies the next day. Coincidence? Curtis Mayfield is paralyzed while performing. Madonna's "Justify My Love" video is banned from MTV for being obscene. 2 Live Crew is arrested for performing obscene lyrics. Milli Vanilli is exposed for lip-syncing as the most-obscene infraction of all. Camper Van Beethoven, The Eurythmics, and Wang Chung break up.

## The 11 Best-Selling Albums of 1990:

1. Janet Jackson - *Rhythm Nation 1814*
2. Phil Collins - *...But Seriously*
3. Michael Bolton - *Soul Provider*
4. Aerosmith - *Pump*
5. MC Hammer - *Please Hammer Don't Hurt 'Em*
6. Paula Abdul - *Forever Your Girl*
7. Mötley Crüe - *Dr. Feelgood*
8. Don Henley - *The End Of The Innocence*
9. The B-52's - *Cosmic Thing*
10. Billy Joel - *Storm Front*
11. Milli Vanilli - *Girl You Know It's True*

# Hit Songs:

- "Been Caught Stealing" - Jane's Addiction
- "Black Velvet" - Alannah Myles
- "Blaze Of Glory" - Jon Bon Jovi
- "Cradle Of Love" - Billy Idol
- "Gonna Make You Sweat" - C+C Music Factory
- "Groove Is In The Heart" - Deee-Lite
- "Hold On" - Wilson Phillips
- "The Humpty Dance" - Digital Underground
- "I Remember You" - Skid Row
- "Ice Ice Baby" - Vanilla Ice
- "It Must Have Been Love" - Roxette
- "Mama Said Knock You Out" - LL Cool J
- "Nothing Compares 2 U" - Sinead O'Connor
- "Poison" - Bell Biv DeVoe
- "The Power" - Snap!
- "Pump Up The Jam" - Technotronic
- "U Can't Touch This" - MC Hammer
- "Vision Of Love" - Mariah Carey
- "Vogue" - Madonna

# R.I.P.:

Tom Fogerty (Creedence Clearwater Revival)
Brent Mydland (The Grateful Dead)
Del Shannon
Stevie Ray Vaughan
Andrew Wood (Mother Love Bone)

# 1991

## Big Music Events of 1991:

Janet Jackson is the first artist to have seven singles from the same album chart in the top 5. Michael Jackson signs a 1 billion dollar contract with Sony. Nirvana's *Nevermind*, Pearl Jam's *Ten*, and Red Hot Chili Peppers' *Blood Sugar Sex Magik* are released, ushering in a new generation of music. Kenny Rogers opens his own fried chicken fast-food chain, Kenny Rogers Roasters. The first Lollapalooza is held with Jane's Addiction as the headliner. The electronic album sales tracking system, Soundscan, begins. N.W.A., Devo, The Byrds, Bad English, and The Talking Heads break up.

## The 11 Best-Selling Albums of 1991:

1. Mariah Carey - *Mariah Carey*
2. Garth Brooks - *No Fences*
3. The Black Crowes - *Shake Your Money Maker*
4. C+C Music Factory - *Gonna Make You Sweat*
5. Wilson Phillips - *Wilson Phillips*
6. Vanilla Ice - *To The Extreme*
7. MC Hammer - *Please Hammer Don't Hurt 'Em*
8. Madonna - *The Immaculate Collection*
9. Queensrÿche - *Empire*
10. Whitney Houston - *I'm Your Baby Tonight*
11. R.E.M. - *Out Of Time*

# Hit Songs:

- "Black Or White" - Michael Jackson
- "Crazy" - Seal
- "(Everything I Do) I Do It For You" - Bryan Adams
- "Good Vibrations" - Marky Mark & the Funky Bunch
- "I Touch Myself" - Divinyls
- "I Wanna Sex You Up" - Color Me Badd
- "Losing My Religion" - R.E.M.
- "More Than Words" - Extreme
- "Motownphilly" - Boyz II Men
- "One" - U2
- "O.P.P." - Naughty By Nature
- "Right Here, Right Now" - Jesus Jones
- "Sadeness Part 1" - Enigma
- "Smells Like Teen Spirit" - Nirvana
- "Someday" - Mariah Carey
- "Summertime" - DJ Jazzy Jeff & The Fresh Prince
- "Unbelievable" - EMF
- "Unforgettable" - Natalie Cole & Nat King Cole
- "Wicked Game" - Chris Isaak

# R.I.P.:

Steve Clarke (Def Leppard)

Miles Davis

Freddie Mercury (Queen)

Johnny Thunders

Rob Tyner (MC5)

# 1992

## Big Music Events of 1992:

Nirvana's *Nevermind* knocks Michael Jackson's *Dangerous* out of the top spot on the album charts, symbolizing a changing of popular music. Vince Neil quits Mötley Crüe, becomes a race car driver. Mariah Carey performs live for the first time for *MTV Unplugged*. Rob Halford quits Judas Priest. Sinead O' Connor rips up a picture of the pope on *Saturday Night Live*. "End of the Road" by Boyz II Men breaks the record for the longest single at number one with 12 weeks. The MP3 is invented. Boogie Down Productions, Fine Young Cannibals, Slade, Styx, and Wire break up.

## The 11 Best-Selling Albums of 1992:

1. Garth Brooks - *Ropin' The Wind*
2. Michael Jackson - *Dangerous*
3. Nirvana - *Nevermind*
4. Billy Ray Cyrus - *Some Gave All*
5. U2 - *Achtung Baby*
6. Garth Brooks - *No Fences*
7. Metallica - *Metallica*
8. Michael Bolton - *Time, Love And Tenderness*
9. Hammer - *Too Legit To Quit*
10. Kris Kross - *Totally Krossed Out*
11. Pearl Jam - *Ten*

# Hit Songs:

- "Achy Breaky Heart" - Billy Ray Cyrus
- "All 4 Love" - Color Me Badd
- "All I Want" - Toad The Wet Sprocket
- "Baby Got Back" - Sir Mix-A-Lot
- "Diamonds And Pearls" - Prince And The N.P.G.
- "End Of The Road" - Boyz II Men
- "Finally" - CeCe Peniston
- "I'm Too Sexy" - Right Said Fred
- "I Will Always Love You" - Whitney Houston
- "Jump" - Kris Kross
- "Jump Around" - House Of Pain
- "Life Is A Highway" - Tom Cochrane
- "My Lovin' (You're Never Gonna Get It)" - En Vogue
- "No Ordinary Love" - Sade
- "Real Love" - Mary J. Blige
- "Rump Shaker" - Wreckx-N-Effect
- "Set Adrift On Memory Bliss" - P.M. Dawn
- "Tears In Heaven" - Eric Clapton
- "Tennessee" - Arrested Development
- "Under The Bridge" - Red Hot Chili Peppers
- "Why?" - Annie Lennox

# R.I.P.:

Willie Dixon
Eddie Kendricks (The Temptations)
Jeff Porcaro (Toto)

# 1993

## Big Music Events of 1993:

*The Bodyguard* soundtrack is the first album to sell over 1 million copies in a week, while Whitney Houston's "I Will Always Love You" from the album spends 14 weeks at number one, breaking the record set by Boyz II Men. Prince legally changes his name to a symbol. Depeche Mode has the first online Q&A session with fans on AOL, leaving most fans SOL. Eddie Vedder, Kurt Cobain, Snoop Dogg, and 2pac are all arrested but not at the same time. Echo & The Bunnymen, Pixies, and the Thompson Twins break up.

## The 11 Best-Selling Albums of 1993:

1. Various Artists - *Bodyguard* OST
2. Kenny G - *Breathless*
3. Eric Clapton - *Unplugged*
4. Janet Jackson - *Janet.*
5. Billy Ray Cyrus - *Some Gave All*
6. Dr. Dre - *The Chronic*
7. Spin Doctors - *Pocket Full Of Kryptonite*
8. Pearl Jam - *Ten*
9. Garth Brooks - *The Chase*
10. Stone Temple Pilots - *Core*
11. Michael Bolton - *Timeless: The Classics*

# Hit Songs:

- "Again" - Janet Jackson
- "Another Sad Love Song" - Toni Braxton
- "Are You Gonna Go My Way" - Lenny Kravitz
- "Cryin'" - Aerosmith
- "Dazzey Duks" - Duice
- "Dreamlover" - Mariah Carey
- "Everybody Hurts" - R.E.M.
- "Fields Of Gold" - Sting
- "Hip Hop Hooray" - Naughty By Nature
- "I Can't Help Falling In Love With You" - UB40
- "I'd Do Anything For Love (But I Won't Do That) " - Meatloaf
- "Informer" - Snow
- "No Rain" - Blind Melon
- "Nuthin' But A 'G' Thang" - Dr. Dre
- "Ordinary World" - Duran Duran
- "Runaway Train" - Soul Asylum
- "Two Princes" - Spin Doctors
- "What's Up?" - 4 Non Blondes
- "Whoomp! (There It Is)" - Tag Team

# R.I.P.:

Dizzy Gillespie
Mick Ronson (David Bowie)
Mia Zapata (The Gits)
Frank Zappa

# 1994

## Big Music Events of 1994:

Bryan Adams is the first Western artist to perform in Vietnam since the Vietnam war. Alice In Chains' *Jar Of Flies* is the first EP to top the album sales chart. 2 Live Crew wins a court battle defending their right to release parody music that incorporates other artists' work. Michael Bolton loses his court battle of plagiarism, finding his parody music wasn't funny. Pearl Jam sues Ticketmaster for being dicks. Woodstock '94 buries concert-goers in mud. Jimmy Page and Robert Plant reunite, Jon Paul Jones isn't invited. New Kids On The Block, Uncle Tupelo, and Whitesnake break up.

## The 11 Best-Selling Albums of 1994

1. Ace Of Base - *The Sign*
2. Mariah Carey - *Music Box*
3. Snoop Doggy Dogg - *Doggystyle*
4. Various Artists - *The Lion King* OST
5. Counting Crows - *August & Everything After*
6. Pearl Jam - *Vs.*
7. Toni Braxton - *Toni Braxton*
8. Janet Jackson - *Janet.*
9. Meatloaf - *Bat Out Of Hell II: Back Into Hell*
10. Michael Bolton - *The One Thing*
11. Tim McGraw - *Not A Moment Too Soon*

# Hit Songs:

- "All For Love" - Bryan Adams, Rod Stewart, & Sting
- "All I Wanna Do" - Sheryl Crow
- "All I Want For Christmas Is You" - Mariah Carey
- "Back & Forth" - Aaliyah
- "Black Hole Sun" - Soundgarden
- "Cantaloop (Flip Fantasia) " - US3
- "Can You Feel The Love Tonight" - Elton John
- "Come To My Window" - Melissa Etheridge
- "Fantastic Voyage" - Coolio
- "Gin and Juice" - Snoop Doggy Dogg
- "Here Comes The Hotstepper" - Ini Kamoze
- "I'll Make Love To You" - Boyz II Men
- "Mmm Mmm Mmm Mmm" - Crash Test Dummies
- "Mr. Jones" - Counting Crows
- "Regulate" - Warren G Featuring Nate Dogg
- "Sabotage" - Beastie Boys
- "The Sign" - Ace Of Base
- "Shoop" - Salt-N-Pepa
- "Streets Of Philadelphia" - Bruce Springsteen
- "Whatta Man" - Salt-N-Pepa and En Vogue

# R.I.P.:

Kurt Cobain (Nirvana)
Antônio Carlos Jobim
Harry Nilsson
Kristen Pfaff (Hole)

# 1995

## Big Music Events of 1995:

The Rock and Roll Hall of Fame Museum opens in Cleveland, Ohio. Tupac Shakur's *Me Against The World* is the first album to go number one while the artist is in prison. TLC files for bankruptcy because they had one of the worst recording contracts of all time. Bill Berry has an aneurysm on stage, quits R.E.M. The Grateful Dead perform their final show with Jerry Garcia. Queen release their final album with Freddie Mercury. The Beatles release their first new song in twenty-five years. Oingo Boingo, Kid 'n Play, Bad Brains, and Pink Floyd break up.

## The 11 Best-Selling Albums of 1995:

1. Hootie And The Blowfish - *Cracked Rear View*
2. Garth Brooks - *The Hits*
3. Boyz II Men - *II*
4. Eagles - *Hell Freezes Over*
5. TLC - *CrazySexyCool*
6. Pearl Jam - *Vitalogy*
7. Green Day - *Dookie*
8. Live - *Throwing Copper*
9. Kenny G - *Miracles: The Holiday Album*
10. Various Artists - *The Lion King* OST
11. The Offspring - *Smash*

# Hit Songs:

- "Big Poppa" - The Notorious B.I.G.
- "Boombastic" - Shaggy
- "Breakfast At Tiffany's" - Deep Blue Something
- "Cotton Eye Joe" - Rednex
- "Gangsta's Paradise" - Coolio
- "Hey Man, Nice Shot" - Filter
- "I Wish" - Skee-Lo
- "I'll Be There For You" - The Rembrandts
- "Just A Girl" - No Doubt
- "Kiss From A Rose" - Seal
- "Name" - Goo Goo Dolls
- "One Of Us" - Joan Osborne
- "Only Wanna Be With You" - Hootie & The Blowfish
- "Player's Anthem" - Junior M.A.F.I.A.
- "Run-Around" - Blues Traveler
- "This Is How We Do It" - Montell Jordan
- "Wonderwall" - Oasis
- "You Oughta Know" - Alanis Morissette

# R.I.P.:

Eazy-E (N.W.A.)
Jerry Garcia (The Grateful Dead)
Shannon Hoon (Blind Melon)
Sterling Morrison (The Velvet Underground)
Selena
Bob Stinson (The Replacements)

# 1996

## Big Music Events of 1996:

"One Sweet Day" by Mariah Carey and Boyz II Men sets the record with 16 weeks at number one on the singles charts. MC Hammer files for bankruptcy in celebration. MTV2 is launched, promises to play videos (they don't). The original members of Kiss reunite in full make-up for the first time in over a decade. Sex Pistols reunite for the first time in twenty years, wear no make-up. David Lee Roth reunites with Van Halen for one night, break up the next day. Crowded House, The Stone Roses, Ramones, Lush, and The Kinks break up.

## The 11 Best-Selling Albums of 1996:

1. Alanis Morissette - *Jagged Little Pill*
2. Mariah Carey - *Daydream*
3. Celine Dion - *Falling Into You*
4. Various Artists - *Waiting To Exhale* OST
5. The Fugees - *The Score*
6. Shania Twain - *The Woman In Me*
7. Garth Brooks - *Fresh Horses*
8. The Beatles - *Anthology 1*
9. Hootie & The Blowfish - *Cracked Rear View*
10. The Smashing Pumpkins - *Mellon Collie And The Infinite Sadness*
11. Bush - *Sixteen Stone*

# Hit Songs:

- "6 Underground" - Sneaker Pimps
- "Big Me" - Foo Fighters
- "California Love" - Tupac ft. Dr. Dre
- "Counting Blue Cars" - Dishwalla
- "Crash Into Me" - Dave Matthews Band
- "Don't Speak" - No Doubt
- "Firestarter" - The Prodigy
- "Follow You Down" - Gin Blossoms
- "Ironic" - Alanis Morissette
- "Jealousy" - Natalie Merchant
- "Killing Me Softly" - The Fugees
- "Macarena" - Los Del Rio
- "No Diggity" - Blackstreet featuring Dr. Dre
- "One Sweet Day" - Mariah Carey And Boyz II Men
- "Pony" - Ginuwine
- "The Beautiful People" - Marilyn Manson
- "Tha Crossroads" - Bone Thugs-N-Harmony
- "That Thing You Do!" - The Wonders
- "Un-Break My Heart" - Toni Braxton
- "Virtual Insanity" - Jamiroquai
- "Where It's At" - Beck
- "Who Will Save Your Soul" - Jewel

# R.I.P.:

Ella Fitzgerald
Bradley Nowell (Sublime)
Tupac Shakur

# 1997

## Big Music Events of 1997:

Madonna wins a Golden Globe for acting in *Evita*. Paul McCartney is knighted. Insane Clown Posse's new album *The Great Milenko* is pulled from shelves six hours after its release due to pressure from religious groups. Faygo sales soar. The First Lilith Affair is held with Sarah McLachlan and Jewel as headliners. Garth Brooks plays to 1 million people in Central Park. Black Sabbath reunites with their original line-up. Bob Dylan performs for Pope John Paul II. Elton John performs at Princess Diana's funeral. Cocteau Twins, Dinosaur Jr., The Fugees, and Soundgarden break up.

## The 11 Best-Selling Albums of 1997:

1. Spice Girls - *Spice*
2. No Doubt - *Tragic Kingdom*
3. Celine Dion - *Falling Into You*
4. Various Artists - *Space Jam* OST
5. Jewel - *Pieces Of You*
6. LeAnn Rimes - *Blue*
7. The Wallflowers - *Bringing Down The Horse*
8. Notorious B.I.G. - *Life After Death*
9. Toni Braxton - *Secrets*
10. Puff Daddy and the Family - *No Way Out*
11. Bush - *Razorblade Suitcase*

# Hit Songs:

- "Around The World" - Daft Punk
- "Barbie Girl" - Aqua
- "Barely Breathing" - Duncan Sheik
- "Bitch" - Meredith Brooks
- "Bitter Sweet Symphony" - The Verve
- "Candle In The Wind 1997" - Elton John
- "Criminal" - Fiona Apple
- "Dammit" - Blink-182
- "Fly" - Sugar Ray
- "The Freshman" - The Verve Pipe
- "How Do I Live" - LeAnn Rimes
- "If You Could Only See" - Tonic
- "I'll Be Missing You" - Puff Daddy, Faith Evans, 112
- "Let Me Clear My Throat" - DJ Kool
- "Men In Black" - Will Smith
- "MMMBop" - Hanson
- "One Headlight" - The Wallflowers
- "Semi-Charmed Life" - Third Eye Blind
- "Tubthumping" - Chumbawamba
- "Wannabe" - Spice Girls
- "You Were Meant For Me" - Jewel
- "Your Woman" - White Town

# R.I.P.:

Michael Hutchence (INXS)
Notorious B.I.G.
Townes Van Zandt

# 1998

## Big Music Events of 1998:

A record label pays a Portland radio station $5,000 to play Limp Bizkit, the most requests the band receives all year. Van Halen adds Gary Cherone as their new singer; it bombs bigger than *Showgirls*. Elton John is knighted. George Michael is arrested for misuse of a public restroom. The first MP3 player is released to the public, the music industry braces for Armageddon. *TRL* premieres on MTV; music fans brace for pop Armageddon. Faith No More, Helmet, Porno For Pyros, and Emerson, Lake & Palmer break up.

## The 11 Best-Selling Albums of 1998:

1. Various Artists - *Titanic* OST
2. Celine Dion - *Let's Talk About Love*
3. Garth Brooks - *Sevens*
4. Backstreet Boys - *Backstreet Boys*
5. Shania Twain - *Come On Over*
6. Matchbox 20 - *Yourself Or Someone Like You*
7. Various Artists - *City Of Angels* OST
8. Will Smith - *Big Willie Style*
9. Savage Garden - *Savage Garden*
10. Spice Girls - *Spice World*
11. Usher - *My Way*

# Hit Songs:

- "Are You That Somebody?" - Aaliyah
- "The Boy Is Mine" - Brandy and Monica
- "Closing Time" - Semisonic
- "Doo Wop (That Thing)" - Lauryn Hill
- "The Dope Show" - Marilyn Manson
- "Everybody (Backstreet's Back)" - Backstreet Boys
- "Flagpole Sitta" - Harvey Danger
- "Gettin' Jiggy Wit It" - Will Smith
- "I Don't Want To Miss A Thing" - Aerosmith
- "Inside Out" - Eve 6
- "Iris" - Goo Goo Dolls
- "This Kiss" - Faith Hill
- "My Heart Will Go On" - Celine Dion
- "One Week" - Barenaked Ladies
- "The Rockafeller Skank" - Fatboy Slim
- "Sex & Candy" - Marcy Playground
- "Tearin' Up My Heart" - *Nsync
- "Torn" - Natalie Imbruglia
- "The Way" - Fastball
- "Wide Open Spaces" - Dixie Chicks
- "Zoot Suit Riot" - Cherry Poppin' Daddies

# R.I.P.:

Carl Perkins

Frank Sinatra

Carl Wilson (The Beach Boys)

# 1999

## Big Music Events of 1999:

Napster is born. Metallica cries. David Bowie in turn, releases the first album available to buy over the internet. A University of Oregon student is busted for downloading too much music and is grounded from the internet. Governor Jesse Ventura of Minnesota declares February 15th, Rolling Stones Day. The rock band Bush is sued by their record label for not making another album, no one knows why. Prince has a yard sale, no one knows why. Bruce Dickinson rejoins Iron Maiden, Maiden fans know why. KMFDM, Love & Rockets, The Jesus Lizard, and Pavement break up.

## The 11 Best-Selling Albums of 1999:

1. Backstreet Boys - *Millennium*
2. Britney Spears - *...Baby One More Time*
3. Shania Twain - *Come On Over*
4. *NSync - *\*NSync*
5. Ricky Martin - *Ricky Martin*
6. Garth Brooks - *Double Live*
7. The Offspring - *Americana*
8. Dixie Chicks - *Wide Open Spaces*
9. Limp Bizkit - *Significant Other*
10. TLC - *FanMail*
11. Lauryn Hill - *The Miseducation Of Lauryn Hill*

# Hit Songs:

- "All Star" - Smash Mouth
- "...Baby One More Time" - Britney Spears
- "Believe" - Cher
- "Every Morning" - Sugar Ray
- "Genie In A Bottle" - Christina Aguilera
- "I Try" - Macy Gray
- "I Want It That Way" - Backstreet Boys
- "Kiss Me" - Sixpence None The Richer
- "Livin' La Vida Loca" - Ricky Martin
- "Mambo No. 5" - Lou Bega
- "My Name Is" - Eminem
- "Nookie" - Limp Bizkit
- "Save Tonight" - Eagle-Eye Cherry
- "Say My Name" - Destiny's Child
- "Scar Tissue" - Red Hot Chili Peppers
- "She's So High" - Tal Bachman
- "Smooth" - Santana Featuring Rob Thomas
- "Steal My Sunshine" - Len
- "Sugar" - System Of A Down
- "Waiting For Tonight" - Jennifer Lopez

# R.I.P.:

Rick Danko (The Band)
Curtis Mayfield
Mark Sandman (Morphine)
Dusty Springfield

# BONUS TRACK / THE NEXT BEST 111 ALBUMS OF THE '90S

While my first list of 111 albums was about the albums that greatly affected me, this list attempts to incorporate albums that were important to the decade whether I liked them or not. I included some leftovers of my favorites, too.

1. **A Tribe Called Quest** - *People's Instinctive Travels and the Paths of Rhythm* (1990)
2. **Air** - *Moon Safari* (1998)
3. **Tori Amos** - *Little Earthquakes* (1992)
4. **Aphex Twin** - *Selected Ambient Works 85-92* (1992)
5. **At The Drive-In** - *In/Casino/Out* (1998)
6. **Bad Religion** - *Recipe For Hate* (1993)
7. **Beastie Boys** - *Hello Nasty* (1998)
8. **Belle and Sebastian** - *The Boy With The Arab Strap* (1998)
9. **Big Bad Voodoo Daddy** - *Americana Deluxe* (1998)
10. **Björk** - *Debut* (1993)
11. **Björk** - *Homogenic* (1997)
12. **Black Sheep** - *A Wolf In Sheep's Clothing* (1991)
13. **Mary J. Blige** - *My Life* (1994)
14. **Blur** - *Parklife* (1994)
15. **Boards Of Canada** - *Music Has The Right To Children* (1998)
16. **Brad** - *Shame* (1993)
17. **Billy Bragg And Wilco** - *Mermaid Avenue* (1998)
18. **Garth Brooks** - *No Fences* (1990)
19. **BT** - *Movement In Still Life* (1999)
20. **Built To Spill** - *Keep It Like A Secret* (1999)

21. **Cap'n Jazz** - *Burritos, Inspiration Point, Fork Balloon Sports, Cards In The Spokes...* (1995)
22. **The Cardigans** - *First Band On The Moon* (1996)
23. **Nick Cave And The Bad Seeds** - *The Boatman's Call* (1997)
24. **The Chemical Brothers** - *Dig Your Own Hole* (1997)
25. **Cibo Mato** - *Stereo \* Type A* (1999)
26. **Crowded House** - *Woodface* (1991)
27. **De La Soul** - *De La Soul Is Dead* (1991)
28. **Del the Funky Homosapien** - *I Wish My Brother George Was Here* (1991)
29. **Ani DiFranco** - *Little Plastic Castle* (1998)
30. **Digital Underground** - *Sex Packets* (1990)
31. **Dinosaur Jr.** - *Where You Been* (1993)
32. **Dr. Octagon** - *Octagonecologyst* (1996)
33. **Electronic** - *Electronic* (1991)
34. **Eminem** - *The Slim Shady LP* (1999)
35. **Fatboy Slim** - *Better Living Through Chemistry* (1996)
36. **The Flaming Lips** - *The Soft Bulletin* (1999)
37. **The Flaming Lips** - *Zaireeka* (1997)
38. **Foo Fighters** - *The Colour And The Shape* (1997)
39. **The Fugees** - *The Score* (1996)
40. **G. Love And Special Sauce** - *G. Love And Special Sauce* (1994)
41. **Gang Starr** - *Step Into The Arena* (1991)
42. **Garbage** - *Garbage* (1995)
43. **Happy Mondays** - *Pills 'n' Thrills and Bellyaches* (1990)
44. **Helmet** - *Betty* (1994)
45. **Ice Cube** - *The Predator* (1992)
46. **Indigo Girls** - *Swamp Ophelia* (1994)
47. **Jamiroquai** - *Travelling Without Moving* (1996)
48. **Janet Jackson** - *The Velvet Rope* (1997)
49. **Jimmy Eat World** - *Clarity* (1999)
50. **Jonathan Fire\*Eater** - *Wolf Songs For Lambs* (1997)

51. **Korn** - *Korn* (1994)
52. **The La's** - *The La's* (1990)
53. **Live** - *Mental Jewelry* (1991)
54. **LL Cool J** - *Mama Said Knock You Out* (1990)
55. **Madonna** - *Ray of Light* (1998)
56. **Marilyn Manson** - *Mechanical Animals* (1998)
57. **Mary Lou Lord** - *Got No Shadow* (1998)
58. **Meat Puppets** - *Too High To Die* (1994)
59. **Megadeth** - *Rust In Peace* (1990)
60. **Method Man & Redman** - *Blackout!* (1999)
61. **Alanis Morissette** - *Jagged Little Pill* (1995)
62. **Morrissey** - *Your Arsenal* (1992)
63. **Mother Love Bone** - *Apple* (1990)
64. **No Doubt** - *Tragic Kingdom* (1995)
65. **The Notorious B.I.G.** - *Life After Death* (1997)
66. **Oasis** - *(What's The Story) Morning Glory?* (1995)
67. **The Offspring** - *Americana* (1998)
68. **Ol' Dirty Bastard** - *Return To The 36 Chambers* (1995)
69. **Orbital** - *Orbital 2* (1993)
70. **Outkast** - *ATLiens* (1996)
71. **Outkast** - *Southernplayalisticadillacmuzik* (1994)
72. **Ozomatli** - *Ozomatli* (1998)
73. **Pearl Jam** - *Vitalogy* (1994)
74. **Liz Phair** - *Exile in Guyville* (1993)
75. **Pixies** - *Bossanova* (1990)
76. **PJ Harvey** - *Rid Of Me* (1993)
77. **Primus** - *Frizzle Fry* (1990)
78. **Prince** - *Graffiti Bridge* (1990)
79. **The Prodigy** - *The Fat Of The Land* (1997)
80. **The Promise Ring** - *Nothing Feels Good* (1997)
81. **Public Enemy** - *Apocalypse 91...The Empire Strikes Black* (1991)
82. **Pulp** - *Different Class* (1995)
83. **Quicksand** - *Slip* (1993)

84. **Raekwon** - *Only Built For Cuban Linx...* (1995)
85. **Rage Against The Machine** - *Evil Empire* (1996)
86. **Red Hot Chili Peppers** - *Californication* (1999)
87. **The Roots** - *Do You Want More?!!!??!* (1994)
88. **Saint Etienne** - *Good Humor* (1998)
89. **Santana** - *Supernatural* (1999)
90. **Sebadoh** - *III* (1991)
91. **Tupac Shakur** - *All Eyez On Me* (1996)
92. **Slayer** - *Seasons In The Abyss* (1990)
93. **Slint** - *Spiderland* (1991)
94. **Slowdive** - *Souvlaki* (1993)
95. **The Smashing Pumpkins** - *Gish* (1991)
96. **Elliott Smith** - *XO* (1998)
97. **Sonic Youth** - *Goo* (1990)
98. **Bruce Springsteen** - *Ghost Of Tom Joad* (1995)
99. **Stereolab** - *Emperor Tomato Ketchup* (1996)
100. **Sublime** - *Sublime* (1996)
101. **Sunny Day Real Estate** - *How It Feels To Be Something On* (1998)
102. **Superchunk** - *Foolish* (1994)
103. **Supergrass** - *I Should Coco* (1995)
104. **TLC** - *CrazySexyCool* (1994)
105. **Uncle Tupelo** - *No Depression* (1990)
106. **UNKLE** - *Psyence Fiction* (1998)
107. **Weezer** - *Weezer* (The Blue Album) (1994)
108. **Wilco** - *A.M.* (1995)
109. **Wilco** - *Being There* (1996)
110. **Wu-Tang Clan** - *Wu-Tang Forever* (1997)
111. **Yo La Tengo** - *I Can Hear The Heart Beating As One* (1997)

# THANK YOUS

1. **'80s Hip-Hop** (Beastie Boys, BDP, Eazy-E, Eric B & Rakim, N.W.A., Public Enemy, Run D.M.C.)
2. **'80s Metal** (Cinderella, Def Leppard, Guns N' Roses, L.A. Guns, Metallica, Skid Row, Tesla, Van Halen)
3. **'80s Modern Rock** (The Cure, Depeche Mode, Jane's Addiction, Joy Division, New Order, Pixies, Prince, R.E.M., The Smiths, U2)
4. **'90s Alternative** (Alice In Chains, Beck, Black Crowes, Faith No More, Foos, Garbage, NIN, Nirvana, Pearl Jam, Rage, Smashing Pumpkins, Soundgarden, Tool, Tori)
5. **'90s Hip-Hop** (A Tribe Called Quest, Del the Funky Homosapien, Digable Planets, Snoop Dogg, Dr. Dre, Jay-Z, Nas, Outkast, Roots, Tupac Shakur, Wu-Tang)
6. **'90s Indie Rock** (Fiona Apple, Built To Spill, Heatmiser, Lush, Modest Mouse, Pavement, Primus, Radiohead, Sebadoh, Sleater-Kinney, Elliott Smith)
7. **'00s Artists** (Arcade Fire, Arctic Monkeys, Bon Iver, Bright Eyes, Eminem, The Killers, LCD Soundsystem, The Strokes, The White Stripes, Wilco, The xx)
8. **Electronic** (BT, Chicane, Daft Punk, Massive Attack, Moby, Morcheeba, Orbital, Portishead, Röyksopp)
9. **Jazz** (Chet Baker, John Coltrane, Duke Ellington, Miles, Mingus, Monk, Max Roach)
10. **Punk** (Bad Religion, Black Flag, Buzzcocks, Damned, Fugazi, The Jam, Ramones, Sex Pistols, Stooges)
11. **Rock** (AC/DC, Aerosmith, Boston, Bowie, Cash, Dylan, Eagles, Elvis, Fleetwood Mac, Marvin Gaye, Hendrix, Led Zeppelin, Marley, Petty, Pink Floyd, Springsteen)

Printed in Great Britain
by Amazon

29067404R00166